Latinos of Boulder County, Colorado, 1900-1980

Volume I:
History and Contributions

by   *Marjorie*

Marjorie K. McIntosh   *McIntosh*

Distinguished Professor of History Emerita
University of Colorado at Boulder

Written for: *March,*
Boulder County Latino History Project
                              2016
With assistance from:
Longmont Museum

Endorsed by:
Department of Ethnic Studies,
University of Colorado at Boulder

 **Old John Publishing**
Palm Springs, California

McIntosh, Marjorie K. (Marjorie Keniston)
Latinos of Boulder County, Colorado, 1900-1980
Volume I : History and Contributions / M.K. McIntosh.
332 pages. 229 cm.
Includes bibliographical references and index.

ISBN 978-0-9863873-3-3 (hardcover)
978-0-9863873-2-6 (paperback)

1. Hispanic Americans–Colorado–Boulder County–History.
2. Colorado–History, Local–20th Century.
3. Boulder County (Colorado)–History.

2015961054

References to Internet Web sites (URLs) were accurate at the time of writing. Neither the author nor Old John Publishing is responsible for URLs that may have expired or changed since the manuscript was prepared.

Contents

Cover: Eloisa, Paulina, and Dulcinea Martinez, daughters of a sugar beet worker, on a Sunday morning in Lafayette, 1929. Courtesy of Linda Arroyo-Holmstrom

Foreword

"It is better to die standing than to live on your knees"
Emiliano Zapata (1879-1919)

"No quiero tu lastima"[1] : The Enduring Power of Stories

I have been teaching and writing about the complex histories, mestiza/o cultures, and borderland identities of the Chicana and Chicano community since the 1990s. Even though we are victimized in many ways—by histories of manifest destiny, land grabs, daily and institutional race- and class-based discrimination, gendered violence, nativism and anti-immigrant laws and practices, erasure and demonization in the media—we hate to see ourselves as victims and do not seek to be pitied or patronized. Like other racially oppressed communities, and survivors of violence, we consider pity offensive. We rather seek empathy, compassion, and open-mindedness from those who want to hear about and feel the stories of survival, struggle, and joy that mark our lives as individuals, families, and communities. Like all groups in the United States, we want to create better lives for ourselves and for future generations. We defy and in fact are the diametric opposite to the enduring, a-factual, ahistorical stereotype of the lazy Mexican. Our underpaid and overexploited labor has been and still is essential to the economic and cultural growth of the nation. Colorado, like other states in the Southwest, has attempted to erase, displace, segregate, co-opt, and "white wash" the demography and historical presence of Mexicans, Mexican Americans, and Chicanas/os. That effort was helped by the U.S. Census, which classified Mexicans as "white" until the 1940s.

The two volumes in this set present stories of struggle and the

---

[1] This translates as "I don't want your pity" and is from a song by "Los Tigres del Norte," an ensemble based in San Jose, California.

implacable force of dignity in the Chicana and Chicano community in Boulder County. The singular and collective power of the voices of individuals and families heard in these volumes is profound, complex, and long lasting. The books and their illustrations, drawn from a large archive of interviews, family biographies, photographs, and other source materials (most of them available on the website of the Boulder County Latino History Project) give the reader the privilege to hear, see, and learn about Chicana/o families as they struggle to maintain their cultural identity, language, religion, food, respect for elders, and belief in the power of *familia*. The study gives us the background to the current-day demonization of immigrants from south of the U.S./Mexico border that is central to the fabric of U.S. political life (insuring that politicians, mayors, and governors will get elected and stay elected in office in some states). We learn that the creation of the eponymous "illegal alien" and the practices of racial profiling, assumptions of illegality, and threats and practices of deportation for those who appear Mexican were already visible in Boulder County in the 1920s and 1930s. To go beyond the anecdotal nature of individual statements, the author has used hundreds of newspaper articles and compiled rare quantitative material extracted from previously unused sources.

Studies of Chicana/o history in states like California, Arizona, and Texas explore a range of issues that are specific to each state and its own local cultures and economic patterns. Yet there are moments, laws, policies, and market forces that affect all peoples of Mexican ancestry in the U.S. and shape how the community responds to and adapts to these events and forces. As the Boulder County Latino History Project started the tremendous work of documenting the histories of Latinos in this area, bringing communities together and creating a space for people—especially women—to discuss their stories, their struggles, their ancestors, and to preserve photographic, archival, and other sources, I was curious to see what is shared or unique about a Chicano community on the northern edge of the borderlands. As you read this captivating study, you will encounter themes that resonate from descriptions of other parts of the Southwest. Families displaced by the violence of the Mexican revolution were "pulled" up to fill labor demands in the fields, especially sugar beets, and mines of Colorado (like other states in the Southwest and even Chicago). Mexican immigrant families whose labor was essential to the economic growth of the state moved into ethnically mixed but partially segregated neighborhoods in Boulder, Lafayette, and

Longmont. We watch how how local families survived the violence of the Ku Klux Klan in the 1920s-1930s and the way they started to "fight back" by organizing strikes, encouraging their children to do well in high school, go to college, and become leaders; we see how women and their *comadres* supported each other and maintained the health and religious vitality of the community. The book also shows how Chicanas/os in Boulder County, like other parts of the Southwest and Chicago, had to learn to suppress their culture and language to fit in and survive in an Anglo world, sometimes internalizing forces of shaming because of skin color, language, culture, and religion that differed from the white dominant society. As the saying by the well-loved Emiliano Zapata, who fought to regain the lands and livelihoods of the majority of Mexicans in the 1910 Mexican revolution, states, "It is better to die standing than to live on your knees." You will be bowled over by the eloquence, truth, and enduring power of *dignidad* of the voices in this study. They never let go the pride of being a human being from a civilization that has roots in this continent that existed way before borders were imposed by nation states.

As a member of the Boulder County Latino History Project, I was very privileged to attend and share in a workshop in 2013 with the ten Latina/o interns (college and high school students) and witness and feel the power of *testimonios* and their impacts on these students. For them, hearing and filming the stories of people who might look like their parents, aunts and uncles, grandmothers and grandfathers as they talked about their struggles, successes, and joys, allowed them to look with new eyes at their own young lives and their own struggles with feeling shame and alienation in white dominant spaces. What an illustration of the palpable power of oral histories and their transformative effects! May the collective *fuerza* of these voices educate, move, and inspire you as well. *Mil gracias* to Marjorie for her vision, acumen, tenacity, respect, and infectious charisma for bringing communities together to share their stories.

Con Respeto,

Arturo J. Aldama
Associate Professor and Associate Chair
Department of Ethnic Studies
University of Colorado at Boulder

Author's Preface

I have written these books as a historian and an ally of Boulder County's Latinas/os. When I was young, my family lived in Argentina, and Spanish was my first language. After we returned to the U.S., we often had Latin Americans staying with us. Later, I spent 30 years at the University of Colorado at Boulder teaching history, doing research, and writing.[1] I have also worked at universities in Africa, doing oral history projects and helping one institution set up a local history study.[2]

After retiring from teaching, I wanted to learn something about Latinas/os in Boulder County and their history. But when I went to the library, I found that almost nothing had been written about them: local Latinas/os are virtually invisible in books about this area. I therefore began talking with Latino leaders and organizations to ask if they would be interested in working on a community-based local history project. Their enthusiastic response led to the formation of the Boulder County Latino History Project [BCLHP], with a 15-person Advisory Committee and 14 institutional partners.[3] Over the following year and a half, I helped to coordinate some 80 volunteers plus 10 Latino summer interns—high school and college students—who together assembled an extraordinary amount and diversity of primary source material. Nearly all of the 1,600 sources are available on the BCLHP's website [bocolatinohistory.colorado. edu] or those of local museums and libraries. This book and its companion volume rely upon that wealth of information.[4]

---

[1] E.g., *Controlling Misbehavior in England, 1370-1600* (Cambridge University Press, 1998), and *Poor Relief in England, 1350-1600* (Cambridge University Press, 2012).

[2] *Women, Work, and Domestic Virtue in Uganda, 1900-2003* (co-authored with Grace Bantebya Kyomuhendo, Athens: Ohio University Press, 2006); *Yoruba Women, Work, and Social Change* (Bloomington: Indiana University Press, 2009); and a project on Muslims living in religiously mixed communities along the Ugandan/Kenyan border, Islamic University in Uganda, 2009.

[3] For further information, see bocolatinohistory.colorado.edu. The BCLHP is currently working with K-12 teachers, helping them introduce material about Latinas/os into the curriculum (teachbocolatinohistory.colorado.edu).

[4] McIntosh, *Latinos of Boulder County, Colorado, 1900-1980*, Vol. II, *Lives and Legacies* (Old John Publishing, 2016).

I am honored to have been accepted as a partner and friend by the BCLHP. It has been a special privilege to spend time with many of the people whose lives and families are discussed in these books. I hope their stories and images will be as powerful for you as they have been for me.

Marjorie K. McIntosh
December, 2015

Acknowledgments

This book rests upon the huge accomplishment of the Boulder County Latino History Project [BCLHP] in gathering and preserving primary sources and creating databases of quantifiable information. While I cannot acknowledge individually all of the people who contributed to that work, their names are listed on the project's website.[1] I hope they take suitable pride in what they achieved. Special thanks go to Oli Olivas Duncan, director of the Longmont Hispanic Study of 1987-1988, who before her death in 2013 generously made available to the BCLHP some unpublished interview transcripts and hundreds of photographic slides. Phil Hernandez of the Boulder Hispanic Families project of 2012 played a key role in getting the BCLHP started and categorizing occupations for quantitative analysis. Tom Martinez, Linda Arroyo-Holmstrom, and Janet Perez Romero nobly prepared and digitized 825 family photos and slides to be put onto the BCLHP website.

Several historically focused institutions provided fine assistance. The Maria Rogers Oral History Program of the Carnegie Branch Library for Local History, Boulder Public Library, trained the BCLHP's interviewers and videographers, checked the transcriptions of those interviews, and posted them and the video files on their website.[2] Erik Mason, Curator of Research at the Longmont Museum, provided research assistance and a convenient workspace for one of our interns in summer, 2013; the Museum waived fees for photographs used in these books and hosted events. Wendy Hall of the Carnegie Branch Library, Tony Shockency of the Longmont YMCA, and Carol Taylor of the Boulder Historical Museum were likewise helpful.

Financial and other types of support for the BCLHP and hence for this book came from many sources, as listed on its website. The Community Foundation Serving Boulder County was a constant source of encouragement and backing, and the University of Colorado at Boulder, particularly the Office for University Outreach, provided invaluable assistance. Arturo Aldama of

[1] bocolatinohistory.colorado.edu.
[2] https://boulderlibrary.org/services/local-history/maria-rogers-oral-history-program.

the Department of Ethnic Studies at CU-Boulder was a much appreciated teacher and advisor; Thomas Andrews of the Department of History at CU-Boulder and four anonymous reviewers read the manuscript with care, making important suggestions. Several members of the Advisory Committee of the BCLHP read sections of the book dealing with their own communities. Any errors are my responsibility, and I apologize for them.

Although nearly all of the material included here was provided by people who were associated with the BCLHP or earlier projects, other families have equally interesting stories to tell. I hope they will be able to preserve those narratives. In deciding which particular examples to use in the text and illustrations, I tried to choose representative samples from many different individuals and families. Some photos were too faded to show up well in print.

The most important contributors to the book are the people whose lives and images it portrays. Without their willingness to share their personal histories, Boulder County's Latinas/os would remain hidden from wider view.

Abbreviations and Notes

Abbreviations:

BCLHP   Boulder County Latino History Project

CU-Boulder   University of Colorado at Boulder

LULAC   League of United Latin American Citizens

LHS   Longmont Hispanic Study

LM   Longmont Museum

LPL   Lafayette Public Library

MROHP   Maria Rogers Oral History Program, Carnegie Branch Library for Local History, Boulder Public Library

OEO   Office of Economic Opportunity, part of the "War on Poverty"

WPA   Works Progress Administration (one of the "New Deal" agencies)

Illustration captions:

The captions under the illustrations give only the title of the image. For full references, including credits, see the List of Illustrations at the back of the book.

References in footnotes and Sources:

All footnote references are given in a short form. Full references are provided at the back of the book, under Sources. Section A includes sources dealing specifically with Boulder County Latinas/os. Nearly all of these materials are available online; a URL or other form of access is given for each entry. In the online version of this book, references in section A are hyperlinked directly to the original source. Other kinds of material are listed in section B of Sources.

Chapter 1

Setting the Stage

Since the beginning of the twentieth century, people from Spanish-speaking backgrounds have played essential roles in Boulder County, Colorado. Immigrants from Mexico, northern New Mexico, and southern Colorado provided much of the labor that fueled two of eastern Boulder County's main economic activities prior to around 1940: growing and processing sugar beets; and coal mining. Work in the beet fields required men, women, and children to stay in a stooped position, using short-handled tools, for hours at a time, often under a hot sun. The housing provided for agricultural laborers was generally deplorable. Coal miners engaged in physically demanding and potentially dangerous work in dark tunnels, always facing the possibility of cave-ins or explosions. Some of their families lived in camps next to the mines, with company stores where purchases for food and other supplies were deducted from miners' wages. Although Hispanics faced overt racism especially in the 1920s and 1930s—with armed attacks on their unions, threats of violence from the Ku Klux Klan, exclusion from stores and restaurants, and mass deportation orders—they held together in strong families and maintained their faith that life in this region offered a brighter future for themselves and their children. In the decades between 1940 and 1980, access to education and better employment options contributed to ongoing immigration and brought many Boulder County Latinas/os into the wider community, where they continued to make valuable contributions. Returning veterans in the 1940s and 1950s and Chicano civil rights activists in the later 1960s and 1970s took the lead in tackling discrimination. Latino culture expanded the horizons of a predominantly Anglo county.

This two-volume set describes the history of Latinas/os living in Boulder County between 1900 and 1980. The present book moves through those 80 years by sub-periods, highlighting changes over time as illuminated in many different types of primary materials. The second volume covers aspects of the social, cultural, religious, and educational lives of local Latinas/os, with a greater reliance upon oral history interviews, family biographies, and personal photos.[1] The study focuses upon three Boulder County towns located within 15 miles of each other that display quite different patterns. Longmont was almost entirely dependent upon commercial agriculture and food processing, while coal mining provided the economic basis for the smaller community of Lafayette. Boulder, the county seat, was a commercial center and home to the University of Colorado.

The main part of both books stops around 1980, because after that time the local Latino population became even more complex: immigrants from many different countries and backgrounds joined residents whose families had arrived earlier in the century, and the various groups became more clearly distinguished along economic, educational, and cultural lines. The decades after 1980 will need to be considered fully in a separate work. Each volume has an epilogue, however, which carries us into the early 2010s. The epilogue to this book offers a quick quantitative look at the situation of Boulder County's Latinas/os in that decade, while the second describes the life experiences of the ten young Latino interns who worked with the Boulder County Latino History Project in summer, 2013.

Although these books are local studies, they address broader themes important to historians, sociologists, Chicano/Ethnic Studies specialists, and others who focus on the American Southwest. Among them are issues of migration, labor conditions, racism and discrimination, the impact of war and veterans, and civil rights activity. The volumes also explore four interpretive questions: (1) What were the roles, experiences, and contributions of women? (2) How did people interact within families, looking especially at relations between men and women and between generations? (3) To what extent did Boulder County share patterns with communities that lay closer to the heart of the U.S.-Mexican borderlands or were major cities with large Latino populations; and to what extent was it influenced by a local network that included Denver? (4) How did local Latinas/os define themselves, creating an ethnic identity?

This study is distinctive in several respects. It provides one of the

---

[1] McIntosh, *Latinos of Boulder County, Colorado, 1900-1980*, Vol. II, *Lives and Legacies* (cited hereafter as Vol. II). The same indexing terms are used in both volumes, to make searching easier.

first detailed examinations of Latinas/os living on the margin of the borderlands that extends from the arrival of the initial immigrants until the later twentieth century. Further, many previous books about Latinas/os in the Southwest deal with major cities or rural communities; within Colorado, attention has generally focused on Latinos living in Denver or in villages in the southern part of the state, tied culturally to northern New Mexico. The present volumes, by contrast, describe residents of small and middle-sized towns and their hinterlands, places located within 30 miles of Denver but displaying their own historical patterns. As case studies, they bring to life the experiences of individual people and communities, complementing more general accounts.

The books draw upon an exceptionally rich body of information: the 1,600 primary sources gathered or produced by the Boulder County Latino History Project [BCLHP] in 2013-2014, one of the largest and most varied sets of material about Latinos in any area of the Southwest. Because most of these sources come from members of the community, local residents are themselves the producers of historical knowledge as they describe their family's histories, tell anecdotes about their own lives, and share photos. Personal sources are supplemented by information from newspapers, school records, listings of local residents with their occupations and employers, and U.S. Censuses.

The books are also unusual with respect to their forms of analysis and presentation. They introduce innovative, interactive maps showing where Spanish-surnamed families lived in each of the three towns once per decade between 1904 or 1916 and 1975. They offer a formal quantitative analysis of changing employment patterns over time, 1926-1975, using standard government occupational headings to facilitate comparison with other places. Virtually all of the primary sources cited in these two volumes are available online.[2] Because a URL or other form of access is given for every reference in the printed format, and all references in the online version of the books are live-linked to their sources, anyone who has access to the Web can view the original evidence, without going to a research library or traveling to archives. The study is therefore a perfect educational tool for K-12 and college teachers, enabling students to see the raw material from which historical work is produced.[3]

---

[2] Most are on the BCLHP's website (bocolatinohistory.colorado.edu), while others are on those of museums or libraries.

[3] The BCLHP's website has a special section for educators, containing Primary Source Sets, Lesson Plans, short clips from interviews and films, and other instructional materials: teachbocolatinohistory.colorado.edu.

This introductory chapter first addresses several questions of definition: what terms to use in describing people from Spanish-language backgrounds, what their biological origins and identities were, and what characteristics marked the three communities studied here. It then lays out the intellectual context created by other historical studies, including the four questions that will be traced across the two volumes. The types of primary sources employed here are surveyed next, while a closing section gives a little background about the nineteenth century.

A. Describing People and Communities in Boulder County

Terms and origins

An immediate question that confronts anyone writing about the history of people from Spanish-speaking backgrounds is what terminology to use. The words employed have changed over time, and even now, there is no uniformity in what individual people like to be called. Various groups may prefer to be identified in different ways: people whose families have been living in the Southwest for several generations or centuries, more recent immigrants from Mexico, and arrivals from other countries in Central or South America or Spain itself.[4] The labels "Mexicans," "*Mexicanos*," or "Mexican Americans" were common at least into the 1960s, but they were often disliked by families that had lived in this country for a long time because they implied that all Spanish-surnamed people had arrived fairly recently from Mexico. Spanish-speaking people from New Mexico who moved to Colorado might term themselves "*Nuevo Mejicanos*" to make their own roots clear. Immigrants from other Latin American countries also felt excluded by any term referring to Mexican origins. "Spanish American" was another possible label; the U.S. government used the word "Hispanic" for Censuses and other analyses across most of the twentieth century; and some people called themselves "*Hispanos*." Those words were later rejected by younger people who did not want to privilege the Spanish/European side of their heritage and deny the importance of their indigenous, Native American ancestors.[5]

---

[4] Until around 2000, relatively few people came to this area from the Caribbean islands.

[5] The Mexican term *mestizo*, referring to a combination of Spanish and Indian backgrounds, has not been used in Colorado.

Especially for people involved in the civil rights movement of the later 1960s and 1970s, "Chicano" became the term of choice.[6] This label, derived probably from the Nahuatl pronunciation of *"Mexicano,"* also implied a commitment to political and social change. As "Chicano" came into use, many older or more conservative people disliked the term, which to them implied a kind of militancy they did not support. They preferred to stay with the familiar labels. Further, whereas Spanish usage had traditionally employed words with masculine endings (like *Americanos* or *Mejicanos*) to refer to both men and women, feminists within the Chicano movement insisted upon a verbal distinction to make the roles of women clear (e.g., Chicana and Chicano). More recently, a spelling of "Xicano" has been adopted by some because it is closer to the Nahuatl pronunciation of the word. To be gender neutral, both "Chicano/a" and "Xicano/a" are sometimes written with the ending @ (e.g., "Chican@" = "o" or "a").

In Boulder County, people from Spanish-speaking backgrounds have described themselves in a variety of ways. During the earlier twentieth century, many referred to their place of origin, calling themselves "Mexicans" or "New Mexicans." By the mid-century, the terms "Mexican American," *"Mejicano,"* or "Hispanic" were widely used. Those words have remained common ever since, even among civil rights activists in the later 1960s and 1970s whom we might label "Chicanos." In the early twenty-first century, "Chicano" has lost its political implications among most community members and is now used sometimes by people whose families have been living in the U.S. for some time, especially those with long histories in the Southwest, to distinguish themselves from more recent arrivals. "Chicano" or "Chicana" are regularly used, however, by college/university faculty members and students.

The most common collective word in this region in the 2010s is "Latino," which covers everyone from Spanish- and Portuguese-speaking backgrounds, regardless of their place of origin, length of time in this country, or social/political stance. But that label is not used widely by individuals to describe themselves. In a survey of Spanish-surnamed residents of Boulder County taken in 2001, people used the following terms as ethnic identifiers:

---

[6] See Ch. 6A below.

Mexican/*Mejicano*	31%
Hispanic	30%
Mexican American	19%
Chicano	9%
Latino	7%
Other	4% [7]

In this study, we use several terms to refer to people from Spanish-speaking backgrounds. For the first half of the twentieth century, we describe people generally as "Hispanics" or as having Spanish surnames. When individuals referred to themselves as coming from Mexico, New Mexico, or southern Colorado, we honor those self-definitions. We call people actively engaged in the civil rights movement of the late 1960s and 1970s "Chicanas/os." When speaking of more conservative people in the 1960s and 1970s and for everyone thereafter, we employ the generic label "Latinas/os," though we recognize that the word may be somewhat anachronistic when applied to earlier periods. We use "Latino" as an adjective, but when referring to individuals, we talk of a Latina or Latino and of Latinas/os, to emphasize that both women and men are central to our discussion. For English-speaking people from European backgrounds, we usually employ the unspecific label "Anglos," in preference to the term "whites" that is sometimes used in contrast to "brown" Mexicans.

Uncertainty about terminology ("What do we want to be called?") is associated with questions about cultural and biological identity ("Who are we, and who were our ancestors?"). While it is possible to define Latinas/os as a distinct <u>ethnic</u> group, based usually on the criterion of having a surname derived from Spanish, it is not possible to categorize them in <u>racial</u> terms. The U.S. government has struggled with this problem since the time of the Treaty of Guadalupe Hidalgo of 1848, at the end of the Mexican-American War. The challenge of placing Latinas/os into a single classification based on race or national origin is illustrated by the various terms used by Census takers in Longmont between 1910 and 1940 when describing people from Mexican or New Mexican backgrounds: Mexican, white, black, Indian, or mulatto.[8] The most recent U.S. Censuses have offered a greater range of racial/ethnic categories for Latinos.

Nearly all the people who moved here from Mexico, New Mexico, other American states, and other Latin American countries are racially and

---

[7] *2001 Latino Task Force of Boulder County Community Assessment*, p. 2.
[8] Rebecca Chavez, "Making Them Count," Table 3.

culturally complex. Their forebears may include at least a few ancestors who had moved to the Americas from Spain as well as many indigenous people. Some have African blood, and certain Latino families from New Mexico have Jewish forebears.[9] Until the advent of DNA testing in the past 20 years, most families did not know the actual composition of their biological heritage but relied on stories passed down over time.

A willingness to acknowledge the diversity of one's ancestry has changed over the past few generations. In the mid-twentieth century, some older people in Boulder County whose families had come originally from New Mexico—particularly if they had light complexions and/ or blue eyes—stressed their Spanish roots and thought of themselves as "white." Because of their appearance, they were less likely to face the kinds of discrimination experienced by people with darker skins and more Native American features. The mother of one of the people involved in this project, who had grown up in an economically secure family outside Longmont, generally defined herself as white, Spanish, or from New Mexico. Though she knew that at least one of her grandparents was a Native American, she raised her children to believe that "the lowest creature on God's earth was an Indian." She also distanced her family from recent Mexican immigrants, telling her children not to play with those dark youngsters. Cleo Estrada grew up in the San Luis Valley of Colorado, where her grandparents had moved from northern New Mexico. Her parents were aware they had Indian forebears, but when she was a child "there was tremendous disdain about being related to or having native blood in our families, so people just didn't bring it up."[10]

In the early twenty-first century, having Native American or Jewish ancestry is more readily accepted and openly discussed by local Latinas/os, in part because of DNA testing. Just as some Anglos who thought that all their ancestors came from Northern Europe have been surprised to learn that they have African American and/or Native American antecedents, so too have some Latinas/os been surprised to realize the extent to which their racial heritage is indigenous, not European. A shift towards

---

[9] Some Jews or *conversos* (Jews who had been forced to convert to Christianity at least nominally) emigrated to Mexico from Spain and Portugal in the sixteenth or seventeenth centuries to escape persecution by the Inquisition. They commonly settled first in Mexico City, but as the Inquisition established itself there and gradually spread throughout New Spain, they moved progressively further north, ending up on the farthest edge of colonial Mexico's Santa Fé territory. See Ch. 2B below for a fuller discussion and references.

[10] "Estrada, Cleo, autobiographical information."

interest and pride in the diversity of one's background is illustrated by the number of people interviewed for this project who mentioned their Native American grandparents or great-grandparents or who identified with indigenous culture.[11] David Young is the son of Maria Dora Esquivel, a Chicana activist from the 1970s onwards. But David chose as an adult to define himself as a member of the Genizaro Apache group of Colorado and used his Indian name, Atekpatzin, especially for his work as a *curandero* [traditional healer] who draws upon Native American traditions.[12] Edwina Salazar, who grew up in the San Luis Valley, part of an extended family originally from northern New Mexico, explained that her father's family "is actually of Jewish heritage."[13] His *conversos* ancestors had left southern Spain and come to Mexico, gradually moving northwards to stay away from the Inquisition.

Boulder County Latinas/os whose families came from Mexico often emphasized their national heritage, referring to themselves as Mexicans or Mexican Americans even if their family had lived in this country for multiple generations. Candace Arroyo, interviewed in 1977 when she was a student at the University of Colorado, said that when she was growing up in Boulder, "I always said I was a Mexican, because that's what my family always told me I was. That's what I felt I was, because that's the way our family traditions and the culture was for me. . . . My father always raised us to be independent and proud of what we are and what we can do just as human beings, but most of all proud of the fact that we are Mexicans."[14] She did not identify with the term "Chicano" until she went to the university.

The question of whether Latinas/os were "white," "brown," or "red" could be significant at the community level. During the racist 1920s and 1930s, light-complexioned Latinas/os in Longmont generally avoided ill treatment. The little towns of Lafayette and Louisville were superficially similar coal mining communities lying just a few miles apart from each other. Both had many residents who had immigrated from Italy as well as ones from Mexico/New Mexico. Yet over the course of the twentieth century, racial/ethnic definitions diverged. In Lafayette, Hispanics came be grouped with Italians, and the neighborhood where they all lived

---

[11] See Ch. 2B below and Vol. II, Epilogue.

[12] Young, David Atekpatzin, interview, 2013. For *genizaros* (abducted Native American children who were raised in Spanish-speaking families), see Ch. 2B below.

[13] Salazar, Edwina, interview, 2013.

[14] Arroyo, Candace, interview, 1977.

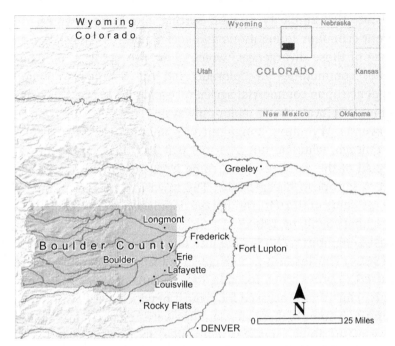

Map 1.1. *Boulder County, showing places mentioned in the text*

was integrated. In Louisville, however, the dominant social groups categorized Mexicans as "brown"—unlike the "white" Italians (who came generally from southern Italy and might be quite dark skinned)—and Hispanics faced greater segregation and racism.[15]

Three Boulder County communities

The three towns examined in this book—Longmont, Lafayette, and Boulder—fall within the same geographical region and are separated by only 15 miles. As Map 1.1 shows, they are located on the plains, at the western edge of the American high prairie. They lie just to the east of the Rocky Mountains, with their 14,000-foot peaks; the Continental Divide defines the western boundary of Boulder County. The histories of the little mountain towns, based initially on "hard rock" mining for gold and other minerals, and the county's other small communities will not be considered here.

---

[15] See, e.g., Perez, Arthur, interview, 2013. In a similar situation in a southern California citrus area, immigrant Italian workers were structurally positioned by the 1930s as "white," while Mexicans were defined as non-white and faced greater discrimination (Alamillo, *Making Lemonade*, pp. 6 and 38).

Despite the similarity of their setting, our three towns had quite different economic foundations and social features. They were chosen because of those divergences, which allow this study to be compared to other communities in Colorado and the Southwest. Longmont's dependence upon commercial agriculture and food processing was made possible by its location on a major railway line running north from Denver to Cheyenne, Wyoming. Longmont was founded in 1871 by investors from Chicago, who laid out a formal plat and then sold memberships. Nearly all of the early residents came from German, Swedish, or other northern European backgrounds. The town had no more than around 6,000 residents until 1940, though the population grew rapidly from then on, reaching 43,000 by 1980.[16]

Most Longmont residents fell into one of two categories prior to the mid-1960s. The leading group consisted of farmers who owned the land used to grow crops for sale, local businessmen, and people who ran the plants that processed food, most of which were owned by larger corporations. Some of these elite families were descendants of the original settlers of the town, and they controlled its economic, political, and cultural life. They were all white and spoke English at least by the second generation. Separated from that dominant group by quite a large gap were the many unskilled workers in the sugar beet fields and processing plants. Although the initial beet workers came from diverse national backgrounds, by the 1920s and 1930s they were primarily Mexicans or New Mexicans.[17] That economic and cultural separation contributed to an unusually high and overt level of racism in Longmont from the 1920s until at least the 1950s, including segregated seating in theaters and signs on some businesses that said "White Trade Only."[18]

Lafayette relied on coal mining. Founded in the 1880s by Mary Miller, who had homesteaded in the area with her husband, the little town was immediately adjacent to several of the early mines and not far from many of the later ones. It housed a mixed population of mining families, mainly Italians and Hispanics, though some of the earlier miners had come from eastern/southeastern Europe. Many of its residents had moved into town from the camps that provided housing next to individual mines. Lafayette had no more than around 2,000 residents until 1950 and only

---

[16] For the total population of each town, 1900-2010, see App. 1.1.

[17] See Ch. 3A below for the nationality of beet workers over time. For minimum numbers of Latino residents, 1900-1975, see App. 1.2.

[18] See Chs. 4B and 5C below.

9,000 in 1980. Social interactions in Lafayette were less economically and ethnically divided than in Longmont and Boulder. The town contained very few people with any wealth; its few stores were locally-owned and small. Miners had to work together and rely on each other for safety when underground, and some of their unions were integrated. That sense of comradeship apparently carried over into their families' lives and the interactions between neighbors.[19]

The town of Boulder had contrasting features. As well as being the home of county government, it was a commercial center, providing supplies for people living and working in the mountains and in nearby communities on the plains. Moreover, from 1876—the year when Colorado achieved statehood—Boulder was the home of the University of Colorado, the major public institution of higher education in the Rocky Mountain region. Boulder was usually about twice the size of Longmont, with 6,000-13,000 residents between 1900 and 1940. Growth increased thereafter, especially in the later 1960s and 1970s, reaching 77,000 by 1980.

Boulder had just a few dozen Latino residents until the 1960s. The modest homes of these families were initially concentrated in a small area lying between "University Hill" and downtown, alongside the river and railroad tracks.[20] Their lives were quite isolated from the rest of the community: they had little contact with the university except as employees, or with the business world except as customers. Until the 1950s, the town was racist and elitist, with no place in its self-image for working people. In the 1960s and 1970s, however, the number, diversity, and educational level of Boulder's Latino population increased markedly. This development when joined with greater discomfort about segregation among some white residents served to open opportunities with respect to employment and housing.

B. The Intellectual Context and Primary Sources

Historical works that provide an intellectual context for this study

By setting this work of local history into a broader intellectual framework, we can identify aspects of the story that resemble patterns observed elsewhere as well as elements that are atypical. The general

---

[19] See Chs. 3B and 4B below, and Vol. II, Ch. 2B.
[20] See Vol. II, Ch. 2B for this neighborhood.

context for this study comes from the fine work done by scholars in two arenas: (1) the history of the Southwest, including Colorado; and (2) the experiences of Chicanos/Latinos. Among geographically defined studies, David Weber's work on the Southwest provides a solid understanding of the generations before around 1900.[21] Histories of Colorado and adjoining regions published between the 1950s and 1970s, including those prepared by LeRoy Hafen, the State Historian for 30 years, feature lively accounts; the *Colorado Magazine* (now *Colorado Heritage*) and *New Mexico Historical Review* include articles on a wide range of topics.[22] Whereas work done on Colorado's history before around 1980 generally paid relatively little attention to women, people of color, or workers, the best recent studies are far more inclusive.[23]

The extensive body of work on Chicanos/Latinos is more directly relevant to this study. Two examples illustrate the contributions and some of the approaches taken by Chicano scholars. Rodolfo Acuña's textbook *Occupied America*, first published in 1972 and revised repeatedly since then, exemplifies the blending of solid academic research and social commitment that characterizes much work in Ethnic Studies. Acuña's book provides a clear narrative structure and thoughtful analysis based—especially in its earlier editions—upon a model of "internal colonialism."[24] Like many works published in the opening stages of the development of the field of Chicano Studies, the initial versions of *Occupied America* were criticized by Chicana scholars for privileging male voices, ignoring women's contributions to the movement, and excluding topics such as families and sexuality.[25] Manuel Gonzales's book, *Mexicanos*, reflects a somewhat different social/political position. Unlike scholars raised in the *Movimiento* tradition of the 1960s and 1970s, Gonzales paints a sympathetic picture

---

[21] E.g., Weber, *The Mexican Frontier, The Spanish Frontier*, and *Foreigners in Their Native Land*.

[22] E.g., Hafen, *Broken Hand*, Hafen, ed., *The Mountain Men*, Hafen and Hafen, *The Colorado Story*, and Lecompte, *Pueblo, Hardscrabble, Greenhorn*.

[23] E.g., Montoya, *Translating Property*, and Andrews, *Killing for Coal*.

[24] That approach argues that Chicanos living in the southwestern U.S. were a colonized group, brought by military force (the Mexican-American War) under the control of an Anglo-dominated society and government; Latinos' economic resources, primarily their labor, were then utilized to the benefit of American capitalism. For criticisms and alternative definitions of this model, see, e.g., Gilbert Gonzáles, "A Critique of the Internal Colony Model," and Barrera, *Race and Class in the Southwest*, pp. 174-219.

[25] E.g., Segura, "Challenging the Chicano Text," and Deena Gonzáles, "Gender on the Borderlands."

of the emerging Mexican American middle class during the 1940s and 1950s and of groups willing to make certain accommodations to Anglo culture, such as LULAC [the League of United Latin American Citizens].[26]

Some valuable work has been done on the history of Hispanics and Latinas/os in Colorado. Two collections of descriptive essays were published in 1976, the year of Colorado's Centennial celebration. *Hispanic Contribution to the State of Colorado*, edited by José de Onís, and *Hispanic Colorado*, edited by Evelio A. Echevarria and Jose Otero, focus on southern areas of the state settled initially by New Mexicans or people coming from Spain: the San Luis Valley, on the western side of the Sangre de Cristo Mountains; and Huerfano and Las Animas Counties to the east of that range. The authors are especially interested in the Spanish/Mexican/New Mexican presence prior to the early twentieth century and in the survival of traditional folklore, art, and religious practices. The essays edited by Vincent de Baca in *La Gente*, published in 1998, extend through the twentieth century, and some offer a more theoretical approach. Jody and Gabriel Lopez's *White Gold Laborers* describes Latinas/os in the town of Greeley, not far from Boulder County, and a recent collection edited by Arturo Aldama and others, *Enduring Legacies*, brings together historical studies and sophisticated cultural analyses of Colorado's people of color.

The four interpretive questions explored throughout this volume and the next build upon more specialized scholarly work. For the first topic—women's experiences—Vicki Ruiz offers a useful conceptual framework and comparative information. Ruiz argues that a key feature of Latinas' lives was their ability to integrate activities within the home, work, and community.[27] She stresses mutual assistance among Latinas, with relatives, *comadres*, and neighbors, and introduces the concept of "cultural coalescence" to describe how Latinas "navigate across cultural boundaries," though limited by racial and ethnic prejudice.[28]

Closer in geographic focus to the present study is Sarah Deutsch's examination of Spanish-speaking people from New Mexico who settled in southern Colorado in the decades after 1880. Between 1900 and 1940, some of them moved northwards to the South Platte Valley, including a small part of Boulder County. Deutsch shows how New Mexicans attempted to maintain the village economies and social and

---

[26] Manuel Gonzales, *Mexicanos*, esp. pp. 181-190 and 224-225.
[27] Ruiz, *From Out of the Shadows*, pp. xii-xiv and 4-6 for this and below.
[28] Ibid., p. xiv.

cultural traditions brought from their home communities. She argues that women suffered a loss of status and social integration when they came to northern Colorado, whether their families were temporary workers who lived in the area only during the agricultural season or had settled here year-round. Whereas Hispanic women had been at the center of village life in New Mexico and were still active participants in the settler communities in southern Colorado, they became "isolated and peripheral" when living on Anglo-owned farms or in Anglo towns in the north.[29]

A second issue addresses relationships within Latino families, especially between husbands and wives and between elders or middle-aged people and their younger relatives. It thus examines both gender-based and generational components of family life. For these topics, we have some important studies of more recent families, especially those struggling with economic and/or migration-related challenges, but they lack a historical perspective.[30] Conversely, several analyses of young Latinas/os in the past pay only secondary attention to their family relationships.

A third question concerns the southwestern borderlands and the extent to which experiences of Boulder County's Latinos—living on the northern edge of that area—resembled those of people in more heavily Latino communities. A narrow geographical definition of the borderlands, including only those states of the U.S. and Mexico that adjoin the national boundary, would of course exclude Boulder County entirely: it lies 650 miles north of the Mexican border and 300 miles north of New Mexico. But "borderlands" is a term open to many meanings. Some analyses of the Southwest consider how this region has developed distinctive, dynamic, and often transnational characteristics in such areas as economic activity, demographic patterns, social institutions, and cultural life.[31] The borderlands were

[29] Deutsch, *No Separate Refuge*, p. 12 and ch. 6.

[30] E.g., Zambrana, *Latinos in American Society*, Angel and Angel, *Hispanic Families at Risk*, and Falicov, *Latino Families in Therapy*. For below, see Escobedo, *From Coveralls to Zoot Suits*, Alvarez, *Power of the Zoot*, and Muñoz, *Youth, Identity, Power*.

[31] For studies using a more inclusive definition, see, e.g., Cadava, *Standing on Common Ground*, Castañeda, ed., *Gender on the Borderlands*, Foley, *Mexicans in the Making of America*, Hernández, *Working Women into the Borderlands*, Martin, *Borderlands Saints*, and Martinez, ed., *U.S.-Mexico Borderlands*. Especially during the 1960s and 1970s, the borderland states acquired yet another meaning for some Spanish-surnamed residents, who regarded the area they termed *Aztlán* as their homeland (John Chávez, *The Lost Land*, pp. 1-5 and ch. 7).

also a region of unusual intercultural contact, ethnic or racial mixing, and hybridization. Using a broader definition, Boulder County in the twentieth century was situated on the far northeastern margin of a socio-cultural region that extended through New Mexico and in some respects down into Mexico itself.[32] It was also influenced to some extent by participation in a more localized network that included the Latino population in Denver, some 30 miles to the south, and a small agricultural community in Fort Lupton, 10 miles southeast of Longmont.[33] How, then, did Boulder people resemble or differ from people living in predominantly Latino areas of states like New Mexico and Texas and the *barrios* of major cities?

The final topic examined here is how Boulder County's Latinos defined their ethnic identity, how they described themselves and their relationship both to the Anglo world around them and to their own cultural heritage. During the 1940s, 1950s, and early 1960s, many Hispanics elsewhere in the Southwest sought to characterize themselves and their culture.[34] As part of what is sometimes labelled "the Mexican American generation," they wanted to create their own identity rather than accepting the generally negative descriptions imposed upon them by Anglos.[35] Some urban and largely middle class, educated Mexican Americans believed that Latinos would benefit from selective adoption of Anglo approaches, rather than defining themselves as part of an entirely distinct culture and then having to deal with the resulting alienation and discrimination. Many of these people were active in moderate political or social organizations that worked for the general betterment of all Hispanics, such as LULAC. In another response, young Mexican Americans in some of the major southwestern cities—both men and women—dressed in "Zoot Suit" or *pachuco* clothing and strutted their stuff on the streets and in dance halls and jazz clubs.[36] By forming their

[32] Deutsch refers to a Hispanic "regional community" that stretched across New Mexico and Colorado in the early twentieth century (*No Separate Refuge,* pp. 9-10), Acuña presents the histories of New Mexico and Colorado as intertwined (*Occupied America,* e.g., p. 191), and the editors of *Enduring Legacies* assume that Colorado forms part of the borderlands (pp. 1-20).

[33] For examples of interactions within this network see Vol. II, Chs. 4B and 5A.

[34] E.g., John Chávez, *The Lost Land,* ch. 6, esp. pp. 113-114 and 126-127, and Gutiérrez, *Walls and Mirrors,* chs. 4-5, plus the references in notes 35 and 36 below.

[35] E.g., Rosales, *Chicano!,* ch. 6, and Manuel Gonzales, *Mexicanos,* pp. 181-190, for this and below.

[36] Alvarez, *Power of the Zoot,* pp. 2-10, and Escobedo, *From Coveralls to Zoot Suits,* ch. 4; cf. Ch. 5C below.

own groups that were visually distinguished from the mainstream, they defined themselves as separate and claimed dignity in a society that did not accept them. As we shall see, concern about identity in Boulder County took different forms.

Sources

In describing the history of Boulder County's Latinos and investigating the issues described above, we are fortunate to have an unusual array of primary sources.[37] Several clusters of material were generated by previous initiatives but recovered, converted into modern formats, and put online by the BCLHP in 2013-2014. A project called "Boulder's Chicano Community: Where Is It?" tape-recorded 13 interviews in 1977-1979, mainly with older people, and made 2 movies.[38] In the summer of 1979, Latino teens from migrant worker families conducted 12 interviews with local people, took photos, and prepared a booklet called *El Aguila*. A group led by Oli Olivas Duncan set up the Longmont Hispanic Study [LHS] in the late 1980s. Duncan published a little book called *We, Too, Came to Stay* in 1988, with transcripts of interviews with 10 local people, photos, and some information about the history of Mexico and Latinas/os in the Southwest.[39] The LHS also gathered 600 photographs from members of the Latino community and converted them into slides for use in presentations about their findings.[40] Duncan later interviewed or

[37] Primary sources are defined as those produced by people living at the time they describe or by people who have been given first-hand accounts by relatives or friends about their experiences. Such sources may include interviews, written descriptions, photos, physical objects, or newspaper articles that are contemporary with the events they report. Primary sources may be personal and qualitative, like oral history interviews and family biographies, or listings that lend themselves to quantitative or numerical analysis, such as records about school children and their parents, or City Directories giving the names and occupations of residents. Secondary studies are written after the period they describe, drawing upon primary sources to create a composite picture. General histories of Colorado and textbooks are examples of secondary studies.

[38] In 1991, one of the movies was shown to a community group, followed by a panel discussion about what had changed in the intervening 15 years. Audio tapes of the original interviews had been stored at the Carnegie Branch Library for Local History in Boulder, and individual local people had kept copies of the two films and a home movie of the 1991 discussion. The BCLHP translated/transcribed those interviews that had previously not been done and made DVDs of the films.

[39] That title refers pointedly to the standard history of Longmont, called *They Came to Stay*, which pays scant attention to Latinas/os.

[40] In 2013, these slides, which were not labeled or identified, were loaned to the BCLHP, which digitized them, gave them simple descriptive titles, and held a viewing session with Longmont seniors, who were able to name some of the people shown.

obtained short family biographies from another 10 people for a planned second edition of *We, Too, Came to Stay*; she had prepared rough transcripts of those materials and generously given them to the BCLHP before her death in fall, 2013. In 2012 the Boulder Hispanic Families project collected family photos and biographies for an exhibit at the Boulder Public Library and prepared a house-by-house map showing where Latino, Italian, African American, and other families lived in the Water + Goss Streets neighborhood in 1955.[41]

Other organizations were meanwhile gathering additional information. The Maria Rogers Oral History Program at the Carnegie Branch Library for Local History, part of the Boulder Public Library, and an oral history project in Lafayette interviewed 14 other Latinas/os between 1975 and 2013, for which tapes, videos, or transcripts were preserved. In 1989, the Lafayette Historical Society, directed by James Hutchison, published a volume as part of the community's 100th anniversary.[42] The group solicited family biographies and wrote up brief accounts of important events by year. Twenty-eight of the biographies were about Latino families, and the annual descriptions described some others. Meanwhile, the Longmont Museum was building a fine collection of photographs, many of which are available on its website; the Lafayette Public Library likewise acquired some old photos, including ones from the local Miners Museum, and is putting them online.

Volunteers with the BCLHP produced a good deal of new material in 2013-14. They conducted interviews with 41 Latinas/os and transcribed them. Those interviews plus previous ones yield a total of 100, a large number for Latinas/os living in one relatively small county. Further, they cover an unusually long time span. Some of those done in the late 1970s were with elders born around 1900; some of those from 2013 were with high school and college students born in the 1990s. The interviews thus span three or even four generations.

Because much of the information presented in this study comes from oral history interviews or biographies written by family members about their earlier relatives, we face the question of the reliability of such sources.[43] An interviewer's questions and responses can affect what

---

[41] For this neighborhood, see Vol. II, Ch. 2B.

[42] *Lafayette, Colorado: Treeless Plain to Thriving City.*

[43] For a convenient introduction to the extensive literature on the benefits as well as the drawbacks of such material, see Perks and Thomson, eds., *Oral History Reader.*

speakers say, and interviewees' memories are by no means infallible. Descriptions of one's own life or those of relatives are sometimes shaped by nostalgia or—whether consciously or not—a desire to present people in the most favorable light, perhaps leading to exaggeration of achievements or exclusion of potentially embarrassing material. Historians may not have an opportunity for direct confirmation or refutation of statements made by one person in a situation remembered by someone else.[44] We must therefore always remember that statements made by individuals about themselves or their families should not be accepted simply at face value.

As scholars who rely upon oral history have noted, the best way to address the potential flaws with subjective personal sources is to set such narratives against other types of evidence, as this study does. If people's individual impressions can be checked against more neutral sources, differences sometimes emerge.[45] To produce a broader narrative and correct for individual variation, the BCLHP combed through microfilms of early newspapers, finding hundreds of useful articles. Scans of slides made by the LHS plus 225 new photos loaned by local people in 2013 resulted in a total of 825 visual images stretching from the early twentieth century to the early twenty-first.

Particularly interesting—because less often used in local studies of people of color—is the quantitative information generated by the BCLHP. Volunteers spent hundreds of hours plowing through sources that lend themselves to numerical analysis, pulling out information about people with Spanish surnames and entering into it spreadsheets. They used three main types of evidence: (1) U.S. Census records, 1900-1940, which describe where all local residents were born, their age and family position, and what kind of work they did; (2) *Polk's City Directories* for our three towns, 1904-1975, which list the names and addresses of adults in each household, street by street, and in some cases give their occupations and employers; and (3) annual School Census books, 1905-1964, which provide the names, year and place of birth, address, and

---

[44] An interesting example from this study concerns the description given by an older participant about the type of work she did for a particular company five decades before. A younger relative who read her account commented that she often tended to inflate: actually she held a much lower level job, not the skilled position she claimed.

[45] See, for example, the common belief among Longmont residents that housing was traditionally segregated along ethnic lines between the east and west sides of the town, a pattern not entirely supported by quantitative evidence about where people actually lived in various decades (see Vol. II, Ch. 2B).

grade level for children and sometimes information about their parents. The resulting quantitative analyses as presented in tables in this and the second volume are therefore based on extensive but almost certainly incomplete data. The original listings may have missed some people, and the BCLHP's volunteers perhaps failed to recognize certain surnames as Latino; Latinas who married men with non-Latino surnames will also have been omitted, though marriage across ethnic lines appears to have been uncommon in Boulder County until around 1970.

The BCLHP prepared material in other media too. A young film-maker worked with long-term residents to produce a video for each of the three towns, describing sites that have been of historical importance to Latinas/os. A local songwriter and performer re-recorded two of his songs that were emblems of the Chicano student movement in the 1970s but had not been preserved in audio form. The interactive town maps are a unique contribution of this project. *Polk's City Directories* have been employed to generate information about where each Latino-surnamed family lived, displayed as markers on street maps of the three towns, one per decade between 1904 or 1916 and 1975.[46] By clicking on one of the markers, viewers are given the street address, names of adults, and sometimes their occupations and employers. College students are identified separately. Hence it is possible to see where individual families lived and to trace the changing location and density of Latino neighborhoods over time.

C. Some Nineteenth-Century Background

Before we begin a detailed examination of Boulder County Latinas/os after 1900, it will be helpful to survey briefly some features of nineteenth-century history in the regions of Colorado discussed here.[47] Around 1800, the part of Colorado lying on the eastern side of the Rocky Mountains was used seasonally or occasionally by some Utes, Lakotas, and other indigenous peoples; by around 1820 the central section of

[46] See bocolatinohistory.colorado.org, under Interactive City Maps. The Boulder maps start in 1904, the other two in 1916. The idea of creating these maps came from Emmanuel Melgoza, one of the interns with the BCLHP in summer/fall, 2013; he also did the initial work on the databases that underlie them.

[47] General information will not be referenced; for fuller accounts, see, e.g., Abbott et al., *Colorado*, and Ubbelohde, Benson, and Smith, *A Colorado History*.

that area was the base for many Arapahos and Cheyennes. Over time, as Spanish-speakers moved north from New Mexico and as Anglos arrived from the eastern or mid-western U.S., many Native Americans were killed by disease, starvation, or warfare. Those who remained were evicted from their traditional hunting grounds and sent to reservations in the later nineteenth century, despite the many treaties signed—but then broken—by the U.S. government that guaranteed their right to certain territories.

Utes were the primary indigenous group active in the areas of southern Colorado that were settled initially by New Mexican immigrants. (The Utes consisted of many distinct bands, some of which dominated western sections of this state and parts of Utah and far northern New Mexico as well.) The series of treaties between leaders of the various bands and the U.S. government provides a painful illustration of the step-wise removal of Indians from land that was coming into demand for privately owned ranches and farms or mining.[48] The year after the Treaty of Guadalupe Hidalgo of 1848, seven Ute groups signed a peace treaty with the victorious Americans. In 1863, some of their leaders were persuaded (or forced) to abandon their claim to the San Luis Valley, in south-central Colorado, which had previously been a major hunting area. Five years later, another treaty required them to relinquish their right to that part of Colorado Territory that lay east of longitude 107° west (a line running north-south about 30 miles west of the San Luis Valley). In return, their right to all of Colorado west of that line was affirmed. But that guarantee was likewise violated. In 1878 a treaty created two reservations in the southwest corner of the state for those Utes who were still in Colorado—one for the Southern Ute bands, the other for the Mountain Utes—but they were obliged to give up their claim to all other land. The new reservations offered scant economic resources and for many Utes were far away from their previous hunting regions. The final stage came with the defeat of the White River band by the U.S. Army in the Ute War of 1879, leading to the dispossession and forced removal of the White River and Uncompahgre Utes to reservations in the Utah desert and a reduction in the size of Colorado's Southern Ute reservation.

In Boulder County, the main native peoples in the mid-nineteenth century were the Arapahos and the Cheyennes, who had formed a lasting

---

[48] Abbott et al., *Colorado*, pp. 87-93, and "Ute People," Wikipedia, accessed Oct. 6, 2014.

alliance around 1811 before the latter moved into this region. In the Fort Laramie Treaty of 1851, U.S. government officials affirmed the right of the Arapahos and Cheyennes to a large expanse of territory on the great plains between the North Platte River and the Arkansas River; that area included most of what is now Boulder County. As the number of white trappers, prospectors, and settlers increased, however, especially after the discovery of gold in Colorado in 1858-9, conflict between newcomers and native people increased. The number of Arapahos and Cheyennes dropped markedly, due to disease, battles between Indian warriors and U.S. army troops, and the take-over by whites of land formerly used for hunting.

In what became known as the Sand Creek Massacre of 1864, some 700 Colorado Territory militiamen attacked a village and camp led by Southern Arapaho Chief Niwot ("Left Hand") and Southern Cheyenne Chief Black Kettle, who had gathered for what they had been told was a peaceful meeting. By the end of the battle, 170 to 200 Indians had been killed and often mutilated, two-thirds of them women and children, some raped or shot for sport.[49] The last major battle in Colorado between the Arapaho-Cheyenne and U.S. forces was fought in 1869. The remaining Northern Arapahos were relocated to the Wind River Reservation in Wyoming, the Northern Cheyennes to a reservation in southern Montana, and the Southern Arapahos and Southern Cheyennes to a reservation in Oklahoma.

Because native peoples had been almost entirely removed from Boulder County by around 1900, they appear in this study only in passing. Some later Latino residents of this area had indigenous forebears, though not from this immediate region, and we encounter a few references from Spanish-speaking communities in southern Colorado in the early twentieth century.[50] But this project found no mention of native people interacting with Latinas/os in Boulder County itself after 1900. Their absence should not, however, absolve us of the obligation of remembering that this region—whether used by Latinas/os or Anglos— was taken by force or duplicity from its original inhabitants.

The history of Spanish-speaking people in Colorado dates back to explorers from Spain or Mexico who began to enter the area that has

---

[49] Abbott et al., *Colorado*, p. 86.
[50] See Ch. 2B-C below.

become the southwestern U.S.—including this state—in the 1540s.[51] They were followed by settlers, who over time reached the northern part of what is now New Mexico and a piece of southern Colorado. Northern New Mexico was first colonized by Don Juan de Oñate, who created the Province of Santa Fé de Nuevo México in 1598, part of the Viceroyalty of New Spain. The town we know as Santa Fé was founded in 1607 by New Mexico's second Spanish governor, Don Pedro de Peralta; three years later, he made it the capital of the province. Santa Fé therefore has the longest history of any state capital in the U.S. It should be noted that this activity took place 13-22 years <u>before</u> the English "Pilgrim fathers" arrived in Massachusetts!

On the basis of grants from the Spanish crown, colonists moved north from central Mexico and created new villages on land taken from Pueblo or other indigenous peoples. After Mexico achieved independence from Spain in the war of 1810-1821, the northern reaches of the old empire became part of the new republic. The area under Mexican control was defined in 1819, when the U.S. government formally abandoned its claim to land south and west of the Arkansas River, including some of the San Luis Valley and adjacent parts of southern Colorado. Over the next few decades, the Mexican government awarded additional grants of land in those areas.

When the United States annexed Texas (which had always been part of Mexico) in the mid-1840s and invaded Mexico to secure its new state, it triggered the Mexican-American War of 1846-1848. In the Treaty of Guadalupe Hidalgo that concluded that conflict, Mexico ceded New Mexico and the southern edge of Colorado (as well as Texas down to the Rio Grande, Arizona, and parts of Nevada, Utah, and California) to the United States. People living in those areas could either move further south to remain in Mexico or stay where they were, becoming Americans. Hence New Mexicans sometimes comment that they did not cross the border to come into the United States: the border crossed them. The Treaty of Guadalupe Hidalgo also said that those Mexicans who wished to remain in the new country would have full rights as American citizens.[52] The government made some effort to follow through with that promise, such as instructing U.S. Census takers to count people of Mexican/New

---

[51] The summary in this and the next three paragraphs is drawn from Echevarria and Otero, eds., *Hispanic Colorado*, de Baca., ed., *La Gente*, and Aldama et al., eds., *Enduring Legacies*.

[52] That was rather surprising. Few non-whites were eligible for U.S. citizenship at the time, yet many Mexicans had a mixed racial ancestry.

Mexican background as "white" between 1850 and 1920. But nominal citizenship by no means ensured equal treatment in practice.

The Treaty also stated that the U.S. government would respect the previous land grants (*mercedes*) made first by the Spanish crown and later by independent Mexico, though none of those three countries recognized the sovereignty of indigenous peoples. Some of the Spanish and Mexican awards were communal, made to an entire village, while others went to wealthy individuals who then brought in settlers. Five to seven of the grants included land in what was to become Colorado.[53] Most lay to the west of the Sangre de Cristo Mountains—in the San Luis Valley or immediately to the south of it—but the huge Vigil and St. Vrain Grant (comprising 97,000 acres) was located to the east of the Sangre de Cristos, containing the later counties of Las Animas and Huerfano.

By the mid-nineteenth century, settlers from New Mexico and occasionally from Spain were starting to colonize regions of southern Colorado that lay within those grants. They generally tried to recreate familiar patterns of village layout, architecture, and community life in the new settings.[54] At the southern end of the San Luis Valley, the towns of San Luis de la Culebra and San Acacio were founded in 1851 and 1853.[55] On the eastern side of the Sangre de Cristos, New Mexican family groups settled the town of Aguilar and the adjacent valley of Trujillo Creek beginning in the 1860s.[56] The town of Trinidad was named after the daughter of Don Felipe Baca, who with Don Pedro Valdez and 12 other families founded the town in 1861.[57] By 1870, 90% of the 6,400 residents of Las Animas and Huerfano Counties had either been born in New Mexico or were the children of New Mexicans.[58]

But the protection of earlier land grants offered by the Treaty of Guadalupe Hidalgo was not realized on the ground. As Anglo settlers began to move into New Mexico and southern Colorado, they joined a few wealthy Hispanics in going to court to establish their own claims to property. U.S. courts demanded written documentation that met the requirements of American law, not of Mexican law. Because few people

---

[53] Abbot et al. say five (*Colorado*, p. 34); Charles Vigil, "Mexican Land Grants," and Tushar, *People of "El Valle*," pp. 9-18, give larger figures.

[54] Lucero, "Aguilar and Its Western Valley," and Atkins, *Human Relations in Colorado*, pp. 93-95.

[55] Tushar, *People of "El Valle*," pp. 14-15.

[56] Lucero, "Aguilar and Its Western Valley."

[57] LARASA, "Contributions of the Spanish Surnamed American," p. 10.

[58] Abbott et al., *Colorado*, p. 35.

living on the previous grants had sufficient proof of their rights, they were vulnerable. Even if they were able to hold on to the agricultural land at the center of their grants, they commonly lost the right to graze animals and take wood from nearby hills or mountains, provisions necessary to their economic survival. Over the course of the later nineteenth and early twentieth centuries, these problems led to the impoverishment of many villagers and eventually contributed to their migration to other areas, including Boulder County.[59]

Until around 1900, a few Hispanic settlers with large ranches in Las Animas and Huerfano Counties prospered. They were also active in Colorado's emerging state government. Casimiro Barela, who had moved from northern New Mexico to the Trinidad region, became one of the richest stockmen in Colorado Territory and was a director of the Trinidad and San Luis Railroad.[60] Barela served in the territorial and later the state legislature from 1867 to 1912, representing Las Animas County; throughout his career, he worked to preserve Hispanic culture and fight discrimination, helping to guard Spanish-speaking people from the "strange bureaucracy" of Anglos.[61] In the Legislative Assembly of January, 1876, when Colorado became a state, Barela was joined by 12 other Spanish-surnamed legislators, all representing southern areas.[62]

Economic success and political participation remained possible for a few decades longer. Tomás Aquino Rivera, 1849-1916, was the son of a shoemaker from Barcelona, Spain who had emigrated to Santa Fé.[63] Tomás or his father acquired land in Huerfano County, and he prospered as a rancher. In 1882 he was elected to the Colorado Legislature as a representative from Huerfano, Las Animas, and Costilla Counties. But as the number and power of Anglo settlers increased, Hispanics lost out. By 1915, only three men with Spanish names served in the state legislature, and by 1921 there was only a single one, representing Las Animas County. That decline was due in part to loss of land and the increasing socio-economic gap between Anglos and Hispanics; it was compounded by the problems faced by all ranchers and farmers in the region as the result of drought. In Huerfano County, most Hispanic landholders gave

[59] See Ch. 2B below.
[60] LARASA, "Contributions of the Spanish Surnamed American," p. 13. Whether that railroad actually operated is unclear.
[61] Abbott et al., *Colorado*, p. 39
[62] Charles Vigil, "Spanish-Surnamed Americans."
[63] "Salazar, Jose Benito and Isabelle, biography."

up farming during the first few decades of the twentieth century, many of them taking jobs in or associated with coal mines in that area.[64]

Apart from the regions of southern Colorado that had formed part of Mexico, the rest of the future state was part of the expanding United States. In a history well known from standard accounts, traders established regular patterns of exchange with native people during the first half of the nineteenth century, focusing on fur and buffalo hides. Among the stockades built to protect that commerce was Fort St. Vrain, located at the junction of the St. Vrain and South Platte Rivers, slightly to the northeast of Boulder County.[65] The discovery of gold, silver, and other precious metals in the mountains starting in the 1850s led to rapid immigration from elsewhere in the U.S. and other countries. During the latter half of the nineteenth and early twentieth centuries, after the deaths and forced removals of Indian peoples, the plains of eastern Colorado were gradually settled by Anglos, through individual homesteading or planned colonies.

We have no specific evidence that Hispanics lived or worked in Boulder County prior to around 1900. The first Spanish-named person to own land in what is now the town of Longmont was José Maricio Varos, a teamster who had fought in the New Mexico Militia and was awarded 160 acres in 1864 under the Military Bounty Land Grant Act.[66] But Varos sold the property to an Anglo the following year, without ever seeing it. Some of the trappers and traders who frequented Fort St. Vrain probably had Spanish-speaking wives.[67] In the western mountains, the prospectors who sought their fortunes beginning in the 1850s were mainly from European backgrounds, but use of the *arrastre* technique for processing ore may have been introduced by Mexican or New Mexican miners.

We turn now to the historical account. The first three chapters deal with the decades between 1900 and 1940, looking at immigration patterns, the contributions of Hispanics as workers, and the conflict, racism, and violence that shook the 1920s and 1930s. Chapter 5 explores the years between 1940 to 1965, while the next two examine the era of

---

[64] See Ch. 2C below.

[65] Ceran St. Vrain, a leading trader in this area, spent much of his life in New Mexico, married a Latina, and self-identified as Mexican-American, though his father was a Frenchman living in St. Louis.

[66] Duncan, "Hispanic History," p. 4.

[67] LARASA, "Contributions of the Spanish Surnamed American," p. 6.

Chicano identity and activism, 1966-1980. An epilogue takes us briefly into the twenty-first century.

Chapter 2

Early Hispanic Immigration
to Boulder County, 1900-1940

Nearly all of the Hispanics who came to Boulder County between 1900 and 1940 derived originally from Mexico or New Mexico, though some of their families had lived in southern Colorado for several generations before moving further north. Immigration to this area started slowly. The U.S. Census records for 1900 and 1910 include no more than six households headed by people with Spanish surnames or who were born in Mexico in any of the three towns (Longmont, Lafayette, and Boulder) in either year.[1] Beginning in the 1910s, however, the pace increased. The first set of new arrivals came from central Mexico in the 1910s and 1920s, and by the later 1930s they were joined by people moving from the northern part of New Mexico. In this chapter we look first at what was happening in Mexico and northern New Mexico and how those events contributed to the difficult decision to leave one's home, relatives, and friends to undertake a journey to an unknown place. We turn then to people who came to this area from southern Colorado, concluding with some quantitative information about patterns of migration.

A. Immigration from Mexico

Many of the earliest Spanish-speaking arrivals in Boulder County, or the parents or grandparents of people who later moved to this area, were from central Mexican states lying west and northwest of Mexico City. Some came initially as single men, but married couples and whole families came too. The few women who migrated singly or with their

---

[1] See App. 1.2. The towns were all very small in 1900. Longmont's population was 2,201; Boulder's was 6,150; and Lafayette's only 970 (see App. 1.1).

children, sometimes escaping abusive marriages, posed a challenge to familiar gender roles.[2] Mexican migration to northeastern Colorado reflects the existence of an extended trans-national borderland in the Southwest during the early decades of the twentieth century, across which people could move with relative ease.

Interviews and family histories indicate that Mexican immigrants came mainly from three states. The largest group was from Zacatecas, with smaller numbers from Guanajuato and Michoacán and a few from the adjoining states of Jalisco and Durango. (See Map 2.1.) It should be emphasized that none of these states lies close to the border with the United States: this was not merely a matter of traveling a short distance for temporary employment.[3] To the contrary, the nearest place at which one could cross into Texas was 350-500 miles away from those areas; to reach Ciudad Juarez and El Paso, a common entry point into New Mexico and then Colorado, immigrants had to travel 700-950 miles.

The three main Mexican states shared some features with Colorado. Zacatecas had for centuries been famed for its extremely profitable mines, especially silver. By around 1900, however, production had decreased. During the Mexican Revolution of the 1910s, its capital city was the scene of a major battle between government forces and the troops of Pancho Villa, a popular rebel leader, which resulted in Villa's victory but at the cost of thousands of lives on both sides. Guanajuato was likewise a mining center. One of its mines, La Valenciana, had accounted for two-thirds of the entire world's production of silver at its peak, but by the early twentieth century it and many of the other mines had either declined markedly or ceased production entirely. Michoacán, ridged with high mountain chains, featured a mixed economy of mining, forestry products, and agriculture. Because farming in that area generally required irrigation, some immigrants to Boulder County brought useful experience.

Mexico underwent considerable violence during the 1910s and 1920s.[4] The country was torn apart in the 1910s by a revolution against José Porfirio Díaz, the nation's president (and increasingly its dictator)

---

[2] For the special problems faced by female migrants, see Ruiz, *From Out of the Shadows*, ch. 1.

[3] The exceptions were people who lived in the Rio Grande Valley or Ciudad Juarez/ El Paso, where Latino communities existed on both sides of the border and local residents moved back and forth.

[4] For film footage from the Revolution, see "La Raza de Colorado: La Historia."

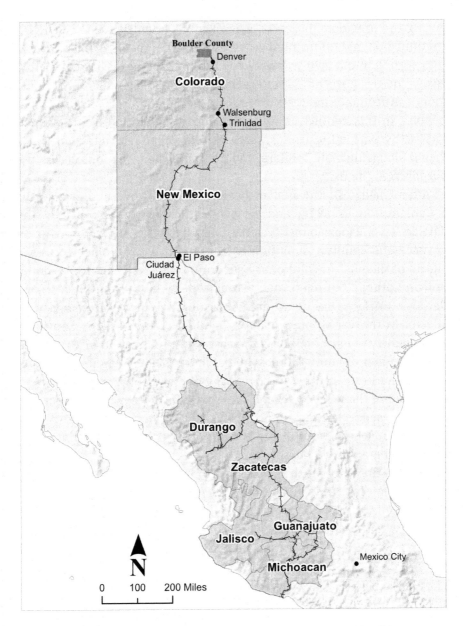

Map 2.1: *Mexican states from which immigrants came to Boulder County, 1900-1940, showing routes of main railroad lines*

during the previous 35 years.[5] Armed conflict, which started in 1910, continued on and off for nine years, as the initial revolt against Porfirio Díaz turned into a civil war between multiple factions with conflicting goals. The U.S. government intervened at several key points to support American economic interests in Mexico, especially control of oil producing regions. In this conflict as in earlier Mexican tradition, some women took active part in the armies. *Soldaderas* travelled with and sometimes fought alongside male soldiers, and they smuggled weapons across the border from the U.S.[6]

After Porfirio Díaz was overthrown, the new government adopted a Constitution in 1917, and a new political party, later called the Partido Revolucionario Institucional, was founded.[7] The Cristero War, an unsuccessful counter-revolution by conservatives who objected to the efforts of the post-Revolutionary government to limit the power of the Roman Catholic Church, brought renewed fighting in the later 1920s. Because warfare was widespread, if sporadic, most Mexicans were affected by the war at some point during the 1910s and 1920s. Some fled their country, at least temporarily, to escape the danger: in 1916, the U.S. Commissioner of Immigration said that more than one million Mexicans were living in the U.S.[8] We know that Boulder County residents were interested in the war, for several newspaper articles in 1916 described its causes, suggested that some local Mexicans were returning to their home country because of it, and laid out the reasons that might lead the U.S. to become involved in the war.[9]

In analyzing why Mexicans decided to leave their homes to venture into a foreign country, scholars often refer to "push" and "pull" factors.[10] The former consisted of problems within Mexico that made life there difficult, while the latter included the availability of work and the possibility of a more successful future for their children in their new home. For

---

[5] As Hart has shown in one of his foundational studies, three interest groups with contradictory class and cultural backgrounds participated in the Mexican Revolution: the elites of provincial towns and *pequeña burguesía* (the "petty bourgeois"); working class people in rural areas; and urban and industrial workers: *Revolutionary Mexico*, pp. x-xv.
[6] Salas, *Soldaderas*, esp. ch. 4. The long history of Mexican female warriors contributed to an emerging Chicana identity in the later 1960s and 1970s (ibid., chs. 6-7).
[7] The PRI monopolized power in Mexico until 2000.
[8] Hamilton, *Footprints in the Sugar*, pp. 265-266.
[9] "Mexicans going south" and "Causes of the Mexican trouble."
[10] E.g., Acuña, *Occupied America*, pp. 154-155.

both kinds of factors, large investors or companies in the U.S., part of an expanding economy that treated Mexico essentially as a colony, played an important role.

Many Mexicans migrated primarily because of economic hardship. As part of his "modernization campaign," Porfirio Díaz opened up opportunities to foreign—mainly American—investors for building railway lines and setting up large-scale commercial agriculture. By around 1900, U.S. investors owned more than a quarter of all land in Mexico, including many of the country's most valuable mining, industrial, and agricultural properties.[11] Mines and factories run by foreign companies had little incentive to concern themselves with the well-being of their workers. In rural areas, most of the millions of *campesinos* (peasants) who had previously held and worked their land through a variety of property systems lost their holdings between 1870 and the end of the century. By 1910, 90% of the *campesino* population was landless. For many of these men and women, the only options were to become paid workers on large *haciendas* devoted to export-based agriculture, or to take industrial jobs if they were available.

These economic problems were compounded by a rising birthrate, which caused the Mexican population to increase by 50% between 1875 and 1910.[12] Population pressure added to the difficult labor conditions on *haciendas* in central Mexico.[13] Due in part to a surplus of labor, real wages dropped during the Porfirio Díaz period, and a growing number of workers were caught up in the system of "debt peonage" which required them to stay with their current employer until they had paid off their debts to him.

By 1910, "famine stalked the dispossessed peasants and working classes" of Mexico.[14] The use of so much land for export purposes had raised the cost of food for domestic consumption. The Revolution caused the Mexican economy as a whole to weaken and made it impossible for the government to provide even the minimal social benefits that had formerly been available. If people no longer had their own piece of land and could not find enough work to support their families, it might be worth the massive dislocation of uprooting themselves and starting from scratch in hopes of creating a better life in the north. A common

[11] Hart, *Revolutionary Mexico*, pp. 158-162 for this and below.
[12] Ruiz, *From Out of the Shadows*, p. 7.
[13] Katz, "Labor Conditions."
[14] Hart, *Revolutionary Mexico*, p. 162.

element of their faith in this better life was that their children would be able to get an education and have a brighter future.

Fighting in Mexico provided additional motivation to leave. Because the conflict became a civil war, support for any of the factions could be dangerous. For those facing physical violence, a "better life" might simply mean a safer existence. Among Boulder County people, Pete Salas's grandfather left Mexico to flee the Revolution; Rich Lopez's grandfather left to avoid conscription in Pancho Villa's army.[15] Captain Manuel Bracamontes, who later came to Longmont, is commemorated by a statue in Zacatecas for fighting alongside Pancho Villa.[16] Al Ramirez's mother slipped out from Guanajuato to San Antonio to escape marrying a much older general, a match arranged by her father.[17] Virginia Alvarez's uncle was hanged during a conflict of the 1920s, and her father left by way of El Paso to escape a similar fate.[18] Some of the Mexicans whose families eventually settled in Longmont brought with them visual souvenirs of the war: photographs of Pancho Villa or officials in the new government.[19] Later, however, personal ties with Mexico weakened, even though social and cultural practices were often sustained.

The primary "pull" factor was the availability of jobs north of the border. Many Mexicans left because they were actively recruited by agents or contractors sent to Mexico by U.S. employers—especially railroad companies, mine operators, and sugar beet producers—to sign up workers.[20] The 15,000 miles of railway lines in Mexico recently constructed by U.S. capitalists made travel from that country to and across the U.S. border easy.[21] Recruitment of Mexican workers was especially common during World War I and after the passage of the Immigration Act of 1924 but before the Great Depression.[22] The 1924 measure was intentionally designed by the U.S. Congress to restrict

---

[15] Conversation with Marjorie McIntosh, Nov. 4, 2013; "Lopez, Rich, notes for his interview."

[16] Gonzales, Alex, interview, c. 1987.

[17] Ramirez, Albert, interview, 2013.

[18] "Alvarez, Virginia, notes for her interview." For another Revolution example, see "Arguello, Alfredo and Donaciana and family, biography."

[19] Included among the family photos gathered by the Longmont Hispanic Study in the late 1980s.

[20] For railroads, e.g., see Garcilazo, *Traqueros: Mexican Railroad Workers*, pp. 48-54.

[21] "Eracism: Exploring the Roots."

[22] The measure was formally titled the Johnson–Reed Act, including the National Origins Act and the Asian Exclusion Act (Pub.L. 68–139, 43 Stat. 153), enacted May 26, 1924.

immigration of people from the Middle East and Southern and Eastern Europe, including Jewish refugees; it prohibited entirely the entry of East and South Asians. Because natives of countries in the Western Hemisphere were excluded from the quota system, American employers who could no longer bring in cheap labor from places like Bulgaria or Italy turned to Mexico. When E. P. Archuleta returned to the Longmont area after serving in the U.S. Army in World War I, he was hired as a labor agent for a Colorado railroad company, recruiting workers in Mexico.[23] At the peak of this practice, more than 2,000 men crossed through El Paso every month to take jobs with the various railroads.[24]

For people who decided to leave Mexico early in the 1900s, entering the U.S. was a great deal easier than it was to be a century later. After 1917, people who crossed the border were supposed to stop, take a literacy test, pay a tax, and be given written documentation, but these requirements were not enforced rigorously. Some stretches of the boundary had no checkpoints at all, so people could just walk across. Even at formal entry stations, some Mexicans were allowed through without question, especially those brought in groups by large employers. Only after the beginning of the Great Depression in 1929 were Mexicans viewed as unwelcome competition for scarce jobs.

The leeway enjoyed by U.S. border agents in deciding who should be allowed to enter and what paperwork they needed to show or receive is illustrated by the experience of David Toledo. Born around 1902, Toledo grew up in a town in Michoacán where he began work as a tailor.[25] But when he was 20 years old, he decided to see what life was like "on the other side." When he reached the border, he put on the one suit he owned, which he had made himself. The officials looked at him and a friend who was travelling with him, who was equally well dressed, and put them into a different group from the people who were obviously manual workers. He and his friend paid an $8 fee and were given a certificate or receipt showing that they had come in legally, with a six-month pass. If he had returned to Mexico, he would have been reimbursed his $8. As it happened, he never went back to his home country and later became an

---

[23] Archuleta had moved to Colorado from Mexico with his parents in 1905, when he was eight years old. When he enlisted for the military during the war, he was assigned to Special Services because of his ability to speak four languages; he used that skill in doing translation and spy work (*They Came to Stay*, pp. 13-14).

[24] Hamilton, *Footprints in the Sugar*, p. 266.

[25] Toledo, David, interview, c. 1978.

American citizen.

Early migration from Mexico to Boulder County followed several different geographic routes. A few families came directly to the Denver/ Boulder/Longmont area. Leslie Ogeda reported that in the 1910s five men from Zacatecas came together to Boulder.[26] The group included her maternal grandfather and two of his brothers, named Zaragoza (later spelled Saragosa), who set up small ranches on the western edge of the town. Eleanor Montour's grandparents emigrated in 1914 from Durango, settling in Lafayette; her grandfather started working in the fields but later became a coal miner.[27] Victoria Gerardo, born in Jalisco in 1894, travelled alone across northern Mexico and through El Paso, Texas, reaching the Lafayette area in 1925; there she met and married Crescencio Martinez, who was employed at the Columbine Mine.[28]

Many of the Mexicans who ended up in Boulder County had gone somewhere else first. The most common pattern was that new immigrants started by working in the coal mines around Walsenburg and Trinidad in southern Colorado. As mining slowed in that area in the 1920s and 1930s, men moved their families north in hopes of finding work in the mines in or near Boulder County. Phil Hernandez's maternal grandparents moved from Zacatecas to the U.S. around 1909.[29] His grandfather, who had been a miner in Mexico, worked initially in the southern Colorado coal fields. During the summers, the whole family did migrant field work, including in eastern Boulder County. Later his grandfather found mining work here, and around 1934 the family settled in the town of Boulder. Linda Arroyo-Holmstrom's paternal grandparents travelled from Mexico first to a community near Trinidad, where her grandfather mined coal, and then to Lafayette, where he worked in the mines during the winter and did handyman jobs during the summer, before moving the family to Boulder.[30] Some immigrants worked in other states before coming to Colorado.[31]

---

[26] Conversation with Marjorie McIntosh, April 13, 2013.

[27] Montour, Eleanor, interview, 2013.

[28] "Martinez, Victoria Gerardo, biography." For other examples of direct early migration, see Alvarez, Teresa, interview, 1976, and Alvarez, Virginia, interview, 2013.

[29] Hernandez, Philip, interview, 2013.

[30] Arroyo-Holmstrom, Linda, interview, 2013.

[31] "Madrigal family of Boulder, biographies" and Gonzales, Alex, interview, c. 1987.

B. Arrivals from Northern New Mexico: A Complex Heritage

The other large group of Spanish-speaking immigrants to Boulder County prior to 1940 came from the villages and small towns of north-central New Mexico and the southernmost part of Colorado's San Luis Valley, which formed part of the same cultural community. Most northern New Mexicans had deep roots within the region, which had been colonized by their ancestors. Those settlers had moved from further south in Mexico, mainly in the seventeenth and eighteenth centuries. Dispossessing many of the indigenous peoples, they created agricultural communities in the hills and mountains around Santa Fé and to the north of it. Northern New Mexico had been part of the Spanish empire and then of independent Mexico since 1598, but because the region was at the very edge of New Spain and the Republic of Mexico, it experienced relatively little control from outside.[32] Santa Fé was 1,200 miles away from the center of the government in Mexico City; some villages were as much as 100 miles beyond Santa Fé, connected only by trails over difficult terrain. Hence these communities were largely free to function as they chose. Although some were located near Pueblo villages and their residents interacted with native peoples, they continued to think of themselves as part of the Spanish or Mexican cultural world.

Some Latinos living in Boulder County in the decades around 2000 could trace their families far back in northern New Mexico. Don Archuleta's father was a direct descendent of Ascencio de Arechuleta, a Basque soldier in the original Oñate colonization expedition of 1598; Ascencio later brought his wife and children with him to New Mexico.[33] The family of Maria Sabina Maes (Cortez) had a line of ancestors stretching back to the Santa Fé area in the 1630s or 1640s.[34] Linda Arroyo-Holmstrom followed her grandmother's relatives back seven generations through southern Colorado into northern New Mexico.[35] Ester Quintana Matheson traced her ancestry even earlier, to Coronado's exploratory expedition to New Mexico in 1540-42 and then to early settlers in the northern part of the province of Santa Fé.[36] When people

---

[32] See Ch. 1C above.
[33] Archuleta, Don, interview, 2009.
[34] Maes, *Following in the Footsteps*, pp. 2-3.
[35] Arroyo-Holmstrom, Linda, interview, 2013.
[36] Conversation with Marjorie McIntosh, April 4, 2013.

asked Ester, rather insultingly, when her family moved to this country, she pointed out that it was before the Mayflower and asked them when their ancestors arrived in the U.S.!

Jessie Velez Lehmann was one of the organizers of the 1977-8 project called "Boulder's Chicano Community: Where Is It?" When she was herself interviewed, Jessie described what she had learned about northern New Mexican life from conversations with older people whose parents or grandparents had moved from that area.[37] Most residents had lived in those villages and little towns for many generations and spoke no English. Nearly all the families held only small plots of land but might have communal access to the surrounding wooded areas. People cooperated, with everyone helping each other to plant and harvest food and maintain their families. They had many practical survival skills, which were necessary in isolated communities. They made their own clothes, butchered and cured their own meat, stored food in cool, earthen cellars, and made tools and kitchen utensils. If they needed something they could not produce themselves, they bartered (trading one kind of goods for another), rather than using money. They knew how to utilize medicinal herbs for treating illnesses, and for more serious physical or emotional problems, they had their own *curandero* or *curandera* (traditional healers). Their midwives delivered babies and looked after new mothers. Many people believed in black or white magic: *la bruja* (a witch or evil woman) was very real. Music was an important part of their culture. They played instruments and sang at baptisms, birthdays, and weddings, to celebrate a good harvest, or just to entertain themselves.[38] We can visualize some of these people and their activities thanks to photos preserved by later relatives living in Boulder County.

Even in the mid-twentieth century, some New Mexican villages retained a strongly communal nature. Secundino Herrera, who moved to Longmont from Mora County in 1951, commented later, "I was used to a small society and to being involved with it—for instance, the educational business and the community business in general—even constructive projects, such as food processing, road work, irrigation systems. I was also in charge of some of these programs myself."[39] But when he got to Colorado, he was expected merely to follow orders from the Anglo

---

[37] Lehmann, Jessie Velez, interview, 1978.
[38] See Vol. II, Illus. 1.13.
[39] Herrera, Secundino, interview, c. 1987.

Illus. 2.1. Espinoza family portrait, 1912, probably in no. New Mexico

Illus. 2.2. Engagement announcement, Pedro and Merenciana Chavez, aged 20 and 17 in 1911, probably no. New Mexico or so. Colorado

farmers who employed him.

Immigrants to Boulder County from northern New Mexico were joined by a few people from small communities at the southern end of the San Luis Valley in Colorado. The San Luis Valley is a large and high plateau surrounded by mountains except at the very south, where it adjoins New Mexico. Settlements in the southern tip of the San Luis Valley had been founded under the Conejos Land Grant, awarded by the Mexican government in 1833, and the Sangre de Cristo Grant of 1843. Both grants completely ignored the rights of the Ute Indians who lived in that area. In 1851, settlers from around Taos, New Mexico founded the town of San Luis de la Culebra, the oldest continuously occupied community in Colorado (though it was part of New Mexico until 1861). More New Mexicans arrived in the region after the Utes were dispossessed in 1868. The town of San Luis and its surrounding villages have maintained many older traditions to the present time.

While many accounts stress the Spanish characteristics, conservatism, and social and cultural cohesiveness of the northern New Mexican and southern Coloradan villages, there was also considerable ethnic, racial,

Illus. 2.3. Farm workers with mules, with adobe building in background,
probably northern New Mexico or southern Colorado

Illus. 2.4. Large group at a traditional wedding, with musicians,
probably northern New Mexico or southern Colorado

and religious diversity among the residents of those communities.[40] Some people had recent European ancestors, and not just from Spain. This is unsurprising if we remember that during the nineteenth century and first part of the twentieth, Santa Fé was situated at the western end of a great overland transportation route that connected the lower Missouri River west of St. Louis with the Southwest. Traders from the eastern and midwestern regions of the U.S. travelled along the Santa Fé Trail, as did immigrants from many European countries. Ancestors of Boulder County people include Tomás Estipol Rivera, who had come to the U.S. from Spain with his three brothers around 1840 and settled in Santa Fé.[41] There he met his wife, a local teacher and lawyer. On one side of Emma Suazo Valdez's family, her grandparents were a mixture of Spanish, French, Mexican, and English forebears.[42] Both William ("Hank") Blazón and Tony Montour got their French surnames from earlier paternal relatives. Conversely, Oli Olivas Duncan's great-grandparents, living in Las Truchas, New Mexico, had seven children by birth but also adopted four children named Hays who came west on an orphan train from New York City.[43]

Many northern New Mexicans had some Native American ancestors, not surprising since Spanish-speaking and indigenous people had lived in close proximity for several hundred years. Whereas until about 20 years ago, many Latinas/os were not comfortable talking about native parents or grandparents, the emphasis of the Chicano movement upon the constructive mixing of indigenous peoples with those of European background has led to more open discussion of the topic. The advent of DNA testing has also demonstrated that many families do indeed have Indian forebears, a matter of interest and even pride for some. Among Boulder County people, one of Emma Gomez Martinez's grandmothers was a Comanche; one of Virginia Maestas's was part Pueblo, part

---

[40] Southern California had an even more diverse population in racial/ethnic terms by around 1900, including American Indians, long-established Spanish-speaking residents, whites, recent immigrants from Mexico, Japan, and China, and a few African Americans. Almaguer argues that race became "the central organizing principle of hierarchical group relations in California," more powerful than class or gender (*Racial Fault Lines*, p. 209 and, more fully, pp. 4-9).

[41] "Salazar, Jose Benito and Isabelle, biography." For another immigrant from Spain, see Maestas, Virginia, interview, 2013.

[42] Valdez, Emma Suazo, interview, c. 1987.

[43] "Olivas, Ralph and Rose, biographical account." For the problems that could arise from such adoptions, see Gordon, *The Great Arizona Orphan Abduction*.

Illus. 2.5. Clefos and Apolonia Vigil,
from northern New Mexico
but living in Alamosa, Colorado, 1930s

Navajo.[44] Augustine Eliseo Cordova had an Apache grandmother, while Cleo Estrada thought that half of her forebears were Utes and Apaches.[45] Several local families who were not from New Mexico likewise had Indian ancestors.[46] Some early photos show people with what appear to be indigenous features, stemming perhaps from the *mestizo* background of their Mexican ancestors or perhaps through more recent relatives. The photograph in Illustration 2.5 above shows the grandmother and great-grandmother of one of the participants in the BCLHP. The family believes they have Indian antecedents, though they do not know from which nation.

Intermarriage between Spanish-speaking and indigenous people was intensified by the abduction of children. In this practice, common through the end of the nineteenth century and apparently even in the early twentieth, Indian or Hispanic children, usually around four to eight

---

[44] Martinez, Emma Gomez, interview, 2013; Maestas, Virginia, interview, 2013.

[45] Cordova, Augustine E., interview, 2013, and "Estrada, Cleo, autobiographical information."

[46] Hank Blazón's maternal grandmother was part Sioux (Blazón, William ["Hank"], interview, 2013); Oli Duncan's paternal grandfather Francisco was born in Texas to an Indian girl and a European father ("Olivas, Ralph and Rose, biographical account").

years old, were kidnapped from their birth families, treated almost as slaves, and raised to be part of the other culture.[47] Western American mythology has emphasized the capture of white children by Indians in the Southwest, and our study does provide a few examples. Andrew Borrego's great-grandfather came from New Mexico to homestead on 100 acres at the base of the Spanish Peaks, northwest of Trinidad; he established his water rights before 1876.[48] That area was the home of Ute Indians, and Borrego family tradition says it was common practice "for the Spanish settlers as well as the Indians to increase their male populations by kidnapping each other's boys." Because the Utes believed that redheads brought luck, and the Borregos were red-haired, three of their sons were taken.[49]

Girls too might be brought up by native families. Don Archuleta's grandmother, Donaciana Manchego, was born in 1848 somewhere in northern New Mexico.[50] When she was about seven years old, she was abducted by a group of Indians fighting the settlers. A few years later a military troop came from Texas to help put down the resistance. One of the soldiers entered a native camp and saw a girl who did not look indigenous. He took her back to Texas to live with his mother, and—when she was fifteen years old—married her. Dolores Silva's Spanish-speaking grandparents lived in Taos prior to their death in a car accident when Dolores's mother was just a baby.[51] She had Indian blood, "but we don't know for sure just what nation they were." The residents of Taos Pueblo adopted the infant and raised her until she was seventeen.

More commonly, however, Indian children were abducted and brought up within Hispanic households. Such people are sometimes described as *genízaros*.[52] Young Native Americans, especially girls, were sometimes kidnapped by bands of armed raiders and sold to Hispanic

[47] See, more generally, Brooks, *Captives and Cousins*.

[48] "Borrego, Andrew, biography."

[49] Family legend also says that Andrew's grandfather, who was raised as a Ute, later made his way home to his birth family, reportedly driving "2,000 fine horses and good blooded cattle" before him (ibid).

[50] Archuleta, Don, interview, 2009. [51] Silva, Dolores, interview, 2013.

[52] The term comes from the practice of the Ottoman Turks to demand an intelligent, strong young boy from each of the Balkan villages within their empire. The boys were taken to Istanbul, trained, and often became part of the elite imperial household guards known as the Janissaries. Spanish and Mexican officials sometimes placed *genízaros* in frontier buffer communities like Abiquiu and Belén (Thomas Andrews, personal communication).

families.[53] There they lived initially as household servants, in most cases gradually forgetting their own culture and absorbing the ways of their new families. As adults they usually married Hispanic men. Leslie Ogeda's paternal grandmother was a Ute who was "adopted" at age six by a family named Archuleta in New Mexico.[54] Oli Olivas Duncan's paternal great-grandmother Cecilia was the daughter of a Comanche chief named White Horse; she was "somehow" raised by a Spanish-speaking family named Roybal.[55] Virginia Maestas's paternal great-grandfather was adopted at age three from the Yaquis of Arizona by a Spanish rancher in New Mexico and as an adult thought of himself as Hispanic.[56]

Other social and cultural interactions with indigenous people were more casual. Roy Maestas recalled going to Taos Pueblo as a child in the late 1910s when his father went to visit people or trade; Roy would play with the native boys though they could not talk to each other.[57] Every Sunday he went to visit his grandparents in San Geronimo, now a ghost town; the Indians in that pueblo taught his father how to make a tea from an evergreen that grows in the mountains that cured his rheumatism. George Abila, who as a child in the 1910s was living in the foothills northwest of Walsenburg, mentioned a Spanish-speaking Apache named José Antonio who used to stay at their ranch.[58]

Another component of northern New Mexico's complex heritage was people of Jewish background, sometimes described as "crypto Jews."[59] They were the descendants of Jews who had been forced to convert to Catholicism in Spain or Portugal in the sixteenth or seventeenth centuries. To escape persecution, they came to Mexico but then had to flee again as an arm of the Inquisition became established in Mexico City. Little by little their families moved further north, to get farther away from powerful and potentially dangerous authorities. For them, the

---

[53] Or children might be stolen from Mexico and carried to New Mexico for sale: e.g., Valdez, Emma Suazo, interview, c. 1987.

[54] Conversation with Marjorie McIntosh, April 12, 2013.

[55] Duncan, "Hispanic History."

[56] Conversation with Marjorie McIntosh, July 31, 2013, and Maestas, Virginia, interview, 2013.

[57] Maestas, Roy, interview, 1978.

[58] Abila, Mr. and Mrs. George, interview, 1978.

[59] That term is not ideal in this context, however, for it suggests that people were deliberately hiding their Jewish faith. In northern New Mexico, many Latinos no longer remembered any Jewish ancestry. For a broader discussion, see Jacobs, *Hidden Heritage.*

remoteness of the isolated New Mexican communities was a plus. Recent DNA testing has found that a number of people in northern New Mexico and some in Colorado's San Luis Valley bear a distinctively Jewish gene. Some of these families have intermarried with Catholics and considered themselves Catholic for many generations, with no cultural memory of Judaism within their histories. A few recognize that certain traditions (such as avoiding pork, lighting candles on Friday evening with the curtains of the house closed, putting small stones on graves, or spinning tops at Christmas) were shaped by earlier Jewish practices.

The ethnic diversity and deep roots of some New Mexican families are illustrated by the research done by Al Ramirez, a retired professor at the University of Colorado at Boulder, about the background of his wife, Vera.[60] Vera was part of the thirteenth generation of a family that had lived in Mexico and New Mexico since the sixteenth century. Some of her ancestors were Jews who had arrived in Mexico in 1590, having escaped from Spain to Portugal and then across the Atlantic. Vera had other relatives who were part of the original Oñate expedition, while a third group included Native Americans who participated in the revolt of Pueblo Indians against the Spanish in 1680, forcing colonists to pull out of the region for many years. After the Spanish re-conquest, her Spanish and Indian ancestors began to amalgamate, a process that continued over the next two centuries.

Most of the northern New Mexican and southern Coloradan villages were economically and ecologically fragile. They generally had only a small amount of agricultural land, and limited rainfall made irrigation necessary if crops were to be grown. A common pattern was for all the residents to work together in maintaining the ditches and deciding how scarce water would be allocated. Animals, especially sheep, were an important part of the local economy, requiring use of the surrounding mountain areas for summer grazing. The need for wood for building and fuel together with *piñon* nuts and other mountain resources put a premium on access to forested hillsides. Most of the communities or their *patrónes* had been granted royal Spanish or Mexican charters, confirming their rights to these secondary areas as well as the central farm land of the village.[61] But because the U.S. government did not honor its promise in the Treaty of Guadalupe Hidalgo to respect the

---

[60] Ramirez, Albert, interview, 2013, and see Ramirez, *Vera's Journey*.
[61] See Ch. 1C above.

earlier charters, other people moved in and claimed title. Gradually the residents lost their property. More than 11,000 New Mexicans migrated to southern Colorado during the first decade of the twentieth century alone.[62]

The situation became desperate for many New Mexican villagers during the 1920s and 1930s. A two-year drought starting in 1917 had already made farming difficult, and the 1920s saw a series of economic recessions, with sharp changes in price. Further, after New Mexico became a U.S. state in 1912, it began to introduce property taxes, a factor that pushed some people over the edge financially. The 1930s offered the double blow of the Great Depression and bad weather. The period of sustained drought during the 1930s, which caused the Dust Bowl in parts of New Mexico and eastern Colorado as well as other states, sharply reduced agricultural yields. For all these reasons, many small farms were no longer able to support a family. Some people who were forced to leave eventually found their way to Boulder County.

Interviews and biographies describe some of the hardships that led Hispanics to abandon their homes in northern New Mexico. Maria Medina was born in Arroyo Seco in 1891, where her father had a small piece of land.[63] She never went to school and could not read or write. After her marriage, she and her husband both did field work around Arroyo Seco. They were resigned to poverty, but life became even more difficult during the Great Depression. They were paid only 50 cents per day for their labor, and it would take three days to earn enough just to buy lard for cooking. They ate only one kind of food until it ran out, and then tried to find something else. During the 1930s they decided to go to Colorado to look for better paying work.

Other New Mexicans had previously held land but lost it during the 1920s or 1930s. Reina Jaramillo Gallegos was from Belén, where her ancestors had received a land grant; when her parents failed to hang on to their property, they moved north.[64] Juan and Josephine Martinez came from families in San Geronimo, Cimarron, and Clayton, New Mexico,

---

[62] Acuña, *Occupied America*, p. 98.

[63] Medina, Maria, interview, c. 1978. Although Maria had lived in the Boulder area for many years prior to her interview, she spoke no English. Her interview is filled with regional usages from northern New Mexico and spoken with a strong local accent.

[64] Gallegos, Reina, interview, c. 1987. By that time, after many years of court battles, the family had recovered title to their land. For later New Mexican grants, see "Homestead Record of Land Patent, 1862" and "Homestead Record of Land Patent, 1915."

where they had a little property.[65] But due to the economic recessions of the 1920s, they had to abandon their land and became migrant workers. One of Oli Duncan's grandfathers was descended from a large landowner in the Chama Valley, New Mexico, but the family gradually lost its property; by the 1920s they were reduced to share-cropping, and during the Great Depression they came to Colorado as migrant farm workers.[66] Her other grandfather still had some land in Chama around 1920, but an epidemic killed all of his animals and those he was tending for other people, leaving him destitute after he had paid his creditors. He moved to Longmont and became a foreman for C. W. Pace, one of the biggest local ranchers.

We can trace the migration patterns of 26 people who left northern New Mexico or the adjacent area of the San Luis Valley between 1910 and 1940, observing where they went after moving away from their original homes. (See Map 2.2.) All these people or their children or grandchildren ended up in Boulder County, but they had often lived in other places first. Seven families or individual people went first from New Mexico to the coal mining area around Trinidad and Walsenburg. Six others began as seasonal agricultural workers in northeastern Colorado, in some cases spending the winters in the San Luis Valley. Seven settled first in the middle San Luis Valley, especially near the little town of Center, where large-scale production and storage/packing of potatoes on commercial farms owned by Anglos offered the possibility of year-round employment. Only six came directly and permanently to Boulder County. Because travel from northern New Mexico was relatively easy, many Hispanics who ended up in this area maintained close ties with their communities of origin and relatives at home. That cultural borderland stayed largely intact across the twentieth century.

The form of transport used by many New Mexicans who traveled north is interesting. American school children commonly learn about the brave settlers who crossed the prairie from the eastern or midwestern U.S. in covered wagons. But we are not told about the immigrants who moved into Colorado from the south, who used the same means of travel. A covered wagon filled many functions when there were no motorized vehicles, or if they were too expensive to buy. It provided shelter while

[65] "Martinez, Juan and Josephine; Marcella Diaz, biography."
[66] "Olivas, Ralph and Rose, biographical account," Duncan, "Some Notes," and Duncan, conversation with Marjorie McIntosh, April 12, 2013, for this and below.

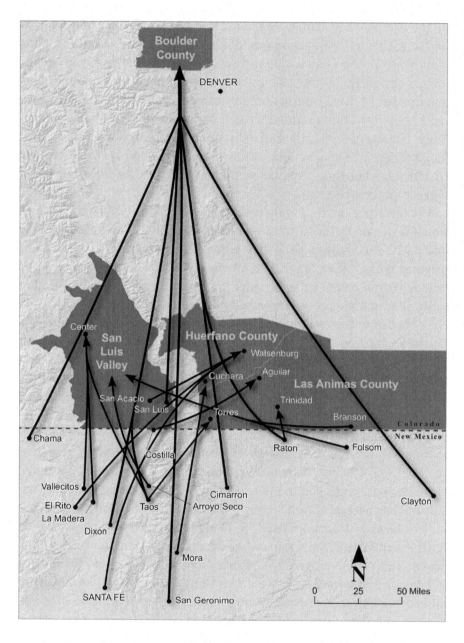

Map 2.2. *New Mexican villages from which immigrants came to Boulder County,*
either directly or after an initial move to southern Colorado

Illus. 2.6. Covered wagon (with old car) like those used by Latino migrants

the family was on the road, it could be pulled by animals that would be useful when they reached a good place to stay, and it carried all the essential household supplies and tools that the family might need later. Roy Maestas, later a Boulder resident, was born in 1909 near Taos, New Mexico.[67] When his parents abandoned their 5-acre tract of land and set off for Colorado, the family travelled in a covered wagon for two weeks before reaching the little community of Torres, west of Trinidad. It took Joseph and Emiliana Borrego a month in their wagon to move to Lafayette in 1912.[68] When Joseph Martinez's parents went north from southern Colorado in March, 1923, the trip took 17 ½ days because they ran into a bad snowstorm.[69] Covered wagons were used by early migrant workers too.[70] We should recognize that these iconic emblems of "The Western Movement" represent "The Northern Movement" as well.

[67] Maestas, Roy, interview, 1978.
[68] "Borrego, Joseph Garfield, biography."
[69] "Martinez, Joseph and Pauline, biography." See also Marquez, Sonia, interview, 2013.
[70] José Esquibel, who later owned pharmacies in Longmont, Boulder, and Denver, moved away from New Mexico with his parents when he was three; they had been living in a covered wagon while doing migrant work there (Esquibel, Jose, interview, 1979). When Juan and Josephine Martinez left their land in New Mexico in the mid-1920s, they travelled with a group of 20-25 other farm workers in covered wagons across northern New Mexico and southern Colorado ("Martinez, Juan and Josephine; Marcella Diaz, biography").

C. Newcomers from Southern Colorado

By around 1930, an increasing fraction of the Hispanic arrivals to Boulder County had lived in southern Colorado before settling here. A few were members of families that had ranched or farmed near the slopes of the Sangre de Cristo Mountains since the second half of the nineteenth century. Maria Sabina Maes's family had homesteaded in the mid-nineteenth century in the area that became known as Maes Creek in Huerfano County.[71] Shortly after her marriage to J. H. Cortez in 1899, the couple and their children began coming to the Longmont area as temporary farm workers; they became year-round residents around 1915. Frank Martinez, born in Huerfano County in 1890, grew up on his father's ranch.[72] In 1911, he came to the Longmont area as a beet worker. Early in the twentieth century George Abila's father was raising grain, hay, and sheep on his 120-acre ranch near the mountains of western Huerfano County.[73] Later the family moved to Walsenburg, because of employment opportunities in the mines and associated industries; from there they travelled to Boulder.

Other families had come initially from Mexico or New Mexico to the coal mining area around Walsenburg and Trinidad. As the mines there declined, they moved north, in some cases becoming migrant agricultural workers in northeastern Colorado before settling in Boulder County. Henry Rosales was born in the Spanish-speaking mining community of Aguilar (between Trinidad and Walsenburg), the son of parents who had immigrated from Mexico.[74] In 1933, his father brought the family to Lafayette, where Henry began work as a coal miner and crop harvester. Another Aguilar native was Emma Gomez (Martinez), born in 1928; her father had come from Mexico in the earlier 1920s, and her mother was from New Mexico.[75] After the family's move to Erie in 1929, her father worked in the coal mines in the winters and did field work in the summers.

---

[71] Maes, *Following in the Footsteps*, pp. 33-34, Cordova, Patsy, interview, c. 1987, and "Cortez, Jose Hilario ("J. H.") and Maria Sabina, biography."
[72] *They Came to Stay*, p. 158.
[73] Abila, Mr. and Mrs. George, interview, 1978. For another farmer, see "Archuleta family, biography."
[74] "Rosales, Henry and Alice, biography."
[75] Martinez, Emma Gomez, interview, 2013.

The former coal miners did not always remain in that type of work once they got to Boulder County. Romolo Martinez was born in Trinidad in 1886, part of a family that had lived in the Southwest for many generations.[76] After working as a miner near Trinidad and Raton, New Mexico for some years, he and his wife moved to Longmont in 1927. In this new setting, Martinez worked first as a carpenter and builder and later became a full-time employee on a local farm. David Manzanares, born in Walsenburg in 1917, came to Lafayette in 1938 looking for work in the mines; his wife Maggie had lived in the town since 1922.[77] Dave was a coal miner near Lafayette for 15 years, serving as president of the local United Mine Workers of America, but then he became a plumber.

Prior to around 1940, some degree of distance and even tension existed between immigrants from Mexico, New Mexico, and southern Colorado. People in the latter two groups were generally better educated than newcomers from Mexico, and they had generally had some previous contact with Anglo culture, even if they came from Spanish-speaking communities. Some New Mexicans, who were accustomed to running their own communities and might be lighter skinned, looked down upon Mexicans, whom they regarded as peasants.[78] But as adults from both groups came to know each other, and as their children and grandchildren went to school together and began to intermarry, those distinctions largely disappeared over the next two generations.

D. Quantitative Evidence about Immigration

The information presented above, drawn largely from family stories, is reinforced by quantitative measures of Hispanic immigration into Boulder County. The U.S. Censuses, taken every ten years between 1900 and 1940, provide valuable information about where residents and their parents were born.[79] Although the U.S. Censuses include a category for "Color or Race," those designations are not useful in identifying people from Spanish-speaking backgrounds, as a variety of terms were used

[76] *They Came to Stay*, p. 159.
[77] "Manzanares, David J. and Marguerite, biography."
[78] For similar tensions in New Mexico itself and other border states during the 1910s and 1920s, see Acuña, *Occupied America*, pp. 90-91 and 180-181.
[79] "Information about Latino-Headed Households in U.S. Census Records for Boulder," "Information about Latino-Headed Households in U.S. Census Records for Lafayette," and "Information about all Latinos in U.S. Census Records for Longmont."

from one census to the next, and even by different census takers in any given year.[80] In order to extract complete information from the Census materials, one must go through long files name by name. For Lafayette and Boulder, our analysis is incomplete, resting on information about households headed by someone with a Spanish surname as listed in Ancestry.com. Fuller information is available for Longmont, thanks to the painstaking analysis of the Census records done by Rebecca Chavez for her M.A. thesis at New Mexico State University.[81] She has included everyone who had a Spanish surname, was said to be Mexican, or was born in Mexico. That means that she has picked up not only household heads but also the children living in those families and boarders or roomers. In the information about birthplaces discussed below, it is important to remember that the evidence is much better for Longmont than for Lafayette and Boulder.

But even the Longmont analysis probably does not include everyone. Census takers may have written some surnames in their English equivalents. Although they went door to door to gather information, some residents—especially if they did not want to interact with a government representative—may have chosen to stay out of sight. Further, it seems highly likely that migrant workers were under-represented, perhaps excluded entirely. Because we cannot determine what fraction of all Hispanics were listed in the U.S. Censuses, we must regard the quantitative data displayed in Appendices 1.2 and 2.1 as showing only general patterns.

No one with a Spanish surname was included in the U.S. Census for 1900 in Longmont or Lafayette, but Boulder had two Hispanic households. An unmarried man from New York State was the co-owner of a farm, and a day laborer from New Mexico lived on university property with his wife and nine children, the oldest of whom was a student. A decade later, Lafayette and Boulder had no Hispanics, but six households in Longmont were headed by Hispanics or had at least one Hispanic living in them. Of the 17 adult men and women listed, eight had been born in Colorado, eight in Mexico, and one in New Mexico.

By 1920, Hispanic immigration was increasing. Lafayette now had 13 households headed by people with Spanish surnames, Boulder had 1, and Longmont had 31 that included Hispanics. The gender balance was almost entirely even. Of the 106 adults recorded, about one-fifth of the

---

[80] See Ch. 1A above.
[81] Rebecca Chavez, "Making Them Count."

men had been born in Colorado, as compared to two-fifths of the women. Some incoming men thus appear to have married women from this state. Two-thirds of the men and half of the women had come from Mexico, presumably reflecting poverty and the violence of the Revolution during the 1910s. Some may have lived in southern Colorado before reaching Boulder County. Only four people were born in New Mexico, implying that economic and weather-related difficulties had not yet become acute there. Four people had arrived from other states in the U.S., and two were from Spain.

The 1930 Census shows a different pattern. The number of people with Spanish surnames had risen sharply, to 294, 2.8 times more than a decade before. There were now somewhat more men than women (56% to 44%), indicating that some of the incoming males were single or had not brought their wives with them. A larger number of both men and women had been born in Mexico than in the previous Census (a total of 92 as compared to 61), probably a sign of ongoing disruption and economic suffering in that county during the 1920s. But the relative percentage of Mexican-born residents had dropped to just over one-third for men and one-quarter for women. A total of 69 men and women had been born in New Mexico, forming around a quarter of all Hispanics. Hard times in that state were obviously taking a toll. The largest group in 1930 consisted of people born in Colorado itself: 40-50% for both sexes. Some of these were presumably the children of people who had arrived from Mexico or New Mexico earlier in the century, while others came from Colorado's older Hispanic communities.

It should be emphasized that as early as 1930, the majority of the Hispanic population of these three towns (69%) had been born somewhere in the United States. Because they were by definition U.S. citizens, as were all future children of foreign-born immigrants living in this country, they should have been freed from any possible problems about their legal status. That was not always the case.[82] Moreover, if we examine where the parents of Colorado-born agricultural laborers and miners in the Longmont Census had themselves been born, we find that half to two-thirds of those parents were born in this country. That means that as early as 1930, the majority of these workers' families had been in the U.S. for at least three generations.

By 1940, the U.S. Census reports 354 Spanish-surnamed adults in

---

[82] See Ch. 4C below.

the three towns, a rise of only 20% over the past decade. The sharply diminished growth rate was probably affected by lack of employment during the Great Depression and possibly by deportation of Mexicans.[83] The proportion of men to women was almost identical to 1930, indicating that some men were still arriving on their own. The number of Hispanic residents born in Colorado had increased significantly (197 as compared to 128 in 1930); they now accounted for more than half of the total, for both men and women. More people had likewise been born in other American states than a decade before, some of them probably the children of migrant workers. The number of men born in New Mexico rose again, the result—one assumes—of the combination of the Great Depression and the terrible drought of the 1930s. The most surprising change was the marked decline in Mexican-born residents. That number had dropped to just 57, down from 92 ten years earlier. First-generation Mexicans now constituted only 16% of all Hispanics living in these towns; more people had been born in New Mexico than in Mexico. As of 1940, 84% of all Hispanics listed here were American-born.

Another source of numeric information is the annual School Census reports required by the state of Colorado from sometime in the late nineteenth century through 1964. On a given day each spring, all schools were required to fill out an entry book that asked for information about every student and sometimes his/her parents. For the children, most listings provide name, home address, birthdate, and grade in school; in some years and towns they also give the child's birthplace, previous school attended, the birthplace (or "nationality") of the parents, and occasionally whether the parents were literate. By searching for Spanish surnames, a labor-intensive task, volunteers with the Boulder County Latino History Project pulled out information about these children and families for one year per decade between 1905 and 1964 and entered it in spreadsheets.[84] The children listed in the school records were said to belong to "resident" families and hence probably excluded migrant workers. Further, we must be cautious in accepting the self-reported information about where parents were born: examination of entries for known people shows that several were listed as having been born in the U.S. who were actually from Mexico. Children's birthplaces seem to be

---

[83] See Ch. 4A and C below.
[84] "Latino-surnamed children in Boulder schools," "Latino-surnamed children in Lafayette schools," and "Latino-surnamed children in Longmont schools." For the limitations of this approach, see Ch. 1B above.

more reliable. Wherever possible the records were sampled for a middle year in each decade. The Longmont lists are complete for that full span, while the surviving books for Lafayette and Boulder are spottier.[85]

Starting in 1925, some of the school books provide information about the children's birthplaces, an indicator of their parents' migration history (see Appendices 2.2 and 2.3). Very few of the children were foreign-born, with the highest proportion (10%) seen in Lafayette in 1925. If they came from Mexican families, most of their parents had already moved to the U.S. before these children were born. In Longmont in 1925 and 1935, just under three-quarters of the Spanish-surnamed students had been born in Colorado; the others were born primarily in New Mexico. By 1945, 93% of Longmont's Hispanic school children had been born in Colorado or New Mexico. In Lafayette in 1935 and 1944, and in Boulder, 1935 through 1955, 89-100% of the children had similarly been born in those two states. This was an overwhelmingly American-born group of children.

We can trace immigration in the previous generation through the 1925 and 1935 School Census books, which indicate where the father and mother of each child were born.[86] In Longmont, nearly half of the children's fathers in 1925 were self-reported as having come from Mexico, with another quarter born in Colorado. Strikingly, however, just over half of the mothers were Colorado natives, with nearly a third from New Mexico. This again suggests that Mexican men were marrying American-born women. By 1935, fewer of the Longmont fathers were Mexican-born, with more from New Mexico, the same pattern visible in the U.S. Census data. In that year, around three-quarters of fathers and mothers alike said they had been born in this country.

The Lafayette and Boulder books record only the "nationality" of the parents. Those born in Mexico are described as "Mexican," people with Spanish names born in the U.S. are called "Spanish," and all other whites are called "American." So we can distinguish between Mexican-born and U.S.-born parents but cannot determine in which states the latter were born. In Lafayette in 1925, just over a quarter of both parents were said to have immigrated from Mexico, but by 1935, the proportion of U.S.-born parents was 78% to 89% for both Lafayette and Boulder.[87]

---

[85] For the grade level and age of school children in the three towns, see Vol. II, Ch. 6 and Apps. 6.1 and 6.2.

[86] See App. 2.4.

[87] See App. 2.4.

A small number of parents and children had been born in American states other than Colorado or New Mexico. Some of those from Texas may have lived in established Hispanic community near the Mexican border, such as Brownsville or El Paso, while others were probably the children of migrant laborers. Children born in Kansas or Nebraska were presumably the offspring of agricultural or railroad laborers, while the fathers of those born in Wyoming may have been beet workers, railroad men, or coal miners.

This chapter has shown that Hispanic immigrants to Boulder County during the first four decades of the century, who came mainly from three countries or states, commonly left their place of origin to escape severe poverty and/or fighting. After their arrival here, they initially formed fairly separate communities in social terms and identified themselves in contrasting ways. Over time, however, the groups moved closer together, in part through their interactions at work. It is the nature of that work that we explore next.

Chapter 3

The Contributions of Hispanic Workers, 1900-1940

The economic growth and prosperity of eastern Boulder County during the early twentieth century rested in large part upon two sectors with heavy demands for labor: agriculture, especially growing sugar beets; and coal mining. By around 1930, though not at the very beginning of the century, most of the workers in local sugar beet fields and many miners were from Spanish-speaking backgrounds. Other Hispanic men and women were employed in different kinds of agriculture, construction, or food processing plants. Without the hard physical labor they provided day in and day out, working under the burning sun in the fields, in dark and dangerous tunnels, or in hot, unventilated factories, Boulder County could not have gained the economic well-being it enjoyed then and subsequently.

The labor demands of agriculture and coal mining are shown in the 1930 U.S. Census. According to that survey, Boulder County had about 32,500 residents, of whom about 9,270 men and 2,280 women worked in "industry," the largest category, which included agriculture and mining.[1] Farming engaged the most people—around 2,600—of whom 1,290 men and 135 women were owners or tenant farmers; 1,130 men and 60 women were regularly employed "wage workers." The breakdown by sex obscures the fact that men were often joined in the fields by their wives and older children. The county's second largest occupation, coal mining, employed 1,125 men and 2 women according to the 1930 Census. Due to the nature of those types of work, many Spanish-speaking families lived on farms or in mining camps, not in the county's towns, through

---

[1] "Farm work and coal mining make most jobs." In Colorado as a whole, agriculture (primarily production of sugar beets and wheat) eclipsed mining as the primary source of economic growth in the early twentieth century: agriculture provided 27% of all jobs by 1920 (Abbott et al., *Colorado*, p. 181).

the 1920s.[2]

The types of jobs most commonly filled by Hispanics depended in part on their background. Thanks to information in the U.S. Censuses of 1920, 1930, and 1940, we can compare type of labor to place of birth for the three largest groups of Spanish-surnamed employees in Longmont and Lafayette: sugar beet workers, general or unspecified agricultural laborers, and coal miners. This analysis shows some degree of occupational stratification.[3] Most Mexican-born men did seasonal work in the beet fields, the lowest paid and least desirable type of employment. Immigrants from New Mexico had a better chance of finding year-round positions with farmers or ranchers or in coal mines, all of which offered somewhat better pay and usually housing. People born in Colorado were the most likely to get relatively good positions. In this chapter, we look first at Hispanic contributions to agriculture and coal mining and then at other types of male employment. A final section considers the work done by women and children.

A. Agricultural Work, Especially with Sugar Beets

Sugar beet production

Starting in the mid-1910s, many Hispanic laborers found employment in the sugar beet fields. In Boulder County, most beet workers were evidently hired as separate families, not as a team of male field hands as was common in some regions. Although it was the husband who signed the contract for a season and received payment after the harvest, the labor of other members of the family—especially during peak agricultural stages—was necessary to fulfilling that contract. Families came to the area early in the spring, living on a given farm and tending a specified number of acres across the growing season. The next spring they signed a new contract, often with a different farmer and sometimes in a different place entirely. Beet working families—especially the women—were generally isolated geographically and socially. They

---

[2] That pattern differs from the national one in which 47% of Mexican-born migrants already lived in urban areas in 1920 (Acuña, *Occupied America*, p. 165).

[3] See App. 3.1. In a parallel division, most owners and managers in the citrus industry of southern California were native-born Anglos; Italian immigrants worked in the packinghouse labor force; and "Mexicans were relegated to field work" (Alamillo, *Making Lemonade*, p. 6).

Illus. 3.1. Vertical rows in a sugar beet field, Longmont, early 20th century

commonly lived in farm buildings at a distance from other people, had few interactions with other Hispanic laborers, and seldom dealt with the wider community apart from the Anglo farmer who employed them.[4]

The process by which sugar beets were grown in very large fields in northeastern Colorado required three ingredients: (1) soil suited to production of this crop; (2) ample water to supplement the often limited rainfall in this generally arid climate, provided by irrigation systems that branched out from the main rivers; and (3) a supply of laborers willing to carry out back-breaking work, moving across a given field multiple times during an extended agricultural season that lasted for around six months.[5] Nearly all of the specific tasks involved in growing beets forced people to work either while standing but bent far over, with their hands near the ground, or kneeling: the hoes and knives provided by

[4] For geographically separated housing and limited social or religious participation until around 1940, see Vol. II, Chs. 2A, 4A, and 5A.

[5] Because only certain parts of eastern Boulder County had suitable soil and water, it was a small producer of sugar beets compared to several other counties in northeastern Colorado. In most years between 1920 and 1927, the area devoted to sugar beets in Boulder was 5,700 - 9,500 acres, whereas its northern neighbor, Larimer County, had 13,500 - 24,100 acres in beets; its eastern neighbor, Weld County, had 42,100 - 86,400 acres (Taylor, *Mexican Labor*, p. 106).

Illus. 3.2. Team of people with a horse-drawn digger, Longmont, 1900

the farmers had very short handles. This physically arduous work was known as "stoop labor," and people who engaged in it commonly suffered from back problems and other joint-related ailments.

In the spring, as soon as the fields were dry enough to be worked, the seeds were planted in furrows, often using a manual beet drill.[6] Larger drills, drawn by a horse or in later periods by a mechanized vehicle, could cover three or four rows at once, digging holes and planting one or more seeds in each. When the seeds had germinated and grown to a height of about four leaves, usually in early June, the field had to be thinned. First it was "blocked, with the weaker plants removed with a hoe so the remaining ones were evenly spaced with 8-12 inches between them. Then each plant had to be individually cropped. Sugar beet seeds are dichotomous, meaning that every seed produces two shoots. To ensure the largest possible beet roots, the smaller shoot from each seed was cut off by hand. That work was especially well suited to children. Twice during the course of the summer, workers used hoes to weed the field and remove any new shoots. Hoeing was usually done over a four- to

---

[6] This paragraph and the next draw heavily on Aguayo, "Los Betabeleros," and Hamilton, *Footprints in the Sugar.*

Illus. 3.3. Men topping sugar beets, Longmont, early 20th century

five-week period. The field was repeatedly irrigated.[7]

Harvesting commonly took place in late September or early October, as late as possible before the first serious frost, to give the beets the longest possible time to grow. A special plow was used to dig deep down under the beets, cutting off the tap root and loosening the dirt around them. Field workers then came through, pulling up each beet by hand and cutting off its large head of leaves ("topping" it) with a long knife.[8] Because the beets were heavy, commonly weighing 3-5 pounds each, workers often grasped them between their knees or thighs, leaving the hands free to steady the beet and do the cutting. Topping resulted in many injuries to people's hands, arms, and legs. The beets were then piled up and carried away in horse-drawn or motorized wagons, each of which held 1 ½ to 2 tons of beets. In Boulder County, some beets were taken directly to the sugar factory in Longmont, while others were hauled to a nearby railway line and dumped into huge piles to be transported by train.[9]

[7] "Beets being irrigated."
[8] "Men and women topping beets" and "Harvesting sugar beets."
[9] "Beets outside Great Western Sugar Factory" and "Beet dump."

Illus. 3.4. *Hauling sugar beets, Longmont, early 20th century*

Illus. 3.5. *Pile of beets at factory, with empty rail cars, Longmont, early 20th century*

Descriptions by former beet workers in Boulder County shed light on what that labor actually involved.[10] Frank Martinez, who started in the beet fields around Longmont as a young man in 1911, recalled that he "crawled all over the county on my hands and knees."[11] He was proud of being a "top-hand," able to thin a quarter-acre of beets by hand in one day, but after several summers of seasonal work, he was glad to be hired on a year-round basis by a farmer with whom he remained for 18 years. Dora Bernal, born in 1911, described the work done by her family (parents and all the children) when they came seasonally from the San Luis Valley to Boulder County's beet fields in the 1920s.[12] After sowing the seeds, they did the thinning, using a tool which she described as a *cabador* and later as an *azadón* (= digger or hoe). The second stage was weeding, which "they called the cleaning, and they said you could fly through this, but there was no flying. You went at a turtle's pace, all covered with grass, pulling and pulling, and you were paid less because they said it was easier the second round. Well, it was not so easy. There were times when the plains were dense with grass, and the grass was so high." Finally came the harvest, "where they claimed you could make great amounts of money per acre. . . . But we could never make what they said."

Mary Martinez talked about her family's work in the beet fields near the small community of Milliken, northeast of Longmont, in the 1920s and 1930s.[13] Her grandparents and their five granddaughters got up at 4 in the morning and worked in the fields all day, regardless of the weather. When they were thinning beets, they dragged themselves along the rows, their knees covered with blisters. She was short, so while topping beets with a machete during the harvest, holding the beet between her knees, she often cut her legs. Her grandparents, whom she described as workaholics, were eager to be sure they had their beets ready when the truck came to pick them up. One fall morning they roused the family even earlier than usual, well before sun-up, but it was so cold that the beets they dug up were frozen by the time the truck arrived.

Beet growing in this area was managed by Great Western Sugar, one of the first companies to control the production of its raw material as

---

[10] For beet workers in Greeley, some 40 miles north of Longmont, see Lopez and Lopez, *White Gold Laborers*, esp. chs. 1-3.

[11] *They Came to Stay*, p. 158.

[12] Bernal, Dora, interview, 1978. This is a translation of her Spanish-language interview.

[13] Martinez, Mary, interview, 1988.

well as the processing.[14] In the contracts Great Western signed each spring with farmers who owned suitable land, the farmer agreed to raise and sell to the company a given number of tons of beets for a pre-determined price per ton. Great Western also provided standard labor contracts for use by all farmers on the western high plains, printed agreements that laid out a uniform scale of pay per acre for workers during the coming growing season.[15] They specified how much laborers would receive for each stage of work, to be paid as a lump sum delivered at the end of the season. As an incentive for high yields, the agreements offered a bonus payment if the weight of the beets harvested exceeded a certain amount per acre. A contracted worker could use whatever family members or friends he could line up to help with the tasks, so long as they were completed at the required times. The labor of women and older children was thus essential to the economic viability of most families. The amount paid was less than the prevailing wage for other kinds of work, but immigrants were seldom in a position to know about other options or to bargain with prospective employers.

To obtain the necessary labor, Great Western initially tried bringing permanent immigrants into northeastern Colorado.[16] The first group consisted of families originally from Germany who had settled in western Russia but were made unwelcome there in the late nineteenth century. These "Volga Deutsch" had often worked previously with sugar beets, either in Europe or through an earlier stay in Nebraska. As the acreage of sugar beet farming expanded rapidly in the early years of the twentieth century, German-Russians no longer provided sufficient labor for the Colorado fields. Further, by 1910, some of them were starting to buy their own farms and grow beets through direct contracts.[17] To fill the resulting gap, Great Western began in the second half of the 1910s to import unmarried Japanese men, some of whom later brought their families. Increasingly, however, they too became independent producers or moved into better kinds of work.[18]

[14] Aguayo, "Los Betabeleros," p. 106.

[15] Although the contracts were written, those employees who were illiterate could not sign them. Esther Blazón's Mexican-born father always confirmed his verbal agreements with farmers through a hand shake, which pledged his honor (Blazón, conversation with Marjorie McIntosh, August 29, 2014).

[16] Hamilton, *Footprints in the Sugar*, chs. 5 and 6, for this and below.

[17] Lopez and Lopez, *White Gold Laborers*, p. 3.

[18] Several Japanese families remained in the Longmont area into the twenty-first century, growing vegetables for market sale and in a few cases becoming land developers (see, e.g., *Actual, Factual St. Vrain Valley*, pp. 30-33).

Until the mid-1910s, relatively few Spanish-speakers from Mexico or the southwestern U.S. were hired for beet field work. Only about 2,800 "Mexicans" were listed by Great Western in 1916 for its operations all through the west-central U.S.[19] But at least a few Hispanics were already employed in Boulder County by 1915, when one was killed in a dispute over a contract for beet work in Lafayette.[20] Alex Gonzales's family came to the Longmont area in 1918 by train from Oklahoma City initially just to harvest beets; in later years, he and his wife worked beets for the whole summer.[21] The Longmont Census for 1920 includes 13 people with Spanish surnames described as beet laborers.[22]

During the 1920s, Great Western undertook more active recruitment of Hispanic workers.[23] Each spring the company sent labor contractors to southern Colorado, New Mexico, Texas, and Mexico, carrying with them a brochure that described life as a beet worker in glowing terms.[24] Great Western also prepared a recruitment film, with sub-titles in Spanish, showing healthy and well-dressed laborers working in the fields, adobe homes with trees in the yard, children attending school, and families enjoying a game of baseball on a weekend afternoon. Once people started coming, word spread informally among Spanish-speaking people in the U.S. and Mexico about the availability of beet work.

Until the late 1920s, if a worker signed on with Great Western, the company paid travel costs for him and usually his family to come to Denver by train. There they would be hired by a farmer for the summer. That process may have been handled through middle-men, though these *padrones* are not mentioned in the local sources; Great Western paid for bilingual interpreters to help with the agreements.[25] At the end of the season the company covered travel for those workers who wished to return home, though some decided to stay in their new surroundings. That arrangement brought a much large number of Hispanics to Boulder County. The 1930 Census for Longmont shows 131 beet workers with Spanish surnames, including men, women, and children.[26]

[19] Hamilton, *Footprints in the Sugar*, p. 272.
[20] "Law and Order."
[21] Gonzales, Alex, interview, c. 1987.
[22] App. 3.2.
[23] Hamilton, *Footprints in the Sugar*, chs. 5 and 6.
[24] Rebecca Chavez, "Making Them Count," pp. 45-46, for this and below.
[25] Newby, *Longmont Album*, p. 78.
[26] App. 3.2.

Later residents of Boulder County described how that system affected their families. When Dora Bernal's parents were hired by Great Western in the 1920s, the whole family went from their home in the San Luis Valley to Fort Garland in a cart pulled by a horse, loaned to them by a relative.[27] The cart carried their necessary items (beds, clothing, and two small leather trunks) to the depot. From there, they took the train to Denver, at Great Western's expense. Lou Cardenas, born in New Mexico in 1918, came to Boulder County when she was ten years old, recruited with the rest of her family by an agent for Great Western.[28] Her parents and their 13 children came to Denver by train with many other workers; from there they were hired and taken to a farm in Niwot, where they were given a dwelling and set immediately to work thinning and hoeing beets.

But for Great Western, it was expensive to hire agents and pay for the travel of workers coming north each summer. The company therefore explored ways of encouraging Hispanic laborers to remain in the area during the winter, ready to accept a new contract and start work as soon as spring weather permitted. One option was for Great Western itself to provide off-season housing. Throughout the northeastern Colorado beet area, Great Western began in the mid-1920s to build *colonias*, clusters of small houses, each with space for a vegetable garden, in which workers could live during the winters, paying a small rent. In towns like Greeley and Fort Collins, the *colonias* housed hundreds of Hispanic families; located outside the main part of town, they formed distinct and often long-lived communities.[29] In Boulder County, however, only Longmont had a *colonia*, and it was small (containing no more than 20 units situated in cramped quarters on the edge of town) and short-lived. Although there are references to it in the later 1920s and 1930s, the *colonia* had apparently shut down by around 1940.[30] In another effort to persuade particularly good workers to remain in the area or at least to return to it the following spring, Great Western gave out gold buttons and hosted a dinner for top employees at the end of each season in the later 1920s; in the early 1930s, the company awarded special certificates to them.[31] Almost without exception, the men known to have received such

[27] Bernal, Dora, interview, 1978. See also Aguayo, "Los Betabeleros," p. 107.
[28] Cardenas, Lou, interview, c. 1987.
[29] E.g., Lopez and Lopez, *White Gold Laborers*, esp. chs. 2 and 16.
[30] See Vol. II, Ch. 2B.
[31] "Best beet thinners get gold buttons," "Beet thinners get gold buttons," and see Illus. 3.6 below.

distinction had Spanish surnames.

Although beet working families too may have disliked moving twice each year, they had to find some way to support themselves and a place to live during the six months between one agricultural contract and the next. People who had migrated from northern New Mexico or southern Colorado might return home for the winter, though employment was generally scarce there too in the colder months. A few people—especially Mexicans—probably survived the winter in poor Hispanic neighborhoods of Denver. The pattern of moving between summer and winter locations, taking a new agricultural job each summer, was what most Boulder County residents meant when describing themselves or their parents or grandparents as "migrant farm workers," not that they moved around following the crops within each growing season.[32]

For farm workers themselves, a better option was to stay in Boulder County throughout the winter, if they could make ends meet. Such arrangements, which made possible more regular schooling for children, became increasingly common across the 1920s. Whereas only 88 families of Hispanic beet workers in the Longmont area had remained in northeastern Colorado during the winter of 1921, 500 families stayed in 1927.[33] Some fortunate men were hired as coal miners in the winters, but many others had to make do with whatever short-term jobs might become available. Marcella Diaz said that when her grandparents were working as beet laborers in the 1920s and 1930s, men were generally able to find only bits and pieces of work in the winters: doing odd jobs, repairing fences, or road construction.[34] Esther Blazón's father never had regular employment during the winters. Their family (her parents and their 14 children) got by thanks to the credit offered by a local grocery store, which they repaid when the family was paid for its beet work at the end of the following summer.[35]

During the 1920s, when labor for beet production was still relatively scarce, some farmers began to offer year-round employment, allowing their best workers to stay in a building on their farm during the colder months even if little labor was needed. The few farmers who grew

[32] See, e.g., Cardenas, Alfonso, interview, 2004, Hernandez, Philip, interview, 2013, and "Olivas, Ralph and Rose, biographical account." More generally, see Kulkosky, "Mexican Migrant Workers."

[33] Taylor, *Mexican Labor*, p. 139.

[34] "Martinez, Juan and Josephine; Marcella Diaz, biography."

[35] Conversation with Marjorie McIntosh, August 29, 2014.

crops other than beets and ranchers who focused on animal raising were also likely to hire laborers on an annual basis, providing some kind of housing. Men who were hired for full-year agricultural positions sometimes stayed with a given farmer for multiple years, though they were free to take a different job at the end of each annual contract. The only agricultural laborers in Boulder County who were truly settled residents were those who were able to save money and rent or even buy their own housing.

Canuto Martinez's experience illustrates the increasing residential stability of beet working families in the late 1920s and 1930s, as well as the labor they performed and the payment they received. Martinez, who had come to southern Colorado in 1909 from Zacatecas, Mexico, worked as a coal miner in the winters, but he and his family did field work in the summers, traveling to wherever employment was available.[36] In 1928, Martinez signed a standard contract with one of Great Western's farmers in western Nebraska for a season's work.[37] He (assisted by his wife and children, who were not mentioned specifically) agreed to carry out the following tasks on 92 acres of sugar beet fields:

"Bunching" and thinning the plants for pay of $9 per acre
Hoeing $2 per acre
One or more weedings $1 per acre
Pulling and topping $11 per acre

If Martinez and his family grew an average of more than 12 tons (24,000 pounds) of beets per acre, he would receive a bonus of $0.50 per acre for each ton over that base. That means that he was expected to produce a base total of 1,104 tons (2,208,000 pounds!) of beets on his 92 acres, for a total season's wage for him and his family of $1,288.

The farmer who signed Martinez's contract agreed to provide him with "a habitable house" and suitable water near at hand, and to carry him and other laborers (one assumes his family), plus their belongings, from the railway station at which they were left off by Great Western to the farm where they would be living.[38] He was not supposed to allow children aged ten years or less to work in the field, but the company—

---

[36] "Martinez, Canuto and Gregoria, biography."
[37] "Contract for Hand Labor, 1928." This agreement was made in June, so the planting had already been done.
[38] For the generally deplorable housing provided for agricultural workers, see Ch. 6B below and Vol. II, Ch. 2A.

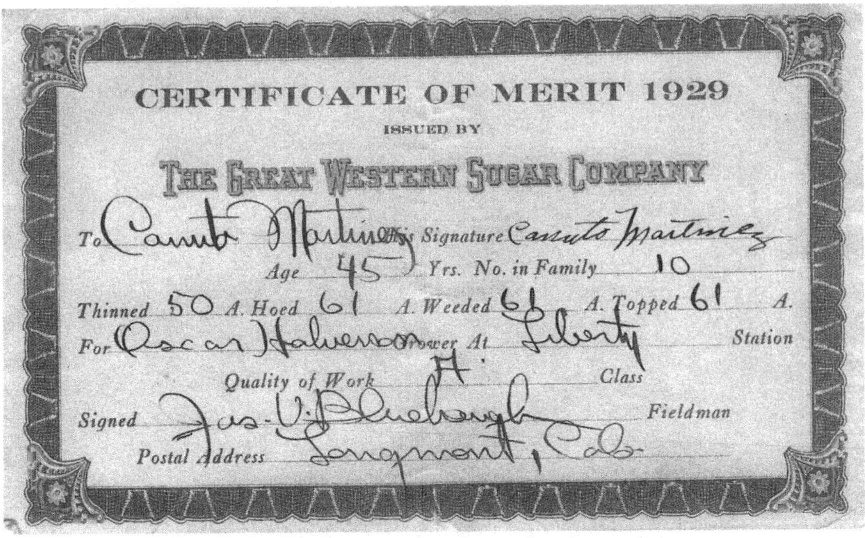

Illus. 3.6. Certificate of Merit to Canuto Martinez, 1929

and presumably its farmers—did not enforce that rule. Should a conflict arise between Martinez and the farmer, it was to be settled by the local Agricultural Superintendent for Great Western Sugar, hardly a neutral party, one might think.

The following summer Martinez and his family took work on Oscar Halverson's beet farm in Longmont, having spent the winter in the Lafayette area, where he was now working as a miner. At the end of the 1929 season, he received a Certificate of Merit from Great Western for his work. Martinez, aged 45 years, together with nine other people in his family, had thinned, hoed, weeded, and topped between 50 and 61 acres at a performance level of "A." The Martinez family moved between different farms in Boulder County for the next few summers before settling permanently in the Water + Goss Streets area of Boulder in the mid-1930s.[39]

Because most beet workers changed location seasonally or annually, transportation was a key issue. As cars and trucks became cheaper, more reliable, and more readily available in the late 1920s and 1930s, they offered great benefits to migrant Hispanic families. Travel was easier and faster than in a covered wagon, and being able to move without relying

[39] See Vol. II, Ch. 2B.

Illus. 3.7. *Elderly couple in front of old car*

Illus. 3.8. *Four children and a baby in front of car*

on train routes gave workers more choice in looking for jobs. When Oli Duncan's grandparents left Chama, New Mexico in the late 1920s to seek work in Boulder County, the family drove north in a Model T Ford.[40]

Having a car or truck also enabled workers to move around on the farm that hired them. Lou Cardenas remembered that when her family received its pay check in 1929 at the end of the first season of working beets near Longmont, her daddy bought a car.[41] He had not driven before but learned quickly, and in subsequent summers the family used the car to travel in the mornings from the house where they were living on the farm to the field where they were to work. (Before buying a car, the whole family had risen at three in the morning to eat breakfast, pack a lunch, and set off on a 2-mile walk to the fields, carrying their food, water, and hoes with them; they reversed that walk at the end of the day.) By around 1940, cars and trucks were also making possible greater social and religious participation for farm workers.[42]

Owning a vehicle has been a source of pride for many Latino families from early in the twentieth century. Cars and trucks are often shown in photos.[43] The image used as the emblem for the Boulder County Latino History Project shows the grandmother and two great-aunts of one of the participants in the project; dressed in their best clothing, the girls, from a beet-working family in Lafayette, sit on the bumper of the family's truck on a Sunday morning in 1929.

By the early 1930s, the Great Depression was causing Great Western to cut back on production. Over the next five years, the company and its farmers reduced the number of employees and the pay per acre several times. Yet widespread unemployment led some Hispanics already in this area and those coming from nearby states to accept beet work even if the cost of travel was not covered and the pay was very low. Declining demand for Hispanic workers is demonstrated in the 1940 Census for Longmont which shows only 25 beet laborers.[44] After that, cheaper cane sugar and other factors lowered beet production even further.

Other types of agricultural work

Although the majority of early Spanish-speaking people who did

[40] "Olivas, Ralph and Rose, biographical account."
[41] Cardenas, Lou, interview, c. 1987.
[42] See Vol. II, Chs. 4A and 5C.
[43] See also Vol. II, Illus. 2.4, "Three boys in matching plaid jackets," and "Two men standing in front of a car."
[44] App. 3.2.

Illus. 3.9. Martinez girls on a truck on a Sunday morning, Lafayette, 1929

agricultural work in Boulder County were employed in the beet fields, a few found different kinds of jobs on farms and ranches. They might be hired short-term to harvest other crops or as full-time workers.[45] Albert ("Paco") Borrego, born in 1906 in New Mexico, came to this area with his parents.[46] One day in the late 1920s, after performing well in some horse races, he caught the attention of C. W. Pace. Mr. Pace, owner of Pace Land and Livestock Company in Longmont and one of the area's largest ranchers, hired young Albert, first as a cowboy and later as a top foreman. He managed the animal side of the ranch, breaking broncos and training horses, and rode the company's entries at the Roosevelt Park Racetrack. Albert also kept up with new farming equipment, able to use and fix any machine. The high point of each year was going to the Denver Stock Show with Mr. Pace. He recalled that they stayed at the Brown Palace Hotel, Denver's grandest, and throughout the show

[45] E.g., "Three men with shocks of grain" and "Harvesting peas."
[46] "Borrego, Albert and Elvinia ("Bea") Martinez, biography," for this paragraph.

Illus. 3.10. E. E. Bernal shearing a sheep

they "wined and dined among the finest and most famous cowboys and cattlemen."

Hispanics were sometimes hired to work with sheep, though Boulder County's flatlands were not commonly used for these animals. People who had come from New Mexico or Huerfano or Las Animas Counties were often experienced with sheep, which formed an important part of local economies there. When Oli Duncan's grandfather moved to Longmont around 1930, he too was hired by Mr. Pace on a year-round basis.[47] His main job was to tend the sheep, but sometimes he supervised work in the fields or raised his own cash crops on acreage rented from the farm. A few Hispanics were in demand as sheep shearers. E. E. Bernal, whose family had "dry farmed" and herded sheep in northern New Mexico and Huerfano and Las Animas Counties, did various kinds of work after he moved to northern Colorado: mining, construction, and farm labor.[48] But even after he settled his family in the town of Boulder, he continued to shear sheep on the side. J. H. Cortez, whose many types of employment over time included herding sheep, likewise kept on shearing after retiring from other work.[49]

[47] "Olivas, Ralph and Rose, biographical account."
[48] "Bernal, E. E. and Eva, biography and photo."
[49] "Cortez, Jose Hilario ("J. H.") and Maria Sabina, biography."

Whereas some of the German-Russian and Japanese immigrants who had been brought to this area to work sugar beets ended up buying their own agricultural land, that pattern was less common among Hispanics. U.S. Census records describe a few Spanish-surnamed men as "farmers," which probably meant farm owners: one in Boulder in 1900; one in Longmont in 1910; four in Longmont and Lafayette in 1920; and seven in those two towns in 1930.[50] By 1940, however, the number had dropped to just three in all the towns together, probably due to the Depression. The Zaragoza (later Saragosa) brothers in Boulder bought land on the western edge of town in the mid-1910s which they used to graze animals and for orchards and gardens, but starting in the 1930s, the one remaining widow gradually sold it off.[51]

A few positions secondarily associated with agriculture were available. A younger relative reported that George Madrigal, who had come from Mexico around 1910, surveyed land in eastern Boulder County.[52] He determined the exact measurements of fields, sometimes helping to resolve disputes between farmers and their employees about how large an acreage had actually been worked. Among the jobs held by Roy Maestas in the 1920s was making pellets in an alfalfa mill.[53]

B. Coal Mining

The experiences of the other major set of early Hispanic workers, those employed in the coal mines in and around southeastern Boulder County, differed in many respects. Male miners (adults and boys in their teens) earned cash wages, and they developed a strong sense of comradery with the men they worked alongside, regardless of national/ ethnic background. Until the 1930s, many miners' families lived in camps of small houses near the mine head, built by the company that owned the mine. Some camps contained as many as a hundred families, coming from southeastern Europe and Italy as well as Spanish-speaking backgrounds. Women in these settings had opportunities for sociability, including at the store that some company camps provided. Yet miners

---

[50] App. 3.2.

[51] Leslie Ogeda, conversation with Marjorie McIntosh, April 12, 2013, and "Saragosa, Pete, Property records."

[52] "Madrigal family of Boulder, biographies." It seems rather surprising that a Mexican immigrant would have been hired for such work.

[53] "Maestas, Pedro (Roy), Ruby, and Abe, biography."

did not form a distinct group from agricultural laborers: during the summers, when the mines did not operate, many families worked in the beet fields.

The coal mines around Lafayette, Erie, and Louisville in southeastern Boulder County formed the primary economic activity of that region. They produced lignite, a soft, brown, "dirty" coal with a relatively low heat content that was used primarily for heating domestic and other buildings in Denver and the surrounding area.[54] Like mines in the southern Colorado coal field (around Trinidad and Walsenburg), production in the northern field (in Boulder and Weld Counties) peaked in the 1910s and gradually declined thereafter.

Across the full history of Boulder County's coal extraction, nearly 50 mines are known to have operated; others lay just across the border in Weld County.[55] In 1920, nearly a million tons of coal were produced in those two counties; in 1930, nearly 30 mines operated in this area, most employing 50 to 100 men each. Yields were already decreasing, however, and demand was dropping due to increased use of oil and gas. By the early 1960s, only six mines, all founded between 1920 and 1949, were still operating. Yet as late as 1975 two dozen Boulder County Latinas/os were working for mining companies.[56]

Although the process of extracting coal varied a little between local mines, depending upon the depth and nature of the seams of coal being worked, the general pattern prior to around 1940 was this. After testing to determine the extent of the site, done by taking core samples, a central shaft was sunk from the surface down to the lowest level of the coal seam. Cages going up and down the shaft transported men and equipment into the mine and brought up coal and "tipple" (rocks and dirt). From the central shaft, miners dug low, narrow tunnels going horizontally along the various levels of the seam. They reinforced the roofs with timber and laid down tracks for the carts that carried material back to the shaft.[57] Mules were initially used to pull the carts but were later replaced by machines. The animals were stabled in a special room at each level and

---

[54] The higher quality coal mined in southern Colorado was put to other uses, including producing electricity, coking smelters and steel mills, and fueling railroad engines. For the relationship between expansion of railroads and coal mining in Colorado, see Andrews, *Killing for Coal*, pp. 51-62. I am grateful to Tom Andrews for clarifying for me many aspects of mining history (personal communication).

[55] "Eracism: Exploring the Roots."

[56] See Ch. 6C below.

[57] "Men in interior of Eagle Mine" and "Men in interior of Vulcan Mine."

Illus. 3.11. Black Diamond Mine, Lafayette, interior, 1942

generally did not return to the surface until they were too old to work. As the tunnels of a given mine spread out, sometimes for several miles, additional shafts might be sunk to lessen the distance that the coal had to be moved underground and to ventilate the underground workings. An extensive array of buildings generally lay above ground.[58] Because demand for heating coal dropped off sharply during the warmer months, mining in this area took place only during the winter.

Colorado's coal miners came from many different national backgrounds. Of 12,894 miners in the state in 1910, 38% were whites born in the U.S., plus 3% African Americans.[59] One quarter of the workers were described as "Mexican," which apparently included everyone with a Spanish surname, regardless of where they were born. Italians constituted 15% of the men, with 11% from other western European countries; 9% came

[58] "Buildings at Industrial Mine," "Tipple at Shamrock Mine," "Simpson Mine, 1900?," "Simpson Mine, 1908," "Simpson Mine, 1909," "Tipple at Standard Mine," and "Tipple and tracks, Standard Mine."

[59] Figures calculated from Rees, "Chicanos Mine the Columbine," p. 18, citing information from Hazel Alice Glenny, "A History of Labor Disputes in the Northern Colorado Coal Mining Fields with Emphasis on the 1927-1928 Strike" (M.A. thesis, University of Colorado at Boulder, 1938), p. 7.

NATIONAL FUEL COMPANY "EAGLE MINE" ERIE, COLO. AUG. 20, 1942

Illus. 3.12. Miners at Eagle Mine, 1942

from eastern or southeastern Europe, and there were a few Japanese miners. Over the following decade, however, the number of Mexican-born miners in Colorado nearly tripled, whereas other foreign-born groups decreased in size.[60]

In Boulder County as early as 1920, nine Spanish-surnamed men in Lafayette and one in Longmont were coal miners.[61] By 1930, those numbers had risen to 12 and 9, and as of 1936, 21 Lafayette men and 6 from Longmont were mining, according to the *Polk's City Directories* of that year.[62] Early U.S. Censuses for Lafayette suggest concentrations of Italian and Southeastern European immigrants as well as families originally from Mexico or New Mexico.[63]

[60] U.S. Census, 1920, as tabulated by Rees, "Chicanos Mine the Columbine," p. 18.
[61] App. 3.2. By 1940, the figures had declined slightly: 15 miners in Lafayette, 8 in Longmont, and 2 in Boulder.
[62] "Occupations and Employers, Three Towns, 1936." *Polk's City Directories*, available in Boulder County's public libraries, list adult residents of each town by street address and give the occupations and employers of some of them. For this project, volunteers entered information into databases about those households headed by people with Hispanic surnames, using as sample years 1904, 1916 (using *Polk's Boulder County Directory*), 1926, 1936, 1946, 1955, 1965, and 1975. The resulting figures are minimum numbers, though coverage is fuller in the later decades. The *Directories* probably missed some people and did not include true migrant workers; our analysis may have failed to recognize some Hispanic names and could not spot any Latinas who married a man with a non-Latino surname, though inter-ethnic marriage was rare in this area until the 1970s. The number of Latinas/os for whom occupations were given in 1904 and 1916 was too small to analyze.
[63] For images, see "Miners at Lehigh Mine," "Miners at Puritan Mine," "Miners at Standard Mine," and "Miners and tipple at State Mine."

We have more specific information about the backgrounds of miners at the Columbine Mine, located a few miles east of Lafayette, during the 1920s.[64] Because there was nothing distinctive about the labor force of the Columbine, these figures probably provide a rough picture of Hispanic miners elsewhere Boulder County too. In Rees's sample of 165 Columbine miners, about half were Hispanic: 28% were born in Mexico, and 24% were Spanish-speakers born in the U.S. Of the others, 24% were American-born English-speakers, 8% came from Western Europe, and 9% from Eastern Europe. Of the 86 Hispanics working at the Columbine, 54% had been born in Mexico, and the rest in the United States. Not all of the 46 miners who had come from Mexico stayed permanently in this country; some crossed the border annually or every few years. The Mexican-born miners were on average two years older than those born in the U.S., and a slightly higher fraction of them were married. Only two of the 25 single miners from Mexico had any relatives in the United States, suggesting that they had come on their own in search of work. Eight of the wives of the 20 married men were still living in Mexico. Of the U.S.-born Hispanic miners, nearly two-thirds were literate only in Spanish or in both Spanish and English; a quarter were literate in English only.

Coal mining was dangerous work. Lesser accidents were common, stemming often from problems with tools or the carts that moved through the tunnels. More worryingly, poorly supported tunnels might allow rocks to fall or could cave in entirely, killing some miners and stranding others on the far side of the blockage. Poisonous gas and accumulations of coal dust sometimes built up if the mine was not adequately ventilated, and it was easy to fall into a vertical shaft, since men were moving about in the dark. The short-term risk of coal dust, which was easily ignitable, was that it would explode; many long-term miners developed "Black Lung Disease" from the dust, though that ailment was not recognized prior to 1940.[65]

An analysis of deaths among coal miners of all ethnicities in Erie and Frederick (across the border in Weld County) between 1900 and 1945 shows the following causes:

---

[64] Rees, "Chicanos Mine the Columbine," pp. 21-28, 68, and 71.
[65] See Vol. II, Ch. 3B.

Falling coal and rocks:	8
Coal car collisions:	6
Falling into shafts:	4
Cave-ins:	1
Unknown or other:	3 [66]

State-maintained records of the deaths resulting from coal mining accidents show that at least 21 Spanish-surnamed miners were killed in Boulder County between the 1910s and 1950s.

1910s:	2 men
1920s:	11 men
1930s:	6 men
1940s:	1 man
1950s:	1 man [67]

The Columbine mine had nine deaths between 1922 and 1945; the Puritan had five between 1922 and 1934. Most of the entries for the first three decades indicate how many children each man left behind. Of 17 men, 9 left between 1 and 6 children each, suggesting that they were living here with their families; the other 8 listed no children, so the men were either unmarried or had not brought their families to Boulder County with them.

The most disastrous explosion in this region took place at the Monarch Mine near Lafayette in 1936, killing eight men, including Joe Jaramillo.[68] At 6:20 am on the morning of January 20, a small night crew was finishing its preparations for the day-shift workers, more than a hundred of whom had already assembled near the main entry point into the mine. Suddenly a powerful blast was heard and felt, and a fireball and smoke erupted from the top of the mine. The explosion reverberated through the mine's miles of underground tunnels, bringing down hundreds of tons of rock, coal, and timber supports; it affected about half of the total area of the mine. Two of the ten-member night crew escaped, but the others were killed: five "by the force of the blast or falling debris," and three men

[66] Adelfang, ed., *Erie*, p. 65.
[67] "Eracism: Exploring the Roots."
[68] The most complete account is William Cohen, "Blast." The next two paragraphs are taken from that description unless otherwise noted. See also "Monarch Mine."

who apparently "succumbed by suffocation from the poisonous gas that erupted following the explosion, called 'after-damp.'"[69] Had the explosion occurred an hour later, after the day shift had gone down in the mine, the casualties would have been far greater. An investigation of the blast failed to establish the exact source of the electric spark that caused the coal dust to explode, but the disaster was attributed to the illegally unsafe conditions that the mine's owner, the National Fuel Company, had allowed to continue for years on end. After rescue efforts were abandoned, the company sealed off the Monarch Mine and closed it permanently.[70]

The bodies of seven miners were found, but despite extensive searching, Joe Jaramillo's was never recovered. Local tradition says that Jaramillo survived the initial blast but went back into the mine to look for his comrades, but the investigative report does not confirm that.[71] Jaramillo, who was in his late 40s, had worked in the Monarch Mine for 20 years. His job was to look after the mules that were stabled in a room leading off one of the tunnels, bringing back the animals tired from work and taking ones that had rested to the place they were needed. At the time of the blast, he was returning two animals to the stable from a distant point in the tunnels. Jaramillo and his wife Josephine had both come to Boulder County from New Mexico (though he was described as "Mexican" in the State Mining Inspector's report of the explosion and as "Mexican Joe" in newspaper accounts). Their four children, born at the Monarch Mine camp between 1919 and 1924, were still living at home and preparing to leave for school when the blast was felt and the emergency sirens began to scream.

Despite the dangers inherent to mining, many men considered it better work than "stoop labor" in the beet fields. Wages were relatively good and the work was steady during the colder months. Many miners continued in that occupation throughout their lives, or as long as they were physically capable of the demanding labor. Until the 1930s, some miners lived in camps next to the central shaft, containing simple wooden houses. The camp around the Columbine Mine was sufficiently large that it was sometimes termed a town in its own right, with the (poorly suited) name of "Serene." Married men could bring their families to live

---

[69] William Cohen, "Blast," p. 3.

[70] A monument to the men who were lost was placed over the mine entrance but later moved to nearby Varra Park when a shopping mall was constructed on the site.

[71] E.g., Noel and Corson, *Boulder County*, p. 97, as compared with William Cohen, "Blast."

with them there, while single men often stayed in boarding houses. Not all miners lived in the camps, however. In October, 1929, Rudolph Ruiz was working at the Puritan Mine but lived with his wife and six children on a farm 2 miles east of Longmont.[72] Later many miners moved their families into one of the nearby towns.

The unionization of Colorado's coal miners was a bitterly disputed issue, leading to frequent conflict with mine operators and sometimes violent strikes in every decade between the 1880s and 1930s.[73] Unions were already functioning as collective bargaining agents in Boulder County prior to 1914 but were then banned; they began organizing again in the late 1920s. The unions gradually achieved some limited benefits for their members, including an award to the family of a man killed at work and pay after an injury.

Miners faced some special financial problems. One was that because the mines only functioned in the winters, their employees had to look for other work during the warm weather. As we shall see, some miners found jobs as seasonal agricultural workers, especially in the beet fields, or in construction. For others, however, the summer involved a series of odd jobs at best. Tom Lopez, the first Latino mayor of Lafayette, remembered that during and after the Great Depression, many miners went into debt during the summer; they then worked to pay off those loans or advances once the mines opened again.[74]

Another issue confronted those families who lived in camps, which were generally located at some distance from towns.[75] If the camp had no store, it was difficult to obtain items that people could not produce themselves. Camps run by the mining company usually provided a store, which stocked basic food and other essential items. Although these stores allowed their customers to buy on credit, with payment deducted from the miners' paychecks, the men and their wives had to pay whatever prices were demanded. The use of credit meant that women had to be thrifty managers of their family's resources, making sure they did not run up against their limit before the next pay day. Merle Travis's song "Sixteen Tons" refers to company stores at coal mines in Appalachia:

---

[72] His five-year-old son fell into an irrigation ditch there and drowned ("Mexican child drowns in ditch").
[73] See Ch. 4A below.
[74] Lopez, Thomas, interview, 1986.
[75] "Houses in camp, Industrial Mine," and see Vol. II, Ch. 2A.

Some people say a man is made outta mud.
A poor man's made outta muscle and blood.
Muscle and blood, skin and bones;
A mind that's weak and a back that's strong.
You load sixteen tons an' what do you get?
Another day older and deeper in debt.
St Peter don't you call me cause I can't go:
I owe my soul to the company store.[76]

Personal narratives provide glimpses into people's experiences as miners. Some highlight the dangers involved. Patrick Arroyo described how his father had helped to stop a terrible fire in the Washington Mine, located east of Erie in Weld County.[77] He talked about starting work himself as a boy, with a description of the interior of the mine and what it was like to descend in the cage that ran up and down the shaft. He told how his hand was shattered between two coal cars when he was trying to couple them. In the 1930s, Juan Francisco Archuleta worked as a "shot-firer," planning out and firing the explosions that loosened coal from the seams.[78] Judging how much powder to use and where to place it required precise mathematical calculation, and after the explosion, he had to ensure that the area was free of harmful gases before other workers were allowed in. Other accounts offer first-person descriptions of mining procedures. Tom Lopez reported how he moved to Lafayette in 1936 to work at the newly opened Morrison mine; he was trained by a slightly older Hispanic miner, Victor Tafoya, and continued to work there until 1956.[79] His narrative gives valuable details about the processes used to extract coal and how they changed over time as power machinery was introduced.

Several records left by Canuto Martinez, the man whose sugar beet contracts we discussed above, tell us how much miners produced, how much they were paid, and how the credit system functioned. Martinez started work in Boulder County mines in the late 1920s, having moved first from Mexico and then from the mines around Trinidad.[80] Altogether

[76] Travis, "Sixteen Tons."
[77] Arroyo, Patrick, interview, 1989.
[78] *The Coal and Metal Miners' Pocket Book*, which he used in his work.
[79] Lopez, Thomas, interview, 1986. See also Martinez, Joe, interview, 1977, and Martinez, Rick, interview, 1975.
[80] "Martinez, Canuto and Gregoria, biography."

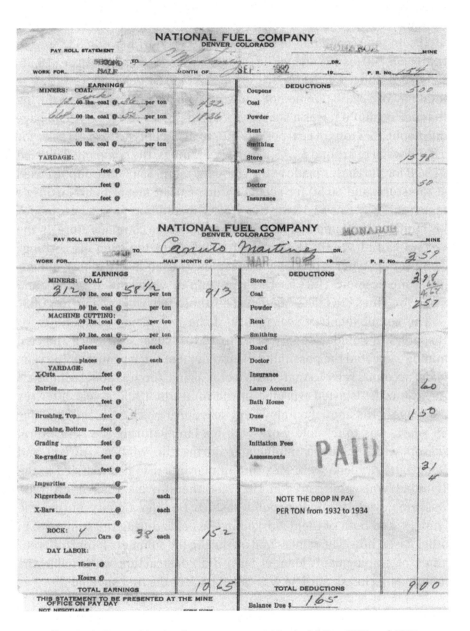

Illus. 3.13. Canuto Martinez's pay statements, Monarch Mine, 1932 and 1934

he mined for 30 winters. One of his grandsons preserved copies of two of Martinez's payroll statements, covering two weeks each, from the National Fuel Company for work at Lafayette's Monarch Mine in the early 1930s. In the second half of September, 1932, Martinez dug 332 tons of coal (= 66,400 lbs.), for which he received wages of 5.5¢ per ton or $18.26. He also produced 12 cartloads of rocks, for 3.6¢ per load, resulting in total pay of $22.58. We do not know how many days he worked during that period, but if it was a standard 6 1/2 days per week, he would have dug about 25.5 tons of coal per day plus nearly a full cartload of rocks, for a daily wage of around $1.75. From his earnings, the company deducted $15.98 for purchases made at the company store, $5.00 for coupons used at the store, and $0.50 for seeing a doctor. That meant that Martinez's take-home pay was $1.10 for two weeks, in addition to free housing for his family in the camp and the items bought at the company store. In the second half of March, 1934, the company deducted from his earnings $2.57 for "powder" (probably the explosive used in the mine), 60¢ for his "lamp account" (fuel for the headlamp he wore underground), and $1.50 for "dues." His take-home pay for those two weeks came to $1.65.

The complementary seasonality of the two major occupations for Hispanics in Boulder County prior to 1940—sugar beet work and coal mining—created the possibility of employment during much of the year. Many accounts refer to that pattern of seasonal/occupational rotation.[81] Alex Gonzales started working in the mines in 1925, a year after his marriage.[82] His annual employment schedule, which he maintained for 29 years, was to do field work with his family during the agricultural season while taking a mining job during the winters. Alfredo and Donaciana Arguello were Mexican immigrants who had married in the Trinidad/Walsenburg area in 1927 and then travelled north.[83] Alfredo was employed in mines around eastern Boulder County during the winters, and both of them worked in the fields during the summers. In other cases, however, miners laid off during the summers found different kinds of employment. Manuel Silva did construction work while the mines were closed, until he was called back at the first snowfall.[84]

---

[81] Alvarez, Teresa, interview, 1977, Martinez, Emma Gomez, interview, 2013, Montour, Eleanor, interview, 2013, "Borrego, Joseph Garfield, biography," "Manzanares, David J. and Marguerite, biography," and "Rosales, Henry and Alice, biography."
[82] Gonzales, Alex, interview, c. 1987.
[83] "Arguello, Alfredo and Donaciana and family, biography."
[84] Silva, Dolores, interview, 2013.

It is not clear whether a combination of mining and sugar beet labor was formally sanctioned by employers. Jim Hutchison, a long-time expert on coal mining in the Lafayette area, said that Rocky Mountain Fuel, the main local mining company, and Great Western Sugar had an agreement that kept workers employed throughout the year.[85] It was to both owners' advantage to have trained people stay in the area, rather than having to recruit and transport new workers each year. But the miners' union apparently opposed a proposal made by sugar beet growers that formal year-long contracts should be issued that combined the two types of seasonal employment.[86] Instead, the union hoped to force the mine owners themselves to hire men for the full year. Labor organizers argued that there was work to be done in the summers, including maintenance of buildings and handling coal that had already been extracted. In practice, however, workers appear to have been hired by the mining companies and individual farmers in separate partial-year contracts, thereby losing the employment security they might otherwise have enjoyed.

C. Other Jobs for Men

Opportunities for other kinds of paid work for Hispanic men were limited. By the early twentieth century, Longmont was beginning its career as a center of food processing. The largest early factory was operated by Great Western Sugar. It was built in 1903 at the request of local farmers who had the land, water rights, and access to labor needed for beet production but lacked a market for their crops.[87] Great Western purchased the factory in 1905. The process of converting raw beets into granulated sugar involved washing and cooking the beets to get a syrup, which was then separated from the beet pulp. The syrup was boiled further until it turned into a thick, dark substance like molasses and then crystalized into sugar ready for sale. Wagons pulled by horses, railroad cars, and later motorized vehicles brought in tons of beets for processing every day. At its peak, the factory processed 3,650 tons of beets daily (about 73 railcar loads).[88] The huge building located on

---

[85] Conversation with Marjorie McIntosh, Jan. 7, 2014.

[86] Leigh Campbell-Hale, conversation with Marjorie McIntosh, March 25, 2013.

[87] *Actual, Factual St. Vrain Valley*, pp. 40-42, and *Longmont 125th Anniversary*, pp. 48-51. For food processing, see also Ch. 5A below.

Illus. 3.14. Great Western Sugar factory, Longmont, 1903-1925

the southeastern edge of Longmont employed workers for all of those stages. The Empson Cannery, founded in 1889, processed local fruits and vegetables; in the early 1920s, Empson merged with the Kuner Canning Factory, increasing production.[89] Several flour mills were built on the outskirts of Longmont at the end of the nineteenth century, eventually employing hundreds of workers.[90]

These plants were not, however, major employers of Hispanics in the first part of the century. In 1919, Great Western built a brick dormitory to house workers in the factory who had been brought up from Mexico, but few local Spanish-speakers worked in the plant.[91] The U.S. Census for Longmont in 1920 lists four workers with Spanish names at the sugar factory and three men as foremen there; a decade later, there was only one.[92] The 1926 *Polk's City Directories* for Longmont, Lafayette,

---

[88] Hamilton, *Footprints in the Sugar*, p. 120.
[89] Scamehorn, *Colorado's Small Town Industrial Revolution*, chs. 2 and 5.
[90] *Longmont 125th Anniversary*, p. 48. There is no indication that Latinos were involved in growing the wheat that supplied these mills, much of it Turkey Red introduced by German-Russians.
[91] *Longmont 125th Anniversary*, p. 51.
[92] App. 3.2.

Illus. 3.15. Men and pumpkins outside Empson Cannery,
Longmont, early 20th century

and Boulder mention no one with a Spanish surname working in any factory or food processing facility, but in 1936, 11 Longmont men were employed at the Great Western plant.[93]

Men were sometimes hired in construction or transportation jobs, but as laborers, not skilled craftsmen. E. E. Bernal built houses for four years after leaving work in the mines, and Romolo Martinez, who came to Longmont in 1927, worked with various builders, "learning to be quite a good carpenter."[94] When work was slow, Martinez made adobe blocks, which he used to build several houses or barns in the Longmont area. The early *City Directories* include one Spanish-surnamed carpenter/ contractor in Boulder and two truck drivers in Longmont in 1936, though other workers may have been included among the many unspecified laborers with no employer given.[95] The U.S. Censuses show one truck driver in Boulder in 1930 and 1940 and two construction workers in

[93] "Occupations and Employers, Three Towns, 1926" and "Occupations and Employers, Three Towns, 1936."
[94] Bernal, Mr. and Mrs. Emerenciano, interview, 1977, and *They Came to Stay*, p. 159.
[95] "Occupations and Employers, Three Towns, 1936."

Lafayette in 1940.[96] In some parts of the American West, many Hispanics found employment in building and maintaining railroads.[97] Among Boulder County people, however, such work was rare until the 1940s.

Hispanics living in eastern Boulder County were seldom involved in the occupation that is often thought to characterize this region: hard rock mining. The mountains along the western side of the county were mined in the nineteenth century for gold and silver and later for such minerals as tungsten and fluorite. Although some mines were still being worked after 1900, we have found no mention of direct Spanish-speaking participation from our three towns. The only person known to have had a connection to mining was Roy Maestas, who moved from the southern Colorado coal fields to Boulder in 1930.[98] His first job in this area was to haul gold, tungsten, and other ores by truck down from the mountains; subsequently he found work as a coal miner.

The U.S. Censuses and *City Directories* reveal a few additional occupations among Spanish-surnamed men. A lawyer, born in Spain, lived in Longmont in 1920; Lafayette had an auto mechanic in 1930; and Boulder had a mechanic and an artist in 1940.[99] In 1936, a Hispanic prize fighter lived in Longmont, shoe shiners lived in Longmont and Boulder, and a manager and a clerk at Shorty's Place lived in Lafayette.[100] Benjamin Madrigal took a job in 1936 with one of the few factories in Boulder—Western States Cutlery—remaining there until 1975.[101]

New types of employment opportunities opened up in the mid-1930s. In an attempt to provide employment for the millions of people who were jobless as the result of the Great Depression, the federal government created the Works Progress Administration [WPA], one of the "New Deal" measures. In its peak year, 1938, the WPA hired 3 million people—men, women, and youth—throughout the country to carry out public works projects (like building roads, bridges, and schools and creating parks) or to engage in the arts. By the time the program closed in 1943, it had created nearly 8 million jobs. The contributions of the WPA were joined by another New Deal program, the Civilian Conservation Corps [CCC]. This program offered employment to people aged 18 to 25

---

[96] App. 3.2.
[97] For the work experiences and community life of Mexican railroad workers in the Southwest, see Garcilazo, *Traqueros*, chs. 3 and 5.
[98] "Maestas, Pedro (Roy), Ruby, and Abe, biography."
[99] App. 3.2.
[100] "Occupations and Employers, Three Towns, 1936." For boxers, see Vol. II, Ch. 4C.
[101] "Madrigal family of Boulder, biographies."

whose families were on relief; they were put to work on government-owned land to conserve and develop natural resources. Between 1933 and 1942 nearly 3 million young people nationally participated in the CCC.

Boulder County's Hispanics were hit hard by the Depression. Those who worked on seasonal contracts had no protection against a decreased demand for labor in agriculture and mining. Racist attitudes led some employers and local government officials to believe that if jobs were scarce, they should go to "real" Americans, not Spanish-speaking immigrants. They did not distinguish between people from Mexico and those from New Mexico/southern Colorado, or between recent immigrants and citizens.[102] But even non-citizens were eligible for WPA and CCC work, and in some areas they qualified for public welfare relief. Although Hispanic farm workers in Colorado sometimes complained that they were dropped from the WPA to provide cheap labor for sugar beet production, in Boulder County New Deal programs had more beneficial consequences.[103]

Their impact is made clear in our quantifiable sources. Whereas the *City Directories* for 1936 make no mention of local people with Spanish surnames employed by local governments or New Deal programs, the U.S. Census of 1940 reveals that such work had become vital to many families. In Longmont, 45 men and 4 women were working for the government.[104] They constituted 38% of all employed adult Hispanic men and half of all Hispanic women. Some were expressly described as participating in WPA or CCC programs; most of the others (like the 32 men working on roads, water projects, reforestation, and town buildings, and the four women in a training course for seamstresses) probably were too. Partial information from the 1940 U.S. Census for the other towns includes six men in Lafayette and three in Boulder who worked on road construction. They too may have been WPA employees.

Personal narratives confirm that some families were kept going thanks to these kinds of employment. Benjamin Madrigal, who had come to this country from Mexico as a baby in 1908, was unable to find regular work after his marriage and move to Boulder in 1931.[105] He was then hired on

---

[102] See Ch. 4 below.
[103] Abbott et al., *Colorado*, p. 286.
[104] As calculated from "Information about all Latinos, U.S. Census Records for Longmont, 1940."
[105] "Madrigal family of Boulder, biographies."

WPA projects, where he helped to construct buildings on the campus of the University of Colorado, build roads in the town and mountains, and create an open-air theater at the top of Flagstaff Mountain, overlooking Boulder. Jake Espinoza, who had lost his job with a railroad elsewhere in Colorado and was doing odd jobs and field work around Lafayette to feed his family, was likewise hired by the WPA.[106] Jake gave credit to U.S. President Franklin Roosevelt, who "established programs and relief for unemployed persons." Manuel Silva, who later became a coal miner, found a place with the CCC when he was in his late teens.[107] He worked in Rocky Mountain National Park, northwest of Boulder, and took care of town parks. As was to be true again in the later 1960s and 1970s, federal government programs made a significant difference for some local Hispanics.

D. The Work of Women and Children

Regardless of their national or ethnic origins, women prior to around 1940 were responsible for extensive domestic work. In an era with no labor-saving devices, women had to perform what may seem to us a huge amount of daily work in the house and sometimes the family's vegetable garden. In wealthy households, many of these tasks were performed by servants, but for poorer people of any ethnicity or race, it was the women of the family who shouldered most of the burden. Female labor at home made it possible for male members of the household to take jobs that brought in a cash income.

Interviews and family histories of Boulder County Hispanics describe these duties more fully. Women cooked and served meals, made or obtained the family's clothing and mended it, and kept the living quarters clean. They washed not only dishes but also all clothes and bedding by hand, having sometimes carried home the necessary water and the fuel for heating it. The wives of most miners and some beet workers raised vegetables and/or chickens, lessening their dependence upon purchased food. Women also needed to plan, organize, and supervise the domestic labor done by their daughters and other members of the household and keep a close eye on expenditures. Older Latinas sometimes expressed

---

[106] "Jake Espinoza at 94."
[107] Silva, Dolores, interview, 2013.

amazement in the 1970s at the amount of hard physical labor performed by their mothers and their ability to help the family get by with little income. The economic survival of the family unit thus relied upon the unpaid and often unacknowledged work of its female members, upon their physical stamina, intelligence, skillful management of domestic tasks, and thrift.

In Boulder County's Hispanic households, women filled other roles as well. They shouldered the primary responsibility for bearing and caring for their children, who were often numerous. They socialized their children, taught them good values, and trained girls in domestic skills; they looked after the health of their families; and they organized home-based religious worship and sometimes offered religious instruction.[108] Grandmothers provided information, practical assistance, and emotional support for younger relatives. Retrospective descriptions from the 1970s and 1980s underscore the economic partnership of the narrators' parents, with their fathers earning money and their mothers managing the household and its expenses. Gender relationships between husbands and wives rested upon an ethic of complementary work for the good of the family. This marital bond was often strong enough to withstand the potentially divisive effects of expanding female education and women's employment outside the home.[109]

Most Hispanic women in the first half of the twentieth century devoted their full efforts to their domestic tasks and made every penny count in large households with generally limited incomes. When Elvinia ("Bea") Martinez Borrego was a child in New Mexico, in the 1910s, she lived first with a grandmother and later with her father and stepmother.[110] She was never able to attend school because she had to work at home, either helping her father in the fields or assisting her stepmother with household chores, including the care of her younger brothers and sisters. She was so small that her father made a special little bench for her to stand on when she was washing dishes or clothing and doing the ironing.

Bea later put that training to good use while she and her husband Albert were living on the Pace Ranch outside Longmont. She was

---

[108] For these topics, see Vol. II, Chs. 1A, 3A-B, and 5B.
[109] See Chs. 5A and 6C below and Vol. II, Ch. 6.
[110] "Borrego, Albert and Elvinia ("Bea") Martinez, biography."

described by her daughter and granddaughter as:

> a professional homemaker, sewing, crocheting, gardening, and cooking for her family. Times were hard during the Great Depression, but she always managed to cook and bake goodies for her family. She made money stretch. Taking advantage of the summer harvest, she canned everything she could for the winter months and always had a cellar full of home-canned goods. She raised her own chickens so they could have fried chicken on Sundays, plus she sold fresh eggs to a local market to bring in a little extra income and sometimes buy treats and an occasional soda for the children. She took in ironing for extra money.[111]

Virginia Maestas told of the housework that had to be done when she was a child in the late 1930s and 1940s.[112] Her parents were agricultural laborers who moved annually with their five children to a new farm in Boulder County. The houses provided by their employers rarely had indoor plumbing, just outhouses. In one house they had a little pump in the kitchen, but normally they hauled water for drinking, cooking, and washing from ditches or an outside well. Because Virginia was the only girl in the family, she did lots of the domestic work. "Beds were made every day, the house was swept every day, ready for company, whether it came or not." On wash days, her brothers would bring in water to heat on the stove, before they left for the fields. Virginia then helped her mother do the laundry, using a washboard. Clofes Archuleta of Boulder heated water for washing on a coal stove, using two large galvanized tubs.[113] To do laundry, she punched a small hole in the bottom of a large can. Through the hole she inserted a long pole, and by pulling the pole up and down, she was able to agitate the clothes and bedding.

When Jennie and Joe Condido Vigil and their six children were living on the Lohr farm east of Boulder around 1950, in a house with two bedrooms, no running water, and a coal stove, Jennie grew and canned or preserved much of their food; she did all the cooking and house cleaning (with some help from her older daughters); and she made most of the children's clothes on a treadle sewing machine.[114] Her sisters supplemented home-made clothing with things they found at second-

---

[111] Ibid.
[112] Maestas, Virginia, interview, 2013. For housing, see Vol. II, Ch. 2A.
[113] "Archuleta family history."
[114] Vigil, Jennie, and others, interview, 2001.

hand and rummage stores. Her daughter Angela remembered, "Every time our aunts came over, we KNEW we were going to get something. Used clothing was a real treat."

Many rural women also worked in the fields at least occasionally, either on land for which their families had a contract or as paid laborers for someone else.[115] Lola Martinez, born in 1913, was one of the ten children of Canuto Martinez and his wife Gregoria. When Lola was in her teens and twenties, she did agricultural work with her parents and siblings during the summers. A nephew later commented, "Her days of hard work in the fields alongside her family gave her special sensitivity to those who need a hand up or an ear to just listen."[116] Angie Munoz, born in Longmont in 1921, grew up in the camp beside the Columbine Mine, where her father worked. At harvest time, her mother and older siblings would all hire out to local farmers, leaving Angie at home to look after the younger children.[117]

Few local Hispanic women were engaged in other kinds of paid work until the 1950s. Just one woman was listed in *Polk's City Directories* for 1926 as employed—a maid in Longmont—though by 1936 the number had risen to nine.[118] In the latter year, women accounted for 5%-7% of all listed workers in each of the towns. The increase in female employment may have resulted from severe need within families due to the shortage of male jobs during the Depression. Longmont's female workers now included two maids, a housekeeper, a seamstress, and an unspecified laborer; Lafayette had one maid and one housekeeper; and Boulder had one maid and one kitchen helper at Community Hospital. Eva Bernal of Boulder augmented her husband's earnings by ironing for pay.[119] Such work—low skilled, poorly paid, and done largely within domestic contexts—was similar to that done by women of all backgrounds at the time, thereby helping to maintain a patriarchal system.

Children often contributed to the economic well-being of their families, especially during the first third of the century. The most common form of labor was with beets, where they worked alongside one

---

[115] In the 1930 U.S. Census, eleven women from Longmont and Lafayette were listed as beet workers and one as an unspecified farm laborer (App. 3.1).

[116] See Vol. II, Illus. 1.7.

[117] "Casias, Angelina and Raymond, biography."

[118] "Occupations and Employers, Three Towns, 1926" and "Occupations and Employers, Three Towns, 1936."

[119] "Bernal, E. E. and Eva, biography and photo."

or both parents. If a mother was in the fields, she probably had no place to leave her children, and even young ones could help to collect the weeds that had been dug up or pile sugar beets. As children moved into their teens, their labor might be essential to their family's ability to complete its contract. Prior to 1938, the use of children in agriculture—which was common among many rural families, regardless of their ethnicity—was generally accepted on the grounds that they were there with their parents. The author of an essay written in 1924 said that Mexican children, "with rare exceptions, work with and under the supervision of their own parents, and except where the parents are ignorant and cruel, may not suffer physically from overwork."[120] He admitted, however, that the children were often kept out of school, especially in the fall, which slowed their advancement.

Hispanics who had worked in the fields as children remembered that life less positively. Merce Vela described the work he did as a child after coming to Longmont with his parents in 1930 as "backbreaking, hard, and heavy."[121] During the harvest, his family would put in 18-hour days: he remembered working far into the night "to beat the first snowfall." His wife Mary, who came to this area in 1926, said that when her family was topping beets, "Dad would get us up at 4 am. We'd work til breakfast, when we'd be all wet from the leaves, we'd change, eat, and go out again." Al Cardenas's parents and their large family of children moved from Aguilar to the area around Erie, where they all worked in the fields. "We did sugar beets, produce, whatever it was on the farms. . . . It wasn't a pleasant job, but that's what we had to do."[122]

The early U.S. Census records for Longmont list few Spanish-surnamed children under the age of 18 as working. In 1910, one 16-year-old boy did odd jobs; in 1920, three boys aged 12 to 16 were described as farm laborers or laborers in beet fields, while a 14-year-old boy worked for an oil company.[123] The Longmont Census for 1930, however, shows that children were now much more heavily engaged in agriculture. A total of 132 adults and children were described as farm laborers, beet workers, or in other agricultural employment. Of that total, 36% were children under

[120] Robert McLean, "Mexicans in the Beet Fields," p. 79.
[121] "Sugar beets brought early Hispanics to Longmont" for this and Mary Vela, below.
[122] Cardenas, Alfonso, interview, 2004. He had eight sisters and four brothers.
[123] "Information about all Latinos, U.S. Census Records for Longmont."

the age of 18. To our eyes, the following figures may be troubling.

Age of child	No. of boys working	No. of girls working	Total no. of children working
6-10 years	7	6	13
11-15 years	11	10	21
16-17 years	9	4	13
Total	27	20	47 [124]

Two other boys aged 16-17 were laborers at the sugar factory or did odd jobs.

The situation changed markedly in 1938 with the passage of the National Fair Labor Standards Act. That law prohibited the use of children under 18 in "oppressive child labor" or dangerous conditions, and it barred children under 16 from working during school hours. An important contributor to the restriction of child labor in agriculture was a novel published in 1935 about beet workers in northeastern Colorado. Hope Williams Sykes' *Second Hoeing* described beet workers who were German-speaking immigrants from Russia, not Hispanics. But its powerful and painful portrayal of the harm done to children by field work, which kept them from attending school and sometimes damaged their health, helped to create pressure for legislation that affected young workers from all backgrounds.

The 1940 U.S. Census for Longmont appears to reflect the new restrictions, though some respondents may simply have refrained from mentioning children who were actually working.[125] Only five teenagers (four boys and a girl, all but one aged 16 or 17) were said to be farm laborers. Two other 17-year-old boys were participating in government employment programs for young people, while three girls aged 16 or 17 worked as maids or housekeepers in private homes. Although some of the people interviewed for this project did agricultural work as children/ teens after the 1938 law, their employment normally took place after school, on weekends, or during school vacations.

Some urban children helped with other kinds of family work. Doris Gonzales, born in 1928, and her siblings lived with her Uncle Pete

---

[124] U.S. Census Records for Longmont, 1930: information as entered by Rebecca Chavez and analyzed by Marjorie McIntosh.

[125] "Information about all Latinos, U.S. Census Records for Longmont."

Saragosa and his family for four years after her mother contracted tuberculosis and was placed in a sanitarium.[126] They shared a big house on the western side of Boulder with three other families. When the 15 children were not in school, they worked in the large vegetable garden and orchards where the Saragosas grew food for sale. The youngsters carried salt shakers in their pockets so they could eat wild or cultivated vegetables during the day, as they were not allowed to come back for a mid-day meal. After Marcella Diaz, who was raised by her grandparents, moved with them to Boulder, she and a young aunt helped her grandmother clean other people's houses on the weekends and in the summers.[127] They turned over their earnings to the family "pot." When her grandmother started a laundry and ironing service out of her home, the girls helped with it too.

While most working children were doing something with relatives, a few had to earn an income on their own. Mines offered employment to some teen-aged boys. In 1919, Joe Arroyo came to Colorado from Mexico with his mother, grandmother, and two sisters after his father's death.[128] He was the only person in the family able to get a job, though he was just 13 years old. He found work in a coal mine, where, after the first three days of using a pick with a cracked handle to hack at the coal face, his hands were so covered with blisters that the skin peeled entirely off. When he looked at the small piles of coal and rocks he had produced despite that pain, he lay down right where he was working and cried. Roy Maestas, born in 1909, moved with his parents from New Mexico to the area west of Trinidad in the late 1910s.[129] He started school in Delagua, where his father worked at a coke oven, but after his father's death when Roy was 14 or 15 years old, he had to leave school and take a job at a mine in order to provide for his mother and younger siblings. At first he loaded and delivered coal, but when he was a little older, he worked as a regular miner. Joe Jaramillo, Jr., the oldest son of the man killed in the 1936 Monarch Mine explosion, had been going down into the mine with his dad since he was seven to help tend the mules.[130] After his father's death, young Joe, then aged 14, left school and took a full-time job at another nearby mine to support his mother and siblings. He

[126] Gonzales, Doris, interview, 2013.
[127] "Martinez, Juan and Josephine; Marcella Diaz, biography."
[128] "Los Inmigrantes."
[129] Maestas, Roy, interview, 1978.
[130] William Cohen, "Blast," for this and below.

spent the rest of his working life—42 years—as a miner.

A job sometimes carried out by young boys was herding sheep. Future Longmont resident Albert "Paco" Borrego was born in 1906 in Clayton, New Mexico.[131] Because his parents could not provide for all their offspring, he and two of his siblings were "rented out" to other people as workers, a practice he said was common among poor families at the time. When he was only eight years old, Albert was hired to tend a flock of sheep. The animals were walked in a drove up to summer grazing areas in the mountains, and Albert was left there alone to protect them. Years later he recalled that "he felt totally abandoned. Isolated, exposed to the elements, sometimes wet and cold, having to fend for himself, and even kill rattlesnakes." His mother came up occasionally to drop off food staples. "When she drove off in the wagon, Albert ran after her, crying, begging to go home. She left him, nonetheless."

Girls normally remained at home until they married, helping around the house, looking after younger siblings or other relatives, and perhaps joining their parents in agricultural labor. Occasionally, however, they might have to take independent paid employment. One of Oli Duncan's great-grandmothers had been a teacher in the Chama Valley of New Mexico, but she became solely responsible for her children after her brutal husband was imprisoned for a murder.[132] Now facing acute poverty, she went to work herself and placed her nine-year-old daughter as a live-in servant with a non-Hispanic family. Mary Martinez, then in her mid-teens, was left on her own with three younger sisters and a 15-year-old aunt when the grandparents with whom they had been living died in the 1930s.[133] The older girls left school and started looking for work to support their household. People did not want to hire them, because they were just girls, so at first they took whatever jobs they could find, like cleaning chicken houses and sorting peas. Later, however, a nearby farmer who needed workers gave them a chance, hiring all of the orphaned girls. A widower with five daughters of his own, he taught them everything they needed to know about a farm. Mary and one of his daughters used to ride horses to bring the cattle back in from the fields, and they learned how to drive mules, use tractors, and handle other machinery. Mary and her sisters continued to work for him for 15 years.

---

[131] "Borrego, Albert and Elvinia ("Bea") Martinez, biography." For another young shepherd, hired out every summer between the ages of 6 and 11, see "Jacob Espinoza, Obituary."
[132] Duncan, "Some Notes."
[133] Martinez, Mary, interview, 1988.

The information presented in this chapter makes clear that Hispanic workers were essential to the economic development of eastern Boulder County through the physically demanding labor they performed. While the primary workers were adult males, sugar beets required the labor of entire families at least in peak periods, and boys might start work in the mines in their teens. Women also organized and carried out—sometimes with the help of their children or other relatives—the domestic work that freed men to earn a cash income, and they exercised the frugality necessary to the family's survival. Marriage was rightly perceived as an economic partnership between the spouses for the good of the whole family. Even in the early twenty-first century, a willingness to work very hard to support one's family, sometimes holding multiple jobs, remained a characteristic of many of Boulder County Latinos and Latinas.[134]

---

[134] See the Epilogue, below, and Vol. II, the discussion of legacies at the end of its Epilogue.

Chapter 4

Conflict, Racism, and Violence, 1910-1940

Whereas the previous chapter noted the difficult working conditions faced by early Hispanics in Boulder County, this one describes even harsher aspects of their lives during the 1910s, 1920s, and 1930s. These decades experienced the severe economic slowdown in Colorado that followed World War I and the more disastrous conditions of the Great Depression. We first examine the role of unions in trying to get better wages and improved working conditions for coal miners and agricultural laborers. When the unions called strikes, owners and local authorities put them down by hiring temporary workers, arresting the organizers, and/or calling in troops. The chapter turns next to the issue of racism. Hispanics faced prejudice in all Boulder County towns around 1920, and that background level of discrimination was made more overt by the Ku Klux Klan. The KKK taught that white people were racially superior; it believed that power should rest in the hands of U.S. male citizens who were members of a Protestant church. In the Boulder area, Klan venom was directed at Hispanics, who were hated not only for their Catholic religion but also because they were brown-skinned and assumed to be immigrants to this country, sometimes wrongly. The final section of the chapter talks about "repatriating" immigrants (sending them back to Mexico) and forced deportations. It is impossible to read this chapter without being struck by the parallels with events in the southwestern U.S. in the early 2010s.

A. Labor Unions and Strikes, 1910-1935

The years between 1910 and 1932 saw considerable activity by labor unions in eastern Boulder County, as was true in much of the state.[1] Union organizers tried to gain members and mobilize them to act as a group in demanding better working conditions and higher wages from employers. If their conditions were not met, unions called strikes, in which their members refused to go to their normal jobs and tried to keep newly hired workers from stepping into their places by mounting lines of picketers carrying protest signs at key entry points. In the Boulder area, unions were most active among coal miners, but in 1932 sugar beet workers too went on strike, one of the earliest farmworkers' strikes in Colorado's history.

Tension over unionization was particularly high in the 1930s, due to the Depression. Owners and operators of coal mines, Great Western Sugar, and the farmers who grew beets all saw their profits decline and were therefore eager to cut labor costs by lowering wages as well as laying off workers. Miners and beet workers claimed they could not support their families on the reduced pay that was offered to them, yet many hesitated to protest actively for fear they would lose their jobs entirely and be unable to find other employment. The force needed to stop strikes was provided by local and state government officials worried about economic and social unrest.

Although we do not have exact figures for how many union members in Boulder County were Hispanic, it is clear that some—perhaps many—were. Personal narratives indicate that some Lafayette miners in the 1920s and 1930s were active in the unions.[2] In the beet workers' strike of 1932, organized by a branch of the Industrial Workers of the World, all of the "agitators" arrested had Spanish names, and they included women as well as men. Labor organizations and their meetings brought Hispanics into contact with a wider group of people and served a social function as well. Some Boulder County miners made good friends with other union members, including people from different national or ethnic backgrounds, continuing to socialize with them after they no longer worked in the mines.[3]

---

[1] Unions were already active among miners elsewhere in Colorado between 1880 and 1903 (Abbott, Colorado, pp. 146-154, and Andrews, Killing for Coal, esp. ch. 5).

[2] E.g., "Archuleta/Ortega family information," "Manzanares, David J. and Marguerite, biography," and Duncan, Erminda "Oli" Olivas, interview, 2013.

[3] E.g., "Madrigal family of Boulder, biographies" and "Archuleta/Ortega family information."

Coal miners

Although coal miners labored in difficult and often dangerous physical settings, many workers considered these jobs more desirable than agricultural employment, in part because in some periods their unions fought on their behalf.[4] Miners and the owners or operators of mines in northern Colorado had repeated conflicts between 1910 and 1935, a period when many Hispanics were moving in from Mexico, New Mexico, and southern Colorado.[5] The lengthiest confrontation, and probably the most difficult for workers, was "the Long Strike" of 1910 to 1914.[6] It was called initially by the United Mine Workers of America [UMWA] in response to the efforts of northern Colorado mine operators to eradicate the UMWA from their coal fields, located mainly in Boulder and Weld Counties, despite having signed contracts with the union the past few years. The UMWA then extended the strike to the southern coal fields, around Trinidad and Walsenburg.

The Long Strike brought violence as well as economic hardship to the union miners. At its very beginning, operators of mines in the northern fields obtained help from local sheriffs in guarding the sites and protecting the non-union workers hired by the companies to keep the mines running; more than 100 deputies and detectives from Denver provided additional force.[7] In 1912, a gun battle broke out near Lafayette between union and non-union miners, with at least 1,000 shots fired and one man wounded.[8] By April, 1914, about 3,000 miners had left work in Lafayette and the nearby coal towns of Erie, Louisville, Marshall, and Superior. The union had by then run out of funds to help support its striking members, so individual families suffered badly. Their entire communities must have been affected too, for those five towns had a combined population of no more than 5,000 people, and the majority of their working males were miners.

To keep operations going, the mining companies brought in strike breakers (known as "scabs" by union members) to go into the mines and work, crossing the picket lines maintained by union members. Some of the men had been brought up from Mexico specifically for that purpose.

[4] See Ch. 3B above.
[5] See Ch. 2 above.
[6] Smith, *Once a Coal Miner*, chs. 8-10.
[7] Adelfang, ed., *Erie*, p. 68.
[8] "Ten Day War."

At the Hecla Mine, on the edge of Lafayette, the Northern Coal and Coke Company built housing for its strike breakers and put up a fence around the compound, to protect them from union men. A nearby tower housed searchlights and a machine gun. When angry strikers outside the compound shot out the searchlights, the guards fired the machine gun at them but apparently did not hit anyone. Boulder County Sheriff Martin P. Capp, who tried to provide protection for the strikers, told the *Boulder Camera*, "The mine operators are the most intemperate men I have ever dealt with."[9]

The Long Strike culminated in April, 1914 with the Ludlow Massacre in southern Colorado.[10] It took place near a mine operated by the Colorado Fuel and Iron Company, owned by John D. Rockefeller, Jr. There the Colorado State Militia attacked a tent city in which 1,200 striking miners and their families were staying. Some 39 people were killed, including women and children who were burned to death in their tents. Don Archuleta of Longmont recalled that his aunt Lola and her husband John Espinoza, a miner, were almost victims of the massacre.[11] They were living in the tents along with the other strikers, but because they suspected that troops were about to be brought in, they crawled down into an arroyo and worked their way out of the camp just in time.

When news of the Ludlow disaster reached Lafayette, local miners sent help to the southern camp. Fighting broke out in Boulder County too, with both strikers and strike breakers wounded. Sheriff Capp worked valiantly to maintain peace, preventing further deaths. When the governor announced he was sending a militia force into the area, Capp tried to keep it out, until eventually Federal troops came in to restore order. The strike finally ended late in 1914, though the demands of the union had still not been met. Until the later 1920s, most Colorado mines banned members of the UMWA from employment.

A strike in 1927 called by the I.W.W. (Industrial Workers of the World, a socialist/communist union known as the "Wobblies") likewise ended in death, this time at the Columbine Mine on the edge of Boulder County.[12] The Columbine, owned by the Rocky Mountain Fuel Company,

---

[9] Ibid.

[10] For background and a full account, see Andrews, *Killing for Coal*.

[11] Archuleta, Don, interview, 2009.

[12] "The Columbine Incident," and, more fully, Campbell-Hale, "Remembering Ludlow." The I.W.W. had already aroused fear in Colorado. As part of the "Red Scare" of 1919, its local headquarters in Denver and Pueblo were raided by the police and its organizers run out of town (Abbott et al., *Colorado*, pp. 269-70).

was located just a few miles ENE of Lafayette; its housing camp was known as "Serene." The Columbine was the only mine in the northern Colorado fields that continued to operate during the 1927 strike, due to the importation of scab workers. Union miners therefore focused their efforts here. The strike had widespread support: one meeting in Lafayette was joined by as many as 4,000 people, including community members and miners from other places.[13]

Because strikers were picketing the Columbine so energetically, Governor Billy Adams at the request of the owners sent in the newly formed State Law Enforcement Agency, a militia force, to protect the mine and strike breakers and curb the picketing. The troopers were under the command of a veteran of the Ludlow Massacre. On November 21, 1927, some 500 supporters of the strike—townspeople as well as miners and their families—came to a protest meeting at the mine. When conflict broke out, the troopers opened fire on the protesters, killing 6 people and wounding 60 others, both men and women.

The Columbine Strike and Massacre were long remembered by people living in this area. John Ortega had moved from the southern Colorado coal fields shortly before the strike started and was living in the Serene camp with his wife Mary and their five children.[14] During the strike, the gates to the fence that surrounded the camp were sometimes locked, with no one allowed in or out. The Ortegas helped with the union's relief efforts. Donated clothing was sent in from other places, and a joint committee of strikers and community people distributed it to needy families. David Toledo likewise joined the Columbine strike; because he had no income, he learned how to be a barber to support himself.[15] Sally Martinez, whose family was living in the camp when she was ten years old, recalled going out every morning before school during the strike with her friend Virginia Amicarella to march with the pickets.[16] She was at home when she heard the sound of shooting, which killed or wounded so many.

Trouble was brewing again in spring, 1932, during a period when

[13] Smith, *Once A Coal Miner*, p. 170. This may have been the time when two of Canuto and Gregoria Martinez's mining sons were arrested as strikers. Family lore has it that Gregoria marched off to the jail and got them out, without paying bail ("Martinez, Canuto and Gregoria, biography").

[14] "Ortega, John, family of, biography."

[15] Toledo, David, interview, c. 1978.

[16] "Salazar, Jose Benito and Isabelle, biography." After the strike, her father was laid off permanently.

the Rocky Mountain Fuel Company had again signed on with the UMWA, in part to avoid dealing with the I.W.W. Due to the Depression and declining demand for heating fuel, the company had recently cut miners' wages, as had happened several times before. Mine operators in the northern Colorado fields had previously banded together to lower wages to the same level, to reduce their costs without causing unprofitable competition between them. The *Lafayette Leader* reported on May 7 that the state Labor Commission had denied permission to mine operators in the northern fields to cut wages further.[17] But the operators, including Rocky Mountain Fuel Company, had nonetheless gone ahead and reduced miners' pay by another 15%. Although the Labor Commission objected to this action, it lacked the power to enforce its decision. Over the next few weeks, miners in Lafayette and elsewhere held meetings to protest the pay cuts.[18] On May 27 the Lafayette paper noted that the State Industrial Commission had just rejected yet another application from the northern Colorado lignite coal operators, this time to reduce the basic pay of miners from $6.72 to $5 per day, a drop of 26%.[19] The commission "held there was no justification for a reduction in the wage scale," but it could not force adherence to its decision.

Quite different views about miners' wages must have been presented in Boulder on May 24, 1932, when Miss Josephine Roche, who had just become principal owner of the Rocky Mountain Fuel Company, addressed the Economic Round Table and the Young America Group at the University of Colorado. The *Boulder Camera* quoted the University's paper as saying,

> Miss Roche is a famous lecturer and writer on democracy in industry and one of the most outstanding progressive liberals of the time. She is one of the leading advocates of profit sharing in industry and conducts her own company on a strictly profit sharing basis. She has conducted many experiments in more democratic relations with workers, and the dealings of her company with its miners are outstanding for their fairness.[20]

[17] "Coal miners' wages cut."
[18] Ibid.
[19] "Coal miners' wage cuts denied."
[20] "Josephine Roche speaks tonight." Ms. Roche had a distinguished future career. After running unsuccessfully for governor of Colorado in 1934, she was appointed Assistant Secretary of the U.S. Treasury by President Roosevelt, a position she held until 1937.

That description was well warranted. After graduating from Vassar College in 1908 and receiving a Master's Degree from Columbia University, Ms. Roche did social work for some years. In 1927, however, she inherited shares in the Rocky Mountain Fuel Company from her father. Over the next few years she purchased a majority interest in the company and became its president. She then enacted a variety of pro-labor policies, based upon her philosophy that capital and labor had equal rights, including inviting the UMWA to unionize her mines. In its 1932 article, the *Boulder Camera* wrote that "In the recent price war of the fuel companies of Colorado, Miss Roche refused to reduce the wages of her workers for the purpose of cutting prices, but the workers themselves agreed to make a loan of a portion of their wages to the company in order that it might be able to compete with the others."[21] Few mine workers probably ventured onto the University campus to hear her talk, nor would most mine operators have wanted to listen.

The UMWA had more success in the mid-1930s, thanks largely to the passage of the Wagner Act of 1934.[22] On Sept. 23, 1935 the *Longmont Times-Call* reported that 2,500 mine workers were on strike in the northern Colorado coal field as well as in other parts of the state.[23] In Boulder County, 750 miners were said to be participating. Two days later the paper claimed that the entire northern field was shut down.[24] But this time there was no mention of picketing, and the union's representative in Lafayette allowed maintenance men to keep the mines ready to resume activity, for an agreement with the coal companies was expected soon. The Boulder County Hispanic sources provide no further information about industrial conflict, though some workers remained active in their unions.

Sugar beet workers

Agricultural workers have always been hard to unionize, even though their jobs were often physically exhausting and poorly paid. Laborers were spread out over various farms and fields, rather than being concentrated in a mine or factory. Workers might be hired as

---

[21] "Josephine Roche speaks tonight."
[22] That measure guaranteed the rights of most private-sector employees to unionize, engage in collective bargaining, and if necessary strike; it did not, however, apply to agricultural workers.
[23] "8000 Colorado miners on strike."
[24] "All mines in Northern Colorado closed."

TIMES
and Community

THE TIMES
is served by a direct United Press
wire. Up-to-the-minute news of
the state, nation and world.

NUMBER 32

BEET LABORERS OF LOCAL DISTRICT DENY AFFILIATION WITH THE I. W. W.

ER
IDAY

Century
:nds

MANY ATTEND FARM AUCTION

175 Workers Hold Meeting Thursday Night and Go on Record as Opposed to Formation of Organization Liable to Create Strife

.gmont.
a to the first
: still living
Springs; Irv:
Mrs. L. E.
A. G. Crock-
Mrs. H. W.

A record breaking crowd attended
the John Ehler sale Thursday, and
everything was disposed of at satis-
factory prices.
W. A. Fisher conducted the auction
sale.
Mr. and Mrs. Ehler moved into the
F. W. Saylor residence on Collyer
street. F. W. Baird is moving to the
Ehler ranch.

WAGE SCALE NOT MENTIONED BUT BETTER LIVING CONDITIONS ASKED

As a result of published statements that I. W. W. organizers are busy
among the beet workers of Northern Colorado with the intention of enlisting
them as members of the organization for the purpose of forcing demands
upon the growers thru strikes and otherwise after beets have reached a
critical stage, a meeting of the laborers from what is known as the Longmont
Sanpish speaking people.

y died April
urs later the
nces Bartlett
· came here

BIRTHDAY PARTY HELD FOR MOTHER OF LOCAL PASTOR

s been at the
years and al-
cians do not
ious. An an-
r, was not
red the ex-
ental to her

A birthday party was held at the
Methodist parsonage Friday in honor
of Mrs. Adeline Hollerback, 82 years
old, Denver, mother of Rev. R. F. Hol-
lenback.
Two daughters, Mrs. Ella Layton and
Mrs. A. A. Nall, Denver, are in Longmont for the occasion.

After discussing the situation at
length, a committee composed of W.
Montes, Benjamin Garcia and Ramon
Montes was appointed to wait upon
the newspapers, and thru these publications, convey to the people a denial
of any connection whatsoever with the
I. W. W. In a statement to the editor
of The Times, spoken in good English,
Ramon Montes, as spokesman said:
"We were named at the meeting last
night to visit the newspapers and deny
any connection with the I. W. W. The
contract was not discussed for 1928 as
the farmer does not know what he is
to get for his beets. But the grower
cannot pay more unless he gets more
money. We do want better living quarters and more sanitary conditions and
believe we are entitled to them, but
will try to bring this about in a
friendly way, but we are not members
of the I. W. W."
We were informed by Montes and the
other two members of the committee
that a former meeting was held on Jan.
12 when living conditions were discussed, but no mention was made of the

price to be paid for tending beets the
coming season.
These men are to represent the Longmont colony at a meeting to be held in
Brighton tomorrow when 26 colonies
are to be represented. In speaking of
this meeting the men said:
"We were instructed to leave the
meeting if we discover the I. W. W.
has any part in it, and return to Longmont. In that case we will carry on
our work among ourselves."
In no uncertain language Montes declared that everyone would suffer
should the I. W. W. organize the beet
workers and cause a strike in the beet
fied during the growing season. The
grower would suffer and so would the
laborers," stated one of the men.
When asked if they expect to ask
for more money for labor, the reply
was:
"We are more interested in living
conditions than we are in more money,
but believe this can be brought about
thru a better understanding and a
friendly agreement. We want to cooperate with the grower and the sugar
company."

ART
OF
IIED

IRISH PRESIDENT ARRIVES FRIDAY

(United Press.)
NEW YORK, Jan. 20.—Enthusiastic
and noisy greetings were accorded to
W. T. Cosgrave, president of the Irish
Free State when he landed here today
for a two weeks' visit to the United
States.

eart, former
·ome for life
lthy canning
·e, but under-
·s long as he

HICKMAN ILL FROM FEVER

(United Press.)
LOS ANGELES, Calif., Jan. 20.—
Will Ed. Hickman, slayer of Marian
Parker, developed a high fever today
following an operation to remove
fluid from his spine in connection with
tests being made to support his in-
sanity plea.
Physicians at the jail said the ill-
ness was natural.

.tions receiv-
·e Longmont
·est was for
which went
is located in
·ed that ren-
·, Mont., dur-
ted to $57,-
is now held

APOPLEXY FATAL TO AGED LOCAL RESIDENT THURSDAY

Henry Gephart, 72 years old, died
suddenly late Thursday afternoon at
his home, 735 Martin street, following
a stroke of apoplexy.
Mr. Gephart appeared to be in the
best of health and had returned from

sons, Ernest, Longmont, and Thomas
of La Junta.
The deceased came to Colorado 30
years ago and moved to Longmont in
1908. He was a member of the K. P.
lodge and the Christian church

Illus. 4.1. *"Beet laborers deny affiliation with IWW",
Longmont Times-Call, Jan. 20, 1928*

single men or families by individual farmers, rather than having many people working for a single employer with whom they could negotiate collectively. Migrant workers often moved through multiple areas during a given season and hence were unable to participate actively in any organizations, whether economic, social, or religious. Nor did agricultural laborers receive the protections granted to other workers in the Wagner Act and other New Deal labor legislation of the 1930s.

Hispanic beet workers in Colorado in the 1920s and 1930s were not in a strong position to demand better working conditions and wages from their employers. If they complained to the farmers who were their immediate employers, the farmers said that their hands were tied: Great Western Sugar's contracts dictated the conditions and rewards for work. Great Western said it only negotiated with farmers, not directly with field workers. In 1928, a meeting of beet workers called for better living conditions but did not protest the wage scale. They were also careful to dissociate themselves from the I.W.W., which was then trying to organize agricultural workers.

Four years later, however, when a sub-branch of the I.W.W. called a strike among beet workers in northeastern Colorado and the Arkansas River Valley of southeastern Colorado, some people from Boulder County took part.[25] Both male and female Hispanics were among the organizers of the 1932 strike, which was centered in Weld County, lying immediately to the east/northeast of Boulder County, but included some farms in this area too. Active coverage of the strike in east Boulder County's newspapers indicates that interest was high among their readers, some of whom would have been farmers raising beets for Great Western who relied on Hispanic labor. The articles make no distinction between people born in Mexico and those who had come from New Mexico or southern Colorado: all were simply "Mexicans."

The strike, which started on May 16, was called to protest "what the workers term 'starvation wages' and because of conditions which they say border on 'slavery.'"[26] Between 1924 and 1928, sugar beet laborers had received a minimum rate of $22 - $24 per acre for tending and harvesting the crop during the whole six-month season.[27] In 1931, after the Depression hit, the per acre rate dropped to $19, and in 1932, employers

---

[25] For "radical labor unrest in the Colorado beet fields" more generally, see Vargas, *Labor Rights*, pp. 70-76.

[26] "Beet growers disclaim responsibility for strike."

[27] Taylor, *Mexican Labor*, p. 142.

offered workers only $13 - $15 per acre. The union, claiming that the average beet laborer earned just $150 in a full season, encouraged its members to strike for $23 per acre.

Because this strike has received little historical attention, we will trace its course by means of local newspaper accounts. The first reference was indirect. On May 17, the *Longmont Times-Call* mentioned that three Weld County taxpayers had appeared before the County Commissioners in Greeley to insist that any person who participated in a labor strike be removed permanently from the list of those eligible for county aid.[28] They claimed also that farmers could not afford the higher payments per acre that beet workers were demanding.

The next day the *Times-Call* reported that seven "agitators," all with Spanish names, had been arrested by the Weld County sheriff for intimidating workers and threatening violence.[29] The sheriff claimed that the agitators had been "riding around, talking to groups of laborers here and there, making threats in some places." One of the organizers operated a pool hall in "Ragtown" (apparently a neighborhood in Greeley), which probably served as a social center for Hispanic men, who were not allowed into Anglo-owned bars and restaurants at the time.[30] Most of the other agitators lived in "the Spanish-American colony" (presumably Great Western's *colonia*) on the edge of Greeley.[31] The May 18 article also suggested that when jobs were scarce, they should go to Americans. It commented approvingly that one Japanese truck gardener had decided "to curb strike activities on his own farm in his own manner."[32] When his Mexican cabbage setters were tempted by agitators who tried to persuade them to join the strike, he fired them all "and got a new set of laborers of Anglo-Saxon blood and who would not be hindered by the visits of Mexican strike leaders."

Action against strikers continued. On May 19, the *Times-Call* noted that ten more "strike agitators" had been arrested in Weld County.[33] Three of the five who were jailed for "trespass and disturbance" (urging workers to leave the fields) had Spanish surnames. In response to

---

[28] "No benefits for strikers."
[29] "First arrests in beet strike."
[30] For pool halls, see Vol. II, Ch. 4B.
[31] That *colonia* had been constructed to house Hispanic workers, located at a distance from the rest of the town (Lopez and Lopez, *White Gold Laborers*, esp. chs. 2 and 4-5).
[32] For Japanese people brought in a generation before as sugar beet workers, see Ch. 3A above.
[33] "Beet growers disclaim responsibility for strike."

the workers' demands, the Mountain States Beet Growers Marketing Association, which represented farm owners, denied any responsibility for the conditions that had led to the strike.[34] The participation of Boulder County beet workers in the strike was described on May 20, when an article reported that Longmont police had "received telephone calls that some armed Mexicans had made threats to workers" in the area.[35] Eight Mexicans, who were picketing and trying to keep other workers from taking "scab" jobs in the fields, were arrested on charges of intimidation. When a meeting of workers appeared likely to end in violence, local authorities mustered their forces, but the crowd—though sullen—left quietly.

That same day the I.W.W. committee that was coordinating the strike filed a formal protest with the State Industrial Commission and Governor Adams against the proposed slash in wages, asking that compensation instead be set at $23 per acre.[36] The committee demanded also a guarantee that at the end of the season, workers would indeed be paid the amount they and the farmer had agreed upon, rather than allowing employers to say they could not afford to deliver those wages.

The strike had now become sufficiently widespread and alarming to farmers and local authorities that the state police were ordered into the northeastern Colorado beet region.[37] Although the police were said to be there only "in case further trouble developed," their presence was presumably intended to restrain strike activists. Punitive measures intensified. On May 21, a *Times-Call* article said that picketing charges had been filed against two dozen activists.[38] The arrests near Greeley came after the sheriff had tailed the organizers for hours to see what they were doing. The paper was explicit about the ethnicity of participants: "The strikers, in the main, are Mexicans. Virtually all of the labor leaders arrested have been Mexicans." Interestingly, 6 of the 24 people jailed

---

[34] They claimed that their contracts with Great Western Sugar specified the amount of wages that should be paid to laborers; even with these lower payments, they were expecting a loss on their 1932 beet growing operations. The growers did not support labor contracts that would be unfair to the beet workers, but they could not recommend contracts that "would simply plunge the farmer deeper in debt" (ibid.).

[35] "State police sent to beet area."

[36] "Beet workers protest."

[37] "State police sent to beet area."

[38] "24 more agitators, mainly Mexicans, arrested."

were women. As early as the 1930s, Hispanic women were not only workers, some were activists![39]

On May 25, 18 Hispanic union organizers were given jail terms by a court in Greeley for violating anti-picketing and vagrancy laws.[40] Their leader, J. H. Cordova, aged 42, was sentenced to 30 days in jail, while the others received 15 days for picketing and 5 days for vagrancy. They had all pleaded "not guilty" and appeared in court without legal counsel. Witnesses for the prosecution said the defendants had moved from farm to farm in several districts, using four cars, encouraging workers to join the strike. Although one farmer said that his workers had asked for protection from the agitators, claiming they were talking about kidnapping, burning property, and even murder, the paper noted pointedly that there was no direct evidence of violence or threats.

More alarming to local authorities was a warning on May 21 from a state police officer assigned to the northeastern Colorado district that "foreign labor"—which meant Mexicans—in nearby coal mining areas was entering into the strike and "might cause some trouble among the agricultural workers."[41] (The I.W.W. was one of the few unions that attempted to build solidarity between workers across diverse types of employment.) Because the coal miners were generally more militant and had more experience at organizing, their intervention in the farm workers' strike would have strengthened the latter's ability to maintain their walkout. But that did not happen. By the end of June the strike had petered out, without any concessions by the farmers or Great Western. So many workers were desperate for employment they were willing to accept a lower payment rather than risking all by joining a strike. The failure of the strike may have hindered the development of a shared working-class bond among local Hispanics employed in different sectors of the economy. Fear of labor unrest probably intensified the racist attitudes already held by many Boulder County Anglos.

[39] One wonders if they remembered the *soldaderas* of the 1910s (see Ch. 2A above).
[40] "18 Mexican beet field picketers given jail terms." Of those men, 13 were in their 20s or 30s, but the remainder were older, including one aged 73.
[41] "24 more agitators, mainly Mexicans, arrested."

B. Racism and the Ku Klux Klan, 1910-1940

"I would rather be a Klansman
in a robe of snowy white,
Than to be a Catholic Priest
in a robe as black as night;
For a Klansman is AMERICAN
and AMERICA is his home,
But a priest owes his allegiance
to a Dago Pope in Rome."[42]

Hispanics living in Boulder County between 1910 and 1940 experienced many forms of discrimination. Their position was ambiguous in racial terms.[43] They were not as dark-skinned as most African Americans, but their "brownness" covered a wide range. A few appeared to be "white," with light skins and blue eyes, while others were darker and/or had strongly Native American features. In the eyes of most Anglos, however, they were lumped together as "Mexicans," a group distinct from the white race.

Colorado's leading Anglo residents generally came from Protestant backgrounds in Northern Europe. They were committed to an American ethic of rugged individualism and a desire to get ahead. The early Hispanic arrivals, by contrast, were Catholic, spoke Spanish, and were often poor and relatively uneducated. Although they wanted their children to go to school and have a better future, they commonly placed family or community welfare above their own personal advancement. Many Anglos accepted without question the stereotype of Mexicans as dirty, lazy, and backward, people who were likely to be law-breakers.[44] As the number of people from Spanish-speaking backgrounds coming into Boulder County began to rise in the 1910s, whether from Mexico, New Mexico, or southern Colorado, Anglo concern mounted. Anxiety was particularly strong if these immigrants showed signs of staying in the area, rather than being temporary workers.

---

[42] *Rocky Mountain American*, a Klan paper, April 24, 1925, as quoted in "Colorado Klaverns of the Ku Klux Klan."

[43] See Ch. 1A above.

[44] Local newspapers rarely mentioned people with Latino surnames unless they broke the law, e.g., Mexicans arrested for stealing clothing and a shooting in Lafayette in 1915, and another shooting in Boulder in 1920 ("Law and Order"). For Mexicans as potential criminals, see Rosales, *¡Pobre Raza!*, esp. ch. 4.

Racist attitudes and practices took various forms in the towns we are considering. Evidence about discrimination in Lafayette is mixed. On the negative side, in 1911, during "the Long Strike," a crowd tried to break into the building where Francisco Diaz and his three sons were being held.[45] The men were accused of killing Teddy Wycherley, a Welch miner who was part of the striking union. Wycherley was angry with the Diazes because they had crossed the picket lines to do scab work, and the men got in a fight with fists and knives outside a bar. When Wycherley was killed, the Diazes were put into temporary arrest in the town hall. A crowd then formed, numbering several hundred men and women, who shouted that the Diazes should be lynched. Only the intervention of Boulder County Sheriff Capp saved them and permitted their safe removal to the jail in Boulder. (The Diazes were later found not guilty of murder, because they had acted in self-defense.) This incident, the only mention of a possible lynching in Boulder County, apparently stemmed at least in part from pro-union/anti-scab sentiment. A different form of discrimination was described by Sally Martinez, who came to Lafayette in 1924 when her father began work at the Columbine Mine.[46] She remembers that other children made fun of her for speaking Spanish and bringing tortillas for lunch. Some of the Mexican and Japanese children used to take their lunches down by the creek near the school, to avoid being teased.

But there is also evidence from Lafayette of social interactions between people of diverse nationalities and ethnicities. A police raid in August, 1915 caught 50 Mexicans, Italians, and Russians gambling (shooting craps) in the back room of a local saloon.[47] When Lupie Ortega later described her walk to elementary school in 1928, she said that she, her sister, and her little brother "joined other children from the neighborhood," children named Brugger, Beranek, Dillon, Hurd, and Lastoka.[48] Jim Hutchison, an English-speaker who moved to Lafayette in 1931 when he was in fourth grade, was welcomed at school by Hispanic as well as other children; his closest friend was Ernie Casillas.[49]

Bonds across ethnic lines seem to have been especially strong among Lafayette's miners. Men from all backgrounds had to rely upon each

---

[45] "Sheriff saved prisoners from lynching."
[46] Martinez, Sally, and others, interview, 1990. For embarrassment about food, see also Vol. II, Chs. 3A and 6B.
[47] "Law and Order."
[48] "Walking to School."
[49] Conversation with Marjorie McIntosh, Jan. 7, 2014.

other while working underground. An immigrant from Wales who worked at the Columbine Mine during the 1920s stressed the solidarity among all the ethnic groups employed there: "We were close in those days. It didn't make any difference whether you were a Mexican . . . . He drinks outta your bucket, you drink outta his bucket . . . And that's the way you are, down below there. . . . When you get down there, you're a family."[50] Tom Lopez too remembered the good relationships among miners during and after the Depression, with mutual assistance and close friendships.[51] David Toledo lived for some years in the nearby coal town of Frederick.[52] He recalled that although miners came from many different places (not only Mexico and New Mexico but also Italy, Bulgaria, and France), they socialized together as well as working side-by-side.[53] "Times were different then from now, because these people would get together to celebrate baptisms, birthdays, and weddings. They would have social dances in a hall." In the past, Toledo said, you "would know these people for years, and there would be a sense of harmony."

Boulder discriminated against the few African Americans who lived in the town and against all working people, but it did not display special animosity to the tiny number of Hispanic residents. Dr. Ruth Cave Flowers, an African American who later received a law degree and a doctorate in foreign languages and literatures, moved to Boulder in 1917 to attend the State Preparatory High School (later renamed Boulder High School).[54] After finishing its requirements, she enrolled at the University of Colorado and in 1924 became its second female African American graduate. She recalled that when she came to Boulder, blacks lived "on the wrong side of the tracks," could not buy food at ice cream parlors, and were not admitted to movie theaters. By the mid-1930s, African Americans were allowed into the theaters but had to sit in the balcony.[55] Boulder also had a city ordinance prohibiting workmen carrying lunch pails from walking around the downtown streets.[56] Chuck

[50] Interview with Welchie Mathias, Eric Margolis's Colorado Coalfields Oral History Project, University of Colorado at Boulder Archives, Box 7, Folder 3, as quoted by Rees, "Chicanos Mine the Columbine," p. 51.

[51] Lopez, Thomas, interview, 1986.

[52] Toledo, David, interview, c. 1978.

[53] Ibid.

[54] Polly McLean, ed., *A Legacy of Missing Pieces*, pp. 31-41, and Abbott et al., *Colorado*, p. 222.

[55] "Segregation, 1936," by John Martinez (Vol. II, Illus. 4.6).

[56] As described by Jim Hutchison, in Martinez, Sally, and others, interview, 1990.

Waneka recalled that some of the stores refused to carry overalls or shoes for working men or wait on customers if they were wearing work clothes; Jim Hutchison said that miners were viewed as troublemakers and despised.[57] But in the late 1920s and 1930s, a few Hispanic families moved to Boulder from other nearby communities because it was less racist as well as offering better educational and employment opportunities and being beautiful.[58]

A handful of people with Spanish names were at the University in Boulder, though they seem to have had no contact with local Hispanics. In the late 1870s, the first Board of Regents had included C. Valdez of Conejos County in the southern San Luis Valley, and a few Spanish names appear in student directories from the 1890s through the 1930s.[59] In 1902 the first Hispanic received an undergraduate degree, and in 1907 men with Spanish names graduated from the Law School and Medical School. These were nearly all *ricos*, coming from wealthy families in southern Colorado or northern New Mexico.

In the 1920s, racist views in Boulder County provided fertile soil for the rise of the Ku Klux Klan. The KKK publicly advocated racial discrimination, basing its views on what it claimed were high American principles, and it was prepared to use mob violence to terrify or chase out people it hated or feared. Many Americans in the early twenty-first century think that the Klan was active only in the southeastern part of the United States, directing its hatred and lynchings against African Americans.[60] So it may come as a surprise to realize how powerful the organization was in Colorado, as elsewhere in the West, and to learn that its attacks in our three communities were targeted at Hispanics.

Physical violence against Hispanics was already common in the Southwest. In the five southwestern states between 1880 and 1930, nearly 600 Hispanics were lynched.[61] At least a few Boulder County

---

[57] Both statements in Martinez, Sally, and others, interview, 1990.

[58] E.g., the Maestas family (Maestas, Roy, interview, 1978) and the Martinez family ("Biographical sketch, Emma Gomez Martinez," p. 1). See also Vol. II, Ch. 2B.

[59] Hays, "'A Quiet Campaign of Education.'"

[60] A lynching was when a group of local people took the law into their own hands and hanged someone, without a formal trial. In some cases they broke into a jail cell to remove a prisoner awaiting trial.

[61] For the U.S. as a whole, lynchings of Latinas/os, predominantly men, occurred at a rate of 27.4 per 100,000 between 1882 and 1930. That rate was lower than the 37.1 per 100,000 for African Americans, 1880-1930, but far above that for whites (Carrigan and Webb, "Lynching of Persons of Mexican Origin," Tables 1 and 2).

residents had relatives who were lynched in northern New Mexico; in the large southern Colorado town of Pueblo, two Hispanic railway workers who had been jailed in 1919 on suspicion of killing a policeman during a steel strike were pulled out of jail by an armed mob and hanged on the girders of the Fourth Street Bridge.[62] Ku Klux Klan chapters in Colorado tapped into that tradition of violence and mounting concern among Anglos about the growing number of Hispanics. Although our study found no evidence of lynchings in Boulder County, and apparently the KKK caused few deaths elsewhere in the state, the organization was adept at using threats and occasional property damage against Hispanics and those who defended them.

The Klan, an organization with a secret membership by invitation only, offered many of the same attractions as other men's groups of the time: private handshakes and passwords, elaborate rituals, and special slogans and songs.[63] Klansmen wore a distinctive costume to events: a long white robe that covered everything except their feet, and a headpiece with eyeholes that covered their face and came to a high point above their head. That "regalia" meant that the men wearing the costumes could not be identified, though because the costumes were generally sewn from a sheet and pillowcase, their wives had probably made them and were aware of the men's participation.

The KKK differed from other fraternal groups because it openly preached a message of white male supremacy for Protestant men born in the United States or who had become naturalized citizens. The Klan promoted racial segregation, stressed a literal reading of the Bible, and advocated prohibition of liquor. In Colorado, the Klan directed its activities against immigrants, Latinos, Catholics, and Jews, with secondary attention to the few African Americans living in the state.

The Klan movement in Colorado kicked off in Denver in 1921. It had an elaborate structure of recruiters (called "Kleagles") who operated throughout the state. The group was especially popular among men who felt marginalized by the reforms associated with the Progressive Movement after World War I. By 1924 the Klan was strong enough that it took over the operation of Colorado's Republican Party, replacing existing candidates with its own. In the election of 1925,

---

[62] Duncan, "Some Notes"; Rosales ¡Pobre Raza!, pp. 118-119.

[63] General information in this and the next three paragraphs comes from Chalmers, *Hooded Americanism*, ch. 18, Goldberg, *Hooded Empire*, esp. ch. 4, Goldberg, "Denver," and Smith, *Once A Coal Miner*, esp. pp. 155-161, and will not be individually referenced.

Republicans who were Klansmen or open backers of the Klan were chosen as Governor (Clarence Morley) and for both U.S. Senate seats. Klan-supported candidates, some of them Democrats, were elected to the offices of lieutenant governor, secretary of state, attorney general, superintendents of public schools, a justice of the Colorado Supreme Court, and seven members of the Denver District Court. They controlled the House within Colorado's General Assembly and barely lacked a majority in the Senate. The Klan dominated city councils in some Colorado towns, and Mayor Benjamin Stapleton of Denver—after whom Colorado's main airport was later named—was an avowed member. One week after the 1925 election, the "Imperial Wizard" (the head of the national organization) and a host of other Klan dignitaries arrived in Denver from Atlanta, Georgia to celebrate the victory. They were greeted at Union Station by Governor-elect Morley, amid a crowd of reporters and photographers, before moving on to the Brown Palace Hotel to plan the agenda of the new administration.

The Klan was said to be stronger in Colorado than any other western state. At its peak, it had 30,000-50,000 Klansmen, with 81 chapters (called "Klaverns"). Not all of the men who joined the KKK were virulent racists. Some members probably liked the organization's emphasis on patriotism, the importance of good moral training, and a fundamentalist interpretation of the Bible; others succumbed to peer pressure, a sense that all respectable white men were joining. Such people may have chosen to ignore the Klan's bigotry and to avoid participating in certain activities. But it was deeply racist men who led Boulder County's chapters and implemented their anti-Mexican agenda.

The KKK emerged in Boulder County in 1922. In July, Colorado's Klavern No. 1 (based in Denver) initiated 200 members into a new Klavern in Boulder, in a secret ceremony held on an abandoned road 5 miles north of the town.[64] Fifty cars drove participants to the event. The *Boulder Daily Camera* said that the town had been full of rumors that such an organization was forming. The group swung into immediate action, shoving some kind of written warning under the office door of "a prominent citizen." The initiations in 1922, like all other Klan meetings and ceremonies, took place after dark. The Klansmen formed a half-circle around a huge flaming cross; light came from the headlights or spotlights of cars parked around the group, facing inwards. Each new

[64] "Ku Klux Klan ceremonial administered to Boulderites."

PAGE SEVEN

THE D

Thirty-Second Year

Boulder,

KU KLUX KLAN VISIT BOULDER SWEEPING THROUGH STREETS A MYSTERIOUS, SHROUDED MASS

11 DAYS TO SHOP

READ THE ADS

Three hundred members of the Ku Klux Klan, nearly all of them masked, paraded Pearl street in automobiles Saturday night headed by a float which was illuminated by three torch lights. The parade consisted of sixty-three automobiles, most of them touring cars, and was joined as it passed by a number of cars containing Boulder members of the klan and the curious of the Saturday night automobile crowd.

Circulars, folded and wrapped with a rubber band, were thrown to the people on the streets by men standing in the float. The float was in white and carried the words "Klu Klux Klan." The circulars stated:

"Ku Klux Klan, 100 per cent American.

WE STAND FOR and are pledged upon our sacred honor to uphold the Flag and Constitution of our country.

WE STAND FOR Free Speech, Free Press, Free Public Schools, and Separation of CHURCH AND STATE.

WE STAND FOR the Purity of Womanhood and are Pledged to Protect and Defend the Sanctity of the Home.

WE ARE "ANTI" NOTHING save those principles which are un-Christian and un-American.

WATCH US GROW IN BOULDER

Postoffice Box 321."

Two or three digits of the license tags of each of the cars taking part

ALPHA TAU OMEGA ARE THE INTERFRAT CHAMPS

in the parade were painted over to prevent detection. Such practice is forbidden by law. Most of the members taking part in the parade were from Denver. A much greater number was expected. As a matter of fact, one man whose name rumor quite commonly connects with the Boulder klan, stated there were 143 cars in the parade, and was surprised when told that there were but sixty-three.

Local klansmen in ordinary civilian clothes patroled Pearl street at the intersections of Twelfth, Fourteenth, and Fifteenth and possibly other corners for nearly an hour before the parade. Near these intersections were automobiles, some of them with drivers, who joined the tail-end of the parade. The patrolmen seemed impatient and anxiously watched the traffic.

The parade came from West Pearl and went as far east as Seventeenth. It turned south at this corner to Arapahoe and then went east, presumably on the way back to Denver. The parade was for the purpose of arousing local interest in the Boulder klan.

Bert Lowe, Convicted Of Murder At Greeley Shows Small Concern Wife Seems Satisfied

Greeley, Colo., Dec. 10.—Bert J. Lowe, convicted last night of the murder of his sister-in-law, Fern Skinner, is taking his fate with the same stoic

DONATIONS BEING RECEIVE FOR NEW CHAPTER HOUSE TO BE BUILT IN BOUL

The pledges of Chi Omega the house-building fund a $100 at the annual Christmas party Saturday. Alumnae of the sor gave useful gifts to the house.

Kappa Kappa Gamma, as wel to build in the near future.

Kappas own lots on University nue, not far from Twelfth st The Chi Omegas have not yet chased a site.

Pi Beta Phi has purchased a g of lots at Eleventh and Col where they plan to build some in the future. They will first pose of their chapter house on teenth street.

The annual Christmas parties the Pi Phis, Kappa Alpha Theta Chi Omega on Saturday were h ly attended. A number were from out of town.

MAY ADD TO CHARGES AGAINST MR. DAUGHER

By Associated Press.

Washington, Dec. 11.—Jackson Ralston, counsel for Representat Keller, Republican, Minnesota, has brought impeachment char against Attorney General Daughe wrote Chairman Volstead of house judiciary committee that "may find it necessary to place fore the committee additio charges of high crimes and mis meanors."

Illus. 4.2. "Ku Klux Klan visits Boulder," Boulder Daily Camera, Dec. 11, 1922

member raised his right hand, went down on one knee, and swore an oath to defend the Klan's ideals, including protection of "the flower of white American womanhood."[65] Fear of inter-racial sexual activity lay right beneath the surface.

The Klan became more visible in Boulder later in 1922. In November, six hooded Klan members barged into a meeting of the Salvation Army, describing their goals and trying to recruit new members; they left a large donation, in keeping with their claim to be a charitable organization.[66] The *Daily Camera* commented that although members of the Klan were supposed to be unidentified, "rumor connects several Pearl Street business men with the organization." In late November and December the Klan organized four parades through the town. One included nearly 300 Klansmen, 63 cars (with the numbers on their license plates painted over so no one could identify their owners), and a float covered in white. The figures riding in the cars and on the float, with their bodies and heads draped in white, held up signs saying "Join the Invisible Empire " and "Watch Us Grow in Boulder."

A statement of the organization's goals is found in a poorly printed leaflet published by Boulder's Klavern around that time. This summary of Klan principles claimed that the group "is the incarnation of patriotism—of American ideals and institutions that are endangered by certain elements and sinister forces."[67] True Americans had to be white, and they had to be Protestant Christians: "God sifted the nations of the Old World and sent to our shores men and women of Protestant faith with which to build this republic." The movement wanted to make the Bible the basis of the U.S. Constitution, its government, and its laws; Bible study should be required in all public schools, while parochial schools should be abolished. The leaflet also stressed allegiance to the cross and the flag and said that the Knights of the Klan "stand for the Purity of Womanhood and are Pledged to Protect and Defend the Sanctity of the Home."

The statement contained an only slightly veiled threat of physical harm to opponents of the Klan. "We confess to certain admiration for the

---

[65] "White sheet business brisk during KKK's Boulder reign."

[66] "Boulder Ku Klux Klan rode thru streets" and "White sheet business brisk during KKK's Boulder reign."

[67] See Illus. 4.3 and "Summary of the Principles of the Knights of the Ku Klux Klan," pp. 2-4. The leaflet mentioned that ten months previously a sister organization known as Women of the Ku Klux Klan had been founded.

A Summary of the Principles of the Knights of the Ku Klux Klan

GOD GIVE US MEN!

"God give us men! The Invisible Empire demands strong minds, great hearts, true faith and ready hands.

Men whom lust of office does not kill;

Men whom the spoils of office cannot buy;

Men who possess opinions and a will

Men who have honor; men who will not lie;

Men who can stand before a demagogue and damn his treacherous flattering without winking!

Tall men, sun crowned, who live above the fog

In public duty and private thinking;

For while the rabbi , with their thumb-worn creeds,

Their large professions and little deeds,

Mingle in selfish strife, Lo, Freedom weeps, .

Wrong rules the land, and waiting justice sleeps

God give us men!

Men who serve not for selfish booty,

But real men, courageous, who flinch not at duty;

Men of dependable character; men of sterling worth;

Then wrong will be redressed and right will rule the earth,

God give us men!

BIRTH OF THE KLAN AND A SUMMARY OF ITS PRINCIPLES

IN every community there are three groups of people who are opposed to the Klan. The first group are those of the lawless element, the crooked politician, the shyster lawyer, the bootlegger, the gambler, the dope peddler, the atheist, the white slaver and the rapist.

The second group are those who by virtue of their education are opposed to all Christian progressive organizations, especially those of secret character, a right that is exercised under the Constitution of the United States. By that same Constitution and right we claim the right and privilege to organize a white, native-born, Gentile Christian organization.

The third group opposed to the Klan are those who have based their judgment upon the articles appearing in newspapers, whose editors are either uninformed or misinformed and have not the time or inclination to look into the matter pertaining to the Klan to see if those reports are true.

The old Ku Klux Klan was a benevolent organization or society. At the close of the Civil War the people were troubled by the carpet-bagger, the rapist and those given to pilfering. The chastity of the mother, wife, sister and daughter was imperilled, and their sacred persons were placed in jeopardy to the licentious longings of lust-crazed beasts in human form. You have heard of the night riders of the Ku Klux Klan. When their purpose was accomplished, the Klan voluntarily disbanded.

The new order of today was brought into existence on Thanksgiving night, in the year 1915. Sixteen men climbed up Stone mountain near Atlanta, Ga., in the teeth of a blinding rainstorm, arriving at the top, each man took a boulder, and they built an altar and placed the American flag and the Holy Bible upon the altar, erected the "Fiery Cross" and all knelt in prayer, and this wonderful organization was brought into existence as a result of that prayer meeting.

In 1920 there were less than 5,000 members, today, by virtue of the splendid, patriotic principles it proclaims, there is a membership of nearly ten million. And this in spite of the controlled press of the country which has continued to empty its vials of hatred and falsehood against an order that is plainly needed in our land today to help place Protestantism where it rightfully belongs.

Ten months ago the organization known as the Women of the Ku Klux Klan came into existence. Its membership now numbers over half a million.

A man cannot make application to come into our order. We will investigate him, and if we feel he is eligible, we will offer him an opportunity of coming in. He must be born in the United States. He must be a Gentile. He and his wife must both be Protestants, then there will be no dissension in his home.

The Klan is not anti-Catholic; it is pro-Protestant.

The Klan is not anti-Negro; it is pro-White.

The Klan is not anti-Jew; it is pro-Christian.

The Klan is not anti-foreign; it is pro-American.

The Klan is not anti any race, color or creed. It is simply pro-Christian and pro-American.

The Klan believes in the tenets of the Christian religion. We magnify the Holy Bible as the basis of our Constitution, the foundation of our government, the source of our laws, the sheet-anchor of our liberties, the most practical guide of right living, and the source of all true wisdom. We have in mind the divine command, "Thou shalt worship the Lord thy God." We honor the Christ as the Klansman's only criterion of character.

There are more than 70,000 ministers of the Gospel who had the courage to stand on their convictions and come into the organization. If, during our ceremonial a man find anything un-Christian or not what he can subscribe to, he is permitted to retire with the good will of the Klan.

We are not a political organization. We don't care what a man's politics are if he is a MAN. Anyone who does not remain a MAN amongst MEN after he gets in

Illus. 4.3. "Summary of the Principles of the Knights of the Ku Klux Klan," 1920s, p. 1

patience and law-abiding characteristics of the reputed two thousand Klansmen of Boulder County in the face of long continued abuse, defamation and personal vilification, . . . especially so when fence rails and tar buckets are handy and feathers are so cheap." Carrying a person out of town on a fence rail or dipping him in hot tar and covering him with feathers were common forms of collective attack. Used especially against people of color, they were deeply painful as well as humiliating.

We have visual and written evidence about a mass meeting of the Boulder Klavern held probably in 1922 or 1923. (A newspaper reporter disguised as a Klansman sneaked into the event and wrote a short description to go with the photo he took of it.[68]) The undated photo shows the head of the Boulder group, its "Exalted Cyclops," receiving the Klavern's official charter. This huge state-wide rally was held "in one of nature's amphitheaters in a canyon near Boulder." Boulder's Cyclops and 500 members of its Klavern welcomed 2,000 Klansmen from elsewhere in Colorado and representatives from the group's headquarters in Atlanta. Some of the visitors had driven only from Longmont, Lafayette, and Louisville, but others came from Pueblo and La Junta. Lighting was provided by 500 cars, many of them equipped with spotlights, forming a large circle around the gathering. New candidates—150 of them— were sworn into the Boulder chapter, after which "short addresses were made by leading professional and business men and the substantial agriculturalists and stockmen of the state." The event ended with "an old fashioned Western barbeque." The reporter's photo shows a large group of men dressed in white robes with the characteristic white pointed hoods carrying an American flag, with a 30-foot cross burning in the background.

The Klan reached its local peak in 1924 and 1925, when the Boulder Klavern may have had as many as 1,000 members. Boulder's total population at the time was only about 11,000, including women and children, so the male heads of many households had obviously joined the Klan. The KKK burned crosses on the lawns of Catholic families and was probably responsible for lighting a giant flaming cross one May night on Boulder's Flagstaff Mountain, visible from all the towns to the east. This structure, made of sawdust saturated with oil, was 53 feet high

---

[68] A date of May 31, 1926 was added to the back of the photo in pencil at some later time, but since it describes the image as "a street scene" and does not match the reporter's own text, we should probably discount it; the Boulder Klavern was collapsing by spring, 1926 ("A KKK meeting in Boulder, 1920s, back of photo").

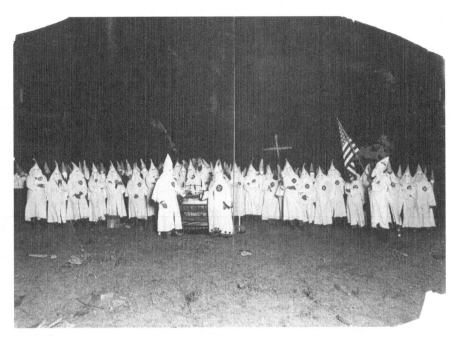

Illus. 4.4. A KKK meeting in Boulder, 1920s

and 25 feet wide.[69] Hooded Klan members walked into a religious gathering in the basement of a Boulder Presbyterian church to advocate Bible study in the public schools.[70] (Though uninvited, they were received with applause.) As the 1925 election approached, the KKK sent out cards to Boulder County voters instructing them how to vote; Klan-backed candidates won many local offices.[71] In that same year, the Klan went after the University of Colorado, due to the Jewish and Catholic professors who taught there. When President George Norlin submitted the University's request to the General Assembly for its annual appropriation of $120,000, Governor Morley—backed by Klansmen in the legislature—demanded that all non-Protestant staff be fired.[72] Norlin refused, whereupon the legislature denied any appropriation to the university for the year.

[69] "Cross burned on Flagstaff Mountain."
[70] "KKK influence was strong here in the 1920s."
[71] "Ku Klux Klan sends election instructions to Boulder County voters"; Goldberg, *Hooded Empire*, pp. 81-82.
[72] Knox, "The Campus and the Klan." The university was able to limp along without an appropriation thanks to a permanent mill levy to support higher education that Norlin had persuaded the General Assembly to pass in 1920.

————o————

NO ALIEN NEWSPAPERS NEEDED IN AMERICA

"One tongue," said John Milton, "is enough for a woman."

He said that because he did not wish his daughter to learn French. He thougth English was good enough for her, as an Englishwoman.

We borrow Milton's thought, to say that one tongue is enough, for an American. And that tongue ought to be the language of America, not the language of some alien land.

The editor of a foreign-language newspaper has just been sentenced in Chicago, for attacking through his journal, the American Army and Navy, in an alien tongue, and disseminating his scurrility within the United States.

Why should we have foreign language newspapers at all?

If a man lives here and makes his money here, and enjoys the blessings that go with life in America, he ought, in all conscience to be willing to learn the language. And he can find enough reading in the newspapers printed in the American language .

These foreign-language papers simply keep alive foreign allegiance and hypheisms and serve as agencies of foreign propaganda in this country. There is nothing American about most of them.

Talk United States!

Illus. 4.5. "No Alien Newspapers Needed," The Rocky Mountain American, May 15, 1925

Illus. 4.6. "Ban on Immigration,"
The Rocky Mountain American,
Apr. 17, 1925

Illus. 4.7. "The Klan Unmasked,"
The Rocky Mountain American,
Feb. 27, 1925

Although by 1925 the main Boulder newspaper was starting to oppose the KKK, or at least make cautious fun of it (editor L. C. Paddock of the *Daily Camera* referred to it as the Komic Kapers Klub), a Klan paper, the *Rocky Mountain American*, was published in Boulder for six months.[73] It spewed out false information and vicious attacks on Catholics, especially foreigners, including the statement that 15 million Catholics in the county were forming military organizations and arming themselves in order to make America Catholic. It argued that no foreign-language newspapers should be published in the U.S. and featured cartoons showing the Klan at work, such as keeping out undesirable immigrants and enforcing laws.[74] One cartoon responded to the objection that Klan members were always covered by showing what lay underneath: Uncle Sam!

The *Rocky Mountain American* encouraged its readers to buy products at local stores approved by the Klan. (It described the new chain stores that were beginning to appear as the work of "unscrupulous Jewish

[73] Smith, *Once A Coal Miner*, pp. 159-60, and Goldberg, *Hooded Empire*, p. 9, for this and below.
[74] See also "Cartoon: The KKK and Law Enforcement."

business magnates.") To demonstrate their support for the organization, business owners placed ads in the paper that described their goods or services in catchy phrases with K's: "Klassy Kut Klothes," "Kash and Karry Shoe Shop," or "Klothing Karefully Kleaned."[75] One store sold "Wizard Sheets" at 98 cents each and "Wizard Pillowcases" at 25 cents each.

The eastern towns of the county had their own Klan chapters.[76] Jack Murphy, a former Boulder County Commissioner born in 1915, remembered being taken to a Klan parade in Longmont when he was 10 or 11 years old.[77] "There were about 2,000 to 3,000 Klan members from northern Colorado—all in their bed sheets—and there were some black horses." Many of the viewers, including young Jack, were "scared to death." Since Longmont had about 6,000 residents at the time, the appearance of so many Klansmen must indeed have been frightening.

The Longmont parade that Murphy remembered was probably the one described in the *Rocky Mountain American* in early June, 1925.[78] The paper said that the procession of local and visiting Klansmen, all in their white robes and marching four abreast, started at 8 pm and was led by officers on horseback; the parade stretched nearly a half mile in length. As the group moved through the main streets of the city, thousands of spectators stood at attention "to show their respect and admiration for the valiant Knights of the Ku Klux Klan as they marched silently by and in perfect order." The procession ended up at a large open space south of the city, where "a huge flaming cross emblematic of the cross of Christ" was erected, together with an American flag. Several hundred new members were initiated into the group, swearing to give their allegiance—and if necessary, their lives—to America and its principles.

Klan members dominated Longmont's government in the mid-1920s. In the election of 1923, only a few Klan candidates were chosen, but in 1925, the group's political efforts paid off: a majority of the city councilors, the mayor, school board members, and various others were elected.[79] The Klan-led city council fired the city engineer, the

---

[75] "KKK influence was strong here in the 1920s."

[76] The KKK was active in other parts of the sugar beet area too. In Greeley, Klansmen marched at night through "the Spanish colony" in 1925, setting fire to at least one cross in the yard of a resident. In Brighton, located 12 miles east of Lafayette, 500 Klansmen joined a parade in 1933, and a "fiery cross" was burned in the fair grounds on 5th Ave. (Donato, *Mexicans and Hispanos*, pp. 53-55).

[77] "Klan had its heyday in county."

[78] "Mammoth Klan parade."

[79] "Ku Klux Klan controlled Longmont in 1920s" for this and the dam, below.

street superintendent, and the fire chief, replacing them with their own sympathizers. One of their ventures was the Chimney Rock dam, which they started against the advice of reliable water engineers and cost the city $130,000 before it was finally abandoned. Klan members flew their flag on the city's official pole and erected an 8-foot cross in electric red lights at the intersection of Main Street and Fourth Avenue.[80] The *Longmont Times-Call*, a Klan supporter, described the cross as "the most effective and beautiful decoration of its kind ever displayed in Longmont." Signs appeared in local stores and restaurants saying "Whites Only," "White Trade Only," or even "No Mexicans or Dogs," and although no actual violence was reported, several men received threatening letters on letterhead with the Klan's insignia.[81]

Oli Olivas Duncan, a local historian of Longmont, was told that sometime in the 1920s, there was a showdown between the Klan and a group of Mexican men.[82] The Klan's rallies were held on the southeast corner of Third Avenue and Martin, which was then an open field. At one nighttime meeting, dozens of armed Hispanic men appeared. They warned the Klan that if any one of them was harmed, all of them would respond. The spokesman for the group was José Hilario Cortez, the informal head of Longmont's Hispanic community, a person to whom local Spanish-speakers turned for advice and help. Mr. Cortez may have learned what happened at Klan rallies from his grandson, Eddie Vigil, who used to sneak out at night with his buddies to watch the meetings from a safe hiding place.[83] But Longmont's Hispanics did not take legal action against discrimination as did people in Greeley, with its large *colonia*. There Mexicans filed a civil rights case in 1927 against restaurant owners for refusing to serve them and organized a boycott of businesses that displayed "White Trade Only" signs.[84]

The Klan was active in the Lafayette area too. The initial meeting was held in 1924 at the "J" barn near Isabelle Road, north of town.[85] The first two members of the local chapter were a dentist and the manager of the Public Service Company; membership grew rapidly over the next two

[80] "KKK influence was strong here in the 1920s" for this and below.
[81] For letters, see ibid. For such a sign, see Illus. 5.12 below.
[82] Conversation with Marjorie McIntosh, July 26, 2013, and see "Cortez, Jose Hilario ("J. H."), and Maria Sabina Maes Cortez, biography." One wonders if this story is an example of embellishment.
[83] "Cortez, Jose Hilario ("J. H.") and Maria Sabina, biography."
[84] Deutsch, *No Separate Refuge*, p. 155.
[85] "Ku Klux Klan in Lafayette."

years, with teachers, town councilors, members of the school board, and even some church pastors signed up. Later the KKK met on a bluff to the southeast of the town, near the Columbine Mine where many Hispanics and Italians worked; large bonfires and the crosses the group erected and set on fire made its presence visible.[86]

The Klan worked inside Lafayette as well. It put up a cross at the intersection of Baseline and South Public Roads and tried to run a few people out of town, coming to their houses wearing their regalia, breaking windows, and threatening them in various ways.[87] A common practice was for Klan members to come into Lafayette's Protestant churches during services, wearing their regalia and leaving a cross burning outside while they gave a speech about the purpose of their organization.[88] The local Klavern treated Lafayette's Catholic Church more fiercely, claiming that it owed its allegiance to the Pope, not to the United States. In 1926, a reporter who was spying on the building that housed the KKK in Lafayette was spotted and kidnapped.[89] With a sack thrown over his head, he was carried to a large Klan rally in the hills somewhere behind the Standard Mine. There some 1,000 white-clad men from various Denver-area Klaverns looked on as he was forced to kneel in front of a wooden altar and threatened with a dagger, after which he was lectured about Klan goals. Finally he was released but had to find his way home by foot in the dark.

The political power of the Klan in Colorado weakened quickly after 1925, at both state and local levels, due to corruption within its leadership, the defection of Mayor Stapleton, and the impact of the few newspapers courageous enough to speak out against it. When Colorado's central organization fell apart late in 1925, Boulder's Klavern voted to leave the national group and remain with Dr. John G. Locke.[90] Locke, the former head of the Colorado unit, was expelled from the Klan for financial misconduct and founded his own group, the Minute Men of America. The Boulder chapter joined the Minute Men in 1926, but that organization soon died out. Yet the hatred the Klan promoted, and the fear it caused,

---

[86] Jim Hutchison, conversation with Marjorie McIntosh, Jan. 7, 2014, "Salazar, Jose Benito and Isabelle, biography," and "Klan had its heyday in county."

[87] Jim Hutchison, conversation with Marjorie McIntosh, Jan. 7, 2014, and "More than 50,000 donned hoods at Klan's height."

[88] "More than 50,000 donned hoods at Klan's height" and "Ku Klux Klan: the invisible empire in Boulder County."

[89] "Ku Klux Klan in Lafayette."

[90] "Boulder Klan fails to take action."

continued. In Boulder, a resident later recalled that during the 1930s a store on 24th Street (now Folsom Avenue) had a racist sign in its front window, and crosses were burned on Flagstaff Mountain as late as 1939.[91]

In Longmont, overt hostility to Hispanics remained strong in the later 1920s and 1930s, though the KKK no longer had a public presence. In 1927, Fred W. Flanders ran successfully for mayor on an anti-Klan platform.[92] When Klan members attempted to march through the downtown later that year, he stopped them. Yet Al Cardenas, born in 1934, described coming into Longmont from Erie as a little boy and seeing signs on the restaurants that said "No Mexicans or dogs allowed."[93] Not until the later 1940s and 1950s were such signs removed.[94] Tony Gomez said that his dad, who was living in Longmont in the 1930s, told him that Mexicans were not allowed to come into many restaurants and stores at all; at others, they had to go around to a back door, off the alley.[95] A hamburger that cost 25 cents for white people would cost 35 or 45 cents for them. The only place Mr. Gomez knew he would be treated well was the City Café, owned by Alex Panfilo Gonzales. As a child in 1938, Virginia Maestas went to a magic show in the Longmont theater but was told that Mexicans had to sit at the very back of the balcony.[96] Some local Hispanics believed that the Klan continued to meet privately for decades longer.[97]

Racism in Longmont may possibly have been directed against African Americans too. Referring to the 1930s, Tony Gomez's dad described large signs over the Johnson's Corners filling stations on Main Street, at the north and south entrances into the town, saying something like, "Nigger, don't let the sun go down on you."[98] Another mention of banners telling blacks to get off the streets before dark came from Al Cardenas; he recalled that these signs said, "Don't let the sunset set on your butt" and that any blacks who violated them would be arrested, in accordance with a city ordinance.[99] Since there were few if any African Americans in

[91] "Historical hatred," and "Ku Klux Klan: the invisible empire in Boulder County."
[92] *Longmont's 125th Anniversary*, pp. 21-24.
[93] Cardenas, Alfonso, interview, 2004.
[94] See Ch. 5C below.
[95] Gomez, Tony, interview, 2009.
[96] Conversation with Marjorie McIntosh, Nov. 24, 2013.
[97] Tony Gomez, for example, reported that his father believed that Longmont was "KKK all the way" (Gomez, Tony, interview, 2009). As late as 2013, several Latinos referred to Longmont as "the Klan capital of Colorado" and thought that a local chapter had met secretly until very recently or was perhaps still active even then.
[98] Gomez, Tony, interview, 2009.
[99] Cardenas, Alfonso, interview, 2004.

Longmont at the time, these notices are puzzling.

A striking example of discrimination in action occurred in Lafayette in the mid-1930s. The episode is surprising, because the little town seemed in general to be fairly well integrated. In 1933, Lafayette's leaders decided to build a swimming pool for children and young people, located west of the high school.[100] The project was sponsored by the Town Board and the Lions Club, with some labor provided through the Federal Relief Program. It was a community-wide effort, with all residents encouraged to contribute a bag of cement or help with the work. The pool was to be like the one at Sunset Park in Longmont, with a concrete swimming area, miniature beach, dressing rooms, and a parking area. Construction began in April, 1933, and after a problem with obtaining water had been solved, was completed the next summer. The pool, operated by the fire department, was officially opened on July 31, 1934.

Two weeks later, however, the Lafayette newspaper reported that a sign had been posted at the entrance saying: "We reserve the right to eject any and all persons without cause. White trade only."[101] Hispanic residents, some of whom had helped to build the pool, were outraged by this policy and decided to turn to the courts. The lawyer they hired, Rose Lueras, prepared a petition claiming that the town had violated the petitioners' equal rights under the Fourteenth Amendment of the U.S. Constitution and demanding that they be allowed to use the pool. After obtaining signatures on the petition and collecting money for legal action, Lueras brought suit in Boulder District Court against the mayor of Lafayette, its town council, fire chief, fire department, town marshal, and city clerk. The pool was closed while the case was being heard. The following summer the District Court judge denied their petition on technical grounds, though he agreed that "race and color should not be made the basis of discrimination."[102] Lueras then appealed the matter to the Colorado Supreme Court. Only in March, 1937 was the suit ended,

---

[100] "Swimming Pool," "Lafayette's 'white only' pool," and "Lafayette's new swimming pool" for this paragraph and the next.

[101] Jim Hutchison recalled that when he was 13, he and his friend Ernie Casillas went to the pool, but Eddie was denied entrance, so they both left (conversation with Marjorie McIntosh, Jan. 7, 2014). Lafayette was not alone in segregating swimming. When blacks in Denver tried to integrate Washington Park's swimming beach in 1932, they were beaten by enraged white swimmers in front of 1,000 onlookers; when the *Denver Post* hired its first black reporter in 1950, he was not allowed to swim in municipal pools (Delgado and Stefancic, "Home-Grown Racism," pp. 739-40).

[102] "Lafayette's 'white only' pool."

with another verdict against the petitioners.

Nevertheless, after those first two weeks in 1934, the pool was never used again. It sat empty during the summer of 1935, and in May, 1936 it was filled in with dirt as part of a new softball field. Sally Martinez commented in 1990 that Lafayette had recently had to spend $8,000 to dig out the old concrete when the Bob Burger Recreation Center was built.[103] Sally's daughter, Sharon Martinez Stetson, the first Latina elected to Lafayette's City Council, described her satisfaction in helping to choose tiles for the swimming pool in the new building, on the very site from which Mexicans had been excluded more than 50 years before.[104]

C. Repatriation and Deportation of Mexicans, 1932-1936

On May 18, 1932, the Boulder County Commissioners passed the following resolution:

> WHEREAS, A number of Mexican families in Boulder County are unemployed, some of which are public charges and there being no prospect of them finding employment and it appears that all of the said families will become public charges of Boulder County, and
> WHEREAS, the Mexican Government has agreed to accept these families and take care of them if Boulder County will transport them to the Mexican border and the Railroad Company has agreed to transport said families for the sum of $8.00 for each full fare and $4.00 for each half fare.
> NOW THEREFORE, be it resolved that there be and is hereby appropriated out of moneys not otherwise appropriated, in the fund for the support of the poor of Boulder County, the sum of $312.00 for the transportation of said families to the Mexican border.[105]

This measure was part of a broader movement between 1930 and 1936 to deport or "repatriate" Mexicans, especially from California and other southwestern states.[106] As the result of large-scale immigration

---

[103] Martinez, Sally, and others, interview, 1990.
[104] Conversation with Marjorie McIntosh, Jan. 15, 2014. Stetson served on the City Council 1986-1995: "Swearing-in, Lafayette City Council, 1989" and "Lafayette Councilwoman Sharon Stetson." See also Illus. 5.13 below.
[105] "Boulder County Commissioners' Resolution."
[106] For this and the following paragraphs, see Balderrama and Rodríguez, *Decade of Betrayal*, esp. pp. 63-88, and Guerin-Gonzales, *Mexican Workers and American Dreams*, esp. ch. 4.

during the 1910s and 1920s, several million Mexicans were living in the United States by 1932. Most of them had taken unskilled, poorly paid jobs: working in fields or mines, or building railroads. Their labor was welcomed in those decades, but as the Great Depression worsened and employment opportunities constricted, many Americans found a convenient scapegoat in these foreign workers. After negotiation with U.S. authorities, the Mexican government offered to pay train fare south from the border to places where returnees could find agricultural work.

In what has been described as a "frenzy of anti-Mexican hysteria," many counties and states decided to cover transportation costs as far as the border in order to send Mexicans back home.[107] That policy, which was promoted at the national level by Secretary of Labor William Doak, was thought to serve two purposes: Mexicans would not compete with American workers for the few jobs available; and local governments would not have to provide relief for destitute Mexican families, support that came out of taxpayers' pockets. A further benefit was that repatriation allowed local authorities to get rid of undesirable people, especially labor union activists.[108]

Although we lack definite figures, as many as one million Mexicans may have been repatriated during the early 1930s.[109] When adult workers left, they were required to take their entire family with them. Because any children born in this country were legally U.S. citizens, their removal may have been illegal, but that was not taken into account. Some Mexicans went home voluntarily, discouraged by their failure to find work and enjoy "the American Dream." Others, however, were in effect forced out of the U.S. by being told they would receive no further relief or would be arrested as agitators if they stayed.

The lives of these families when they reached Mexico were generally very difficult. The new government, still struggling to gain economic solidity after the Revolution of the 1910s, was often unable to honor its promise of employment. Most returnees were therefore left largely on their own, desperately trying to find work and reestablish social ties in a country they had left as many as 20 years before. Young people had a

---

[107] Balderrama and Rodríquez, *Decade of Betrayal*, p. 1.
[108] Doak advocated the deportation of Mexican labor organizers; in California, some of the people sent back were union activists (Guerin-Gonzales, *Mexican Workers and American Dreams*, pp. 79 and 123).
[109] Balderrama and Rodríquez, *Decade of Betrayal*, p. 151, and Escobedo, *From Coveralls to Zoot Suits*, p. 5.

particularly hard time adjusting. If they tried to come back to the U.S., however, they rarely had the birth certificate needed to prove their claim of citizenship. As the American economy began to recover from the Depression, it was hampered by the loss of so many hard-working Mexicans. It is impossible to quantify the contributions that these immigrants and their children might have made to the U.S. in social, political, and cultural terms had they remained.

How are we to interpret the 1932 resolution by the Boulder County Commissioners? Was it a clear example of illegal activity, underpinned by racist attitudes and economic concerns, constituting a clear violation of basic human rights?[110] Or were the Commissioners genuinely trying to help destitute Mexicans return to their families and friends, in a setting where they would be able to find work? To answer those questions, we need to explore what was happening in this area in spring, 1932. Evidence is available in English-language newspapers from Longmont, Boulder, and Lafayette. They reflect only Anglo perspectives, but no Spanish-language papers published in northern Colorado survive from the early 1930s.

The first reference to repatriation came on May 17, 1932, when the *Longmont Times-Call* reported that a trainload of Mexicans would depart that evening.[111] Four trucks carrying Mexican men, women, and children from Larimer County had passed through Longmont on their way to the train station in Denver, the beginning of an expected exodus to their native land. Boulder County's "first consignment" was expected to leave the following week. Claiming that an estimated 700 people from the region would eventually "make the trip," the paper noted that only people who volunteered to leave and could demonstrate that the head of the family had been born in Mexico were eligible. The article said that the cost of train fare to the border at El Paso was being covered "by county commissioners of various northern Colorado counties, charity organizations and the Great Western Sugar company." From Ciudad Juarez onward, the Mexican government would furnish transportation to the farm lands which it was giving to them. That benign account was reinforced the next day by the *Boulder Daily Camera*, which quoted a county welfare worker as saying that "the families came to the county in

---

[110] In California in 2006, the children and grandchildren of families that had been forced out in the 1930s demanded an official apology from the state.
[111] "Train load of Mexicans will leave for homeland tonight." Larimer County adjoined Boulder County to the north.

the hope of getting work in the beet fields, but had been unable to do so. The county is defraying their expenses on the return trip."[112]

A similar perspective is seen in a report printed on May 18 by the *Longmont Times-Call*. This article said that 14 Mexican families from Boulder County, comprising some 75 men, women, and children, would be sent to Denver by train the following day to start their journey.[113] Transportation for these people was being handled by the American Red Cross. Four more families left by train for El Paso on May 24, with another group scheduled to depart later in the week; for all, transportation was paid by the county.[114]

On May 18, the *Boulder Daily Camera* presented a quite compassionate first-person description of families leaving from Union Station in Denver.[115] Harry Casaday said that watching many hundred people being loaded onto trains "for deportation to their native land" was "an affecting sight." Nearly all of the deportees, who included women and children, were from Weld and Larimer Counties. Observing that many of them did not understand "what it was all about," Casaday explained that they had come to Colorado to work in the beet fields, "ignorant of the fact that the state has more laborers than it needs." He felt, however, that the deportations were being conducted "in a humane manner," supervised by state authorities.

These reports suggest that local officials and organizations like the Red Cross were for humanitarian reasons assisting unfortunate Mexican citizens who wished to return to their home country. One wonders, however, why Great Western Sugar was willing to pay to have Mexicans sent home. Other factors were certainly contributing to pressure for repatriation.

An economic motive was mentioned in an article published on June 3 in the *Longmont Times-Call*.[116] Commenting that several hundred people who had been living in Weld County were leaving for Denver that day on their way to Mexico, the account said the county commissioners and other agencies that were paying for transportation "believe that the cost of deporting them is less than the demand upon charity sources would be." That concern parallels the Boulder County Commissioners' reference

---

[112] "County to deport 75 beet workers."
[113] "75 Mexicans leave for Mexico."
[114] "Mexican families deported at county's expense."
[115] "1,500 Mexicans loaded on trains in Denver."
[116] "300-400 Weld County Mexicans leaving."

to "public charges."

The need for welfare assistance was indeed high and growing, in Boulder County as in most of the U.S., due to the ongoing effects of the Depression. On May 25, the *Boulder Daily Camera* reported on a talk given to the Lions Club by E. B. Hill, one of the county commissioners, and Mrs. Anna Powless, the Social Service secretary.[117] Mrs. Powless said that whereas in the past, about 30 families had required assistance for three months in the year, now 100 families were being "kept alive by Social Service funds every month." Each household received between $8.50 and $18 per month. She described 40 of the families, containing 8 to 11 members each, as "transients," presumably referring to Mexican immigrants; they were totally dependent upon Social Service support. Commenting that the county lacked sufficient funds to care properly for "our own Boulder people" and yet was expected to help outsiders as well, she noted that all of the newcomers had been offered transport back to their previous homes, but some had declined.[118]

Many Anglo Coloradans probably resented Mexican laborers on multiple grounds. If they were working, they took scarce jobs away from "Americans" and were likely to be trouble- makers, stirring up unrest among their fellow employees. They participated in mining and agricultural unions, and some were organizers of strikes. The Boulder County Commissioners' resolution was made two days after the beginning of the beet workers' strike; subsequent conveyance of Mexicans out of the area came just as the mine operators were cutting wages once again and the unions were attempting to resist. If, on the other hand, Mexicans were unemployed, hard-working taxpayers had to provide relief. Encouraging or in some cases virtually forcing immigrants to go back to Mexico therefore seemed justified. We do not know the names of the people who left, but it would not be surprising if some were union organizers: miners or beet workers who had been given a choice between repatriation or a jail sentence. Getting rid of these "agitators" may explain why Great Western Sugar was helping to cover transportation costs.

Racism presumably played a role too. Although the views openly espoused by the KKK in the 1920s were no longer being expressed by local governments and newspapers in the mid-1930s, those attitudes

[117] "Relief units swamped by needy's calls."
[118] Unemployed Mexican beet workers had been treated differently in Denver in 1921, when "public hysteria" led the police to put hundreds of them in jail on trumped-up charges of loitering (Rosales, *¡Pobre Raza!*, p. 78).

obviously continued among at least some people, as witnessed by "White Trade Only" signs in Boulder and Longmont and the swimming pool episode in Lafayette. Public statements justifying deportation on economic grounds may have been supported by racially-based fears of Hispanics.

Although efforts at repatriation in Boulder County were concentrated in 1932, government-backed discrimination against Hispanics did not end then. During the new few years, unemployment worsened, and labor unions, some with Mexican leaders, called a growing number of strikes. In a drastic and illegal attempt to stabilize the situation, Colorado's Governor Edwin C. Johnson recommended in 1936 that all "Mexicans" be sent back to their homes.[119] ("Big Ed" was running for Senate that year.) He did not distinguish between immigrants from Mexico, children born in this country, and people whose families had lived in New Mexico for many generations. (As we have seen, by 1930, 69% of the adults with Spanish names living in Longmont, Lafayette, and Boulder had been born in this country and were therefore citizens; by 1940 the proportion had risen to 84%.[120])

Few people responded voluntarily to Governor Johnson's proposal, whereupon he ordered all Mexican beet workers to leave the state. To make sure they did not return, he declared martial law in southern Colorado and sent the National Guard to blockade its border. Troops set up barriers and stopped trains, buses, and automobiles. People who looked "Mexican" were questioned by the soldiers about their origins and financial situation; only those with money were allowed to enter. After strong protests by Mexico's Ambassador to the U.S. and by Hispanic organizations in Colorado and New Mexico, the blockade was lifted. Other organs of Colorado's government nonetheless continued to push for deportation. Relief agencies alone arranged for the expulsion of thousands of Mexicans.[121] Other families probably found their own transportation, though it was a long drive to the Mexican border, some 650 miles south.

---

[119] For "Big Ed's War," in this paragraph and the next, see Delgado and Stefancic, "Home-Grown Racism," pp. 737-739, and Sandoval, "Recruitment, Rejection, and Reaction." A newspaper in one of the Denver suburbs proposed that Mexicans who refused to leave should be placed in concentration camps ("Home-Grown Racism," pp. 737-738).

[120] See Ch. 2D above.

[121] Delgado and Stefancic, "Home-Grown Racism," p. 739.

Emma Gomez (Martinez) provided an eye-witness account of the deportation of Mexicans, evidently in 1936.[122] In a later letter, she described a "scary and sad" experience she had as a young girl, when she and her dad had come into Longmont from Erie to go shopping. As they walked along Main Street, they saw "a parade of old cars and trucks filled with Mexicans and all their household items. Men were clinging to the trucks and standing on the running boards." Emma was frightened, but her father told her to stand close beside him and she would be safe. He was "not molested because he had blue eyes." Her recollection is that these Mexican farm workers were replaced by Anglos.

The full number of Mexicans who left Boulder County in 1932 and 1936—whether willingly or unwillingly—is unknown but was probably fairly small. Figures given in the newspapers for those who went in 1932 total only 18 families, including perhaps 100 - 150 men, women, and children, plus one more group of undescribed size. Many more people, perhaps as many as 1,700, went from Boulder County's eastern and northern neighbors, Weld and Larimer Counties. We do not know how many people were forced to leave in 1936, or how many of them subsequently returned.

It is clear, however, that the departure of Mexican families from Boulder County did not have the same effect upon the local Hispanic community as was often the case in California and Arizona. In those settings, many of the early *barrios* or *colonias* in which Mexican families had found housing, friendship, and neighborly assistance disappeared as the result of massive repatriation during the 1930s.[123] When Mexicans again began to come into the U.S. after the Depression, they formed new residential and social communities.

For our three towns in Boulder County, U.S. Census records show that the total number of Spanish-surnamed households grew slightly between 1930 and 1940.[124] Any decline in the Hispanic population due to repatriation or deportation in 1932 and 1936 was therefore surpassed by new arrivals as well as by natural growth within settled families. But we do see a drop in the number of Mexican-born people living in these

---

[122] "Martinez, Emma Gomez, letter to her children" and "Mexican deportation in the 1930s."

[123] In Los Angeles, which had the largest Mexican population in the country, about 35,000 Mexicans (nearly one-third of the city's total) were deported or repatriated during the 1930s (Escobedo, *From Coveralls to Zoot Suits*, p. 5).

[124] See App. 1.2.

communities across that decade: 92 were listed in the U.S. Census of 1930 but only 57 in 1940.[125] Further, the number of Spanish-surnamed household heads and their spouses listed in *Polk's City Directories* for Longmont remained flat between 1936 and 1946, whereas figures for Lafayette and Boulder show a marked rise.[126] It is possible that repatriation and deportation of Mexicans contributed to the stagnation of Longmont's Hispanic population between 1930 and 1946, but the Depression and economic problems confronting the sugar beet industry were probably the major causes.

We have now completed our description of the main features of the local Hispanic experience during the first four decades of the century. By around 1940, Boulder County contained hundreds of Spanish-surnamed people from Mexican, New Mexican, or southern Coloradan backgrounds who had lived in this area for a decade or more and were ready to start moving into new kinds of economic and community activity. Some had settled into integrated though low-income neighborhoods in the towns, their children were attending school, and the local churches were beginning to welcome them.[127] The regionally-based identities that had previously separated them were breaking down. The great majority of these Hispanic residents were U.S. citizens, most of them spoke English, and they were gaining confidence in dealing with Anglos. In the following chapter we follow their expanded range of activity across the next generation.

---

[125] See App. 2.1.
[126] App. 1.2 for this and below. For *Polk's City Directories*, see Ch. 3, note 62 above.
[127] See Vol. II, Chs. 2A, 6, and 5C.

Chapter 5

Work, Wars, and Confronting Racism, 1940-1965

During the generation between 1940 and 1965, the lives of Boulder County's Hispanics underwent gradual but significant change. Migration into the area continued, with some people arriving from U.S. states other than Colorado or New Mexico and others coming directly from Mexico. Opportunities for employment in the sugar beet fields and coal mines narrowed after 1946, the result of increased mechanization, lowered demand for their products, and competition from other sources. Thanks largely to improved education, Latinos and Latinas began to move into a wider range of occupations. World War II called many local men into the military, as did the Korean War and Vietnam conflict; groups like the Veterans of Foreign Wars and the G.I. Forum provided welcoming social venues after soldiers came back from service. Veterans returning to Longmont were unwilling to accept the forms of overt discrimination that still existed and tore down the "White Trade Only" signs. In Lafayette, Latinas/os became more fully incorporated into the social community, while cultural horizons in Boulder were broadened by the arrival of Latino G.I.s and the introduction of Spanish language classes in the elementary schools. Some young Mexican Americans from established families were now trying to define themselves relative to their own heritage and the prevailing Anglo world.

A. Immigration and Employment

The migration patterns of Hispanics moving into Boulder County during the period between 1940 and 1965 differed from those seen earlier in the century. Whereas nearly all of the new arrivals prior to 1940 had come from Mexico, New Mexico, or southern Colorado, some of those who came in the following generation had previously been living in other U.S. states.[1] Many were farm workers of Mexican background who had been pushed out of employment by ongoing mechanization of agriculture and hoped for better opportunities within a state whose economy was generally healthy. But some of them had difficulty finding jobs in Boulder County too. In the first paid position that Emma Gomez Martinez held in the 1960s, serving as a translator for the city, she worked with Spanish-speaking people who had come from states like Kansas or Nebraska but ended up needing help from the welfare system.[2] A smaller number of new arrivals had moved recently from Mexico.

The newcomers were sometimes regarded as of lower status by Latino families who had previously settled in Boulder County. Thanks to increased interaction between earlier arrivals from Mexican and New Mexican backgrounds at work, in the neighborhoods, and at school, leading to intermarriage between young people, the distinction between those two groups was rapidly dying out. Now, however, another kind of divide appeared, based upon length of residence in the community, educational level, and type of employment. Many Latinos whose families had lived in this area for two or even three generations had gone to school and moved into better kinds of work; their wives and daughters had generally been educated too, and some women were taking paid jobs outside the home. Such families enjoyed a certain degree of financial security, they knew how to function within the local community, and they commonly had fewer children. The new arrivals, by contrast, normally arrived with limited resources, little education, and larger families to support. So they were obliged to take whatever unskilled and poorly paid work they could find.

Many families who had lived in the area for several generations distanced themselves from these newer migrants. Virginia Maestas, who moved to a farm outside Boulder in 1945 and then into the town a few years later, remembers that there was a division at school between American-born Hispanics and people just coming in from Mexico.[3] When Secundino Herrera and his family arrived in Longmont from northern New Mexico as farm workers in 1951, "We found the [established

---

[1] See Ch. 2 above.
[2] Martinez, Emma Gomez, interview, 2013.
[3] Conversation with Marjorie McIntosh, July 31, 2013.

Hispanic] people very different from the Mexican people of New Mexico. They were not too sociable. They kept to themselves. They didn't care to exchange information with migrant people."[4] Divisions among Latinos in Boulder County were to become more marked in the following years.

Due to the arrival of newcomers and a high birthrate among some settled families, the number of Latino adults in our three towns nearly tripled in just 30 years. *Polk's City Directories* for 1936 list a total of 423 adults with Latino surnames.[5] By 1946, Longmont's number had not changed, but Lafayette's had increased by 39% and Boulder's by 49%. The biggest surge came between 1946 and 1955. The total for the three towns rose to 932, with growth of 46% in Lafayette but much higher values in Longmont (103%) and Boulder (93%). Some of Boulder's expansion stemmed from a substantial rise in the number of Latino college students living in the town as listed in the *City Directories*: 9 students in 1946, but 56 in 1955.[6] By 1965, the three towns had 1,219 Latino adults, with growth of 11% in Longmont, 25% in Lafayette, and 70% in Boulder. In that year, however, only 28 students were listed in Boulder (the rest probably lived on campus and hence were not picked up by the *City Directories*), so they did not account for much of the increase; 1965 is also the first year in which Longmont and Lafayette recorded more than just a few college students each.

A key social and economic development was that many families were now moving into urban communities, due in part to the availability of new kinds of jobs. Here they lived in neighborhoods that included other Latinas/os as well as people from different cultural backgrounds. Urban women were able to form more lasting bonds of friendship and mutual assistance with their *comadres*, neighbors and friends as well as family members; men had increased chances for sociability with their peers outside work. Town life and greater economic security enabled more children—both boys and girls—to finish high school.[7] A few families went regularly to Catholic services or sent their children to parochial schools, but some degree of ethnic discrimination within religious contexts continued.

The work done by this expanded population of Latinas/os was more varied than what we observed prior to 1940. Employment in both

[4] Herrera, Secundino, interview, c. 1987.
[5] App. 1.2. For *Polk's City Directories*, see Ch. 3, note 62 above.
[6] "Occupations and Employers, Boulder," 1946 and 1955.
[7] See Vol. II, Ch. 6C. For below, see Vol. II, Ch. 5B.

agriculture and mining was seriously affected by mechanization. Across these 25 years, the need for hand labor continued to drop as machines were introduced that could do the same job more quickly and with greater cost effectiveness. Great Western Sugar reported that whereas it took 10.1 man-hours to produce a ton of sugar beets in 1925, only 4.4 man-hours were required in 1958 and only 2.7 man-hours in 1964.[8] Employment was modified further by a shrinking market for beet sugar, replaced by the cane sugar produced in warmer climates, and by the decreased level of production—or in some cases, the complete closure— of many of the county's coal mines. Because the need for labor in what had been the two major sources of work in Longmont and Lafayette declined drastically across this generation, many Latinas/os sought other local jobs or moved to larger cities, especially Denver.

In many parts of the Southwest, especially Texas and California, the *Bracero* program was a major source of agricultural labor between 1942 and 1964.[9] This arrangement, formulated by joint agreement of the American and Mexican governments, was intended to provide the seasonal workers that U.S. commercial agriculture required without creating new long-term residents. Set up during World War II when Mexican labor was eagerly desired to replace Americans involved in the military or defense industries, the program ultimately conveyed an estimated 2 million Mexicans to the U.S., the largest influx of "guest workers" in U.S. history.

In Boulder County, however, few *braceros* appear to have come. Virginia Alvarez, who was born in Longmont in 1942, remembers going into a little grocery store on Main Street and 2nd Avenue when she was 10 or 12 years old and translating for some *braceros* who were shopping there.[10] The only other reference encountered here concerned Olga Melendez (Cordero)'s father and uncle, who first came to this area as *braceros* in the 1950s or 1960s.[11] It is possible, however, that more *braceros* were present in the county than showed up in this study, because they normally lived on the farms where they worked and had little interaction with more settled families.

Whereas farmers throughout the Southwest had customarily

---

[8] Hamilton, *Footprints in the Sugar*, p. 333.
[9] The fullest discussion is Deborah Cohen, *Braceros*.
[10] Alvarez, Virginia, interview, 2013.
[11] Cordero, Olga Melendez, interview, 2009. The men later returned to Longmont with their families, finding work at the turkey plant.

Illus. 5.1. Emma Suazo thinning beets with a short hoe, Longmont, 1942

required their employees to use hoes with a short handle (*el cortito*), forcing people to work on their knees or stooped way over, by the 1950s and 1960s agricultural workers in California were beginning to demand long-handled hoes.[12] Farmers claimed that the taller hoes, which made it possible to work while standing upright and let workers move more quickly through the fields, were too expensive. Agricultural laborers, however, thought that employers also liked being able to spot who was working and who was resting, by seeing who was crouched down and who was standing up. In Boulder County, Secundino Herrera argued with Lloyd Dickens, his employer for several years in the 1950s, over Dickens' refusal to provide long-handled hoes and machinery that would have decreased the physical demands placed upon beet workers.[13]

Yet the number of resident Latino families continuing to work in the beet fields was diminishing. Lou Cardenas's parents, who had come to the Longmont area in 1929 from New Mexico as beet workers, stayed

[12] Murray, "Abolition of El Cortito."

[13] Herrera, Secundino, interviews, 1979 and c. 1987. See also Ch. 3A above and "Mechanical beet harvester." Some Boulder County farmers were still providing short-handled hoes in the 1970s (see Ch. 6C below).

in the fields into the 1940s, as did Lou and her husband in the early 1940s.[14] But her husband also worked in the coal mines around Lafayette and later took construction jobs in Cheyenne, Wyoming. In the 1940s, Virginia Alvarez still moved around with her parents from one beet farm to another each year, and Esther Blazón preserved a snapshot taken of herself and her sister, aged 6 and 14, taken while their parents were farm workers in this area.[15] By the 1950s, however, many local farmers were shifting to crops other than sugar beets that required less ongoing labor and were more profitable. In the 1946 *City Directories*, only three Latinas/os in Longmont identified themselves as sugar beet workers, though some of the 14 unspecified laborers might also have done such work.[16] In 1955 and 1965, beets were not mentioned at all, and only a few Latino residents indicated they had any other kind of agricultural employment. Work in Boulder County's fields was henceforth done primarily by truly migrant workers, who travelled across multiple regions during the growing and harvesting seasons as their labor was needed.[17]

Owning farm land was rare in the middle decades of the century. In 1946, only three Latinos in Longmont and one in Boulder described themselves as "farmers" (as opposed to farm workers); Boulder had one farmer in 1955.[18] The few people encountered in this study who were able to buy agricultural land had income from sources other than farm labor. Hank Blazón's father bought a farm in Mead, to the northeast of Longmont, in 1942, having come to the area in 1927.[19] Among other types of work, he operated a pool hall in Longmont which became a popular social center for Latino men and presumably produced the funds for his purchase of land. Alex Gonzales, a former miner, was able to buy a farm of 40 acres outside Longmont thanks to profits from the City Café in Longmont, which he bought in 1945.[20]

Some of the Latinas/os who had previously worked on farms found

---

[14] Cardenas, Lou, interview, c. 1987.

[15] Alvarez, Virginia, interview, 2013, and "Esther and Ann Blazón."

[16] "Occupations and Employers, Three Towns, 1946." For below, see "Occupations and Employers, Three Towns, 1955" and "Occupations and Employers, Three Towns, 1965."

[17] See Ch. 6B below. For migrant workers in the fields in 2013, see "Longmont, film of places of historical importance."

[18] "Occupations and Employers, Three Towns, 1946" and "Occupations and Employers, Three Towns, 1955."

[19] Blazón, William ("Hank"), interview, 2013. For pool halls, see Vol. II, Ch. 4B.

[20] Tafoya, Mary Gonzales, interview, 2009, and Gonzales, Alex, interview, c. 1987.

employment in the expanding number of food processing plants in Longmont. Companies may have recognized the desirability of increasing production in a community with a pool of potential laborers willing to accept hard jobs for low pay. For people who had been spending long days in the fields under the hot sun, these jobs may have been seen as an improvement, even though the work was often unpleasant and sometimes dangerous. Wages were better than the earnings of agricultural laborers, work might continue throughout the year, and in some cases the companies provided benefits for their employees. Further, several of the plants hired women as well as men, opening up paid work outside the home. In 1955, 26 men and 12 women from Longmont— 27% of the Latino workers listed in the *City Directory*—were employed by food-related processing plants.[21] The four main factories were all located along the railroad tracks that ran west-east on the southern side of Longmont, an area in which some Latino families were already living.[22] Several of the plants continued to provide employment until the late twentieth century.

The easternmost factory was operated by Great Western Sugar to convert raw sugar beets into sugar for sale. Long after the Longmont area had ceased growing beets itself, the company maintained the processing plant, importing by train great quantities of beets raised more cheaply in other parts of the region. At one time, more than 7,000 farms in three states shipped beets to this facility.[23] The sugar factory hired six Latinas/ os as workers in the plant and one as an interpreter in 1946; ten years later it employed only five, but in 1965 it had thirteen Latino workers, including several mechanics or specialists.[24]

The next big installation, moving west along the railroad tracks, was the turkey processing plant. This huge factory, occupying several blocks adjoining Main Street, was operated first by General Foods, later by Con-Agra, and finally by Butterball.[25] Work in the turkey plant, which was open to both men and women, was physically demanding and caused

---

[21] "Occupations and Employers, Three Towns, 1955."

[22] See Vol. II, Ch. 2B.

[23] *Actual, Factual St. Vrain Valley*, p. 42.

[24] "Occupations and Employers, Three Towns, 1946," "Occupations and Employers, Three Towns, 1955," and "Occupations and Employers, Three Towns, 1965." For the abandoned factory in 2013, see "Longmont, film of places of historical importance."

[25] For photos from the 1960s, see Illus. 6.6, "Turkey plant workers," and "Interior of Longmont Foods turkey plant"; for the disused complex of buildings in 2013, before they were torn down, see "Longmont, film of places of historical importance."

many accidents: employees used sharp equipment to dismember the turkeys, and because the floors and counters were covered with liquids and grease from the turkeys, it was easy to slip and fall. After her marriage in 1941, Mary Martinez—who had previously been doing farm work—took a job at the turkey plant.[26] When Lou Cardenas's husband was fired from his agricultural job and removed from his house after being injured while working, he eventually found a job at the turkey plant.[27] As the turkey plant expanded in the 1950s, it hired more Latinas/os. Its 27 workers in 1955 made it the largest single employer of the Latinos listed in our three towns.[28]

The remaining sources of food-processing jobs for Latinas/os lay further down the railway line. The Kuner-Empson cannery prepared and canned fresh vegetables, known especially for its peas.[29] The cannery employed five Latinos in 1946 and two a decade later.[30] Longmont also had two flour mills, located on the southwestern edge of town. Golden West and St. Vrain Valley Milling Companies hired one or two Latino men and women in 1946, 1955, and 1965.[31] A few other people worked for meat packing plants, rendering companies, and related types of food processing firms. When John Borrego came to Longmont around 1932 from northern New Mexico, he worked first in the fields but in the 1940s was hired as a meat packer.[32]

Work in the mines changed but did not end entirely. Some were still producing coal, while others needed labor to shut down operations or carry out land restoration projects. In 1946, 35 Latinos in Lafayette and 11 in Longmont were employed by a total of eight different mines.[33] In 1955, Lafayette still had 20 coal miners, with four each in Longmont and Boulder.[34] (The residential camps had now been closed: improved private transportation made it possible for men to live in nearby towns

[26] Martinez, Mary, interview, 1979.
[27] Cardenas, Lou, interview, c. 1987.
[28] "Occupations and Employers, Three Towns, 1955."
[29] See "Interior, Kuner-Empson factory" for the cannery in 1946; for its exterior in 2013, after conversion into expensive apartments, see "Longmont, film of places of historical importance."
[30] "Occupations and Employers, Three Towns, 1946" and "Occupations and Employers, Three Towns, 1955."
[31] "Occupations and Employers, Three Towns, 1946," "Occupations and Employers, Three Towns, 1955," and "Occupations and Employers, Three Towns, 1965."
[32] Marquez, Sonia, interview, 2013.
[33] "Occupations and Employers, Three Towns, 1946."
[34] "Occupations and Employers, Three Towns, 1955."

and drive to their jobs.) As late as 1965, 13 men living in Lafayette described themselves as coal miners, as did 6 or 7 each in Longmont and Boulder.[35] Most of the eight mines at which they worked were located just over the Weld County border. The pattern of coupling mining during the cold weather with seasonal farm labor, construction, or odd jobs continued for some time after 1940.[36]

The nature of mining changed even further during these years. Several former miners from Boulder County who were interviewed about the period after 1940 provided detailed descriptions of the new machines and what they did.[37] If a miner was good with equipment and fortunate, he might get higher pay and perhaps be kept on at the mine to handle certain kinds of machinery on a year-round basis. But demand for labor was further reduced by the decreasing profitability of these mines, leading to cut-backs in production and the complete closing of some.

Many Latinos now sought other ways of supporting their families. Defense industries offered possibilities. During World War II, Helen Contrerras Beck's father left his normal routine of doing winter mine work and summer field work to go to California; employed in a navy shipyard, he sent money home to his family.[38] When Roy Maestas could no longer provide for his family on the amount of work offered by the Washington Mine in the early 1940s, he moved his family to Boulder and went to California, where he took a job in a shipyard during the early years of the war.[39] In 1942, Juan Archuleta and his son Arthur went to work at another California shipyard.[40] Tom Lopez, the first Latino mayor of Lafayette, talked about the expansion of defense-related employment opportunities within commuting distance during the Cold War period after 1945: Rocky Flats Nuclear Weapons Plant, a facility south of Boulder operated by Dow Chemical which manufactured plutonium triggers for hydrogen bombs; Rocky Mountain Arsenal, a munitions plant; and Beech Aircraft, which held many military contracts.[41]

Rocky Flats/Dow Chemical became a major employer of Latinas/os

---

[35] "Occupations and Employers, Three Towns, 1965."
[36] "Rosales, Henry and Alice, biography" and Silva, Dolores, interview, 2013.
[37] Lopez, Thomas, interview, 1986, and Martinez, Joe, interview, 1977.
[38] Rough interview notes taken by Oli Duncan, undated, but probably 2007-2009.
[39] "Maestas, Pedro (Roy), Ruby, and Abe, biography."
[40] "Archuleta family history." Arthur was drafted in 1943.
[41] Lopez, Thomas, interview, 1986.

from these towns. Although exposure to radioactive substances was to have fatal consequences for some of its workers in the future, at the time Rocky Flats attracted a wide range of employees, nearly all in jobs that required education or specialized training and hence paid far better than most previous work open to Latinas/os.[42] In 1965, when Dow Chemical was the largest employer of Latinas/os from the three towns as listed in the *City Directories*, 22 people worked at the facility: as electrical engineers, chemical operators, laboratory technicians, inspectors, mechanics, secretaries, security guards, and custodians, as well as unspecified employees.[43]

The University of Colorado hired a small but growing number of both unskilled and skilled workers. Whereas in 1946, only two Latino men were listed as employed by the university (a janitor and an Instructor), sixteen people were hired in 1955: one janitor, five laborers, a truck helper, three food service workers, two clerks (one of them female), and four Instructors (one female).[44] Some of the people listed as laborers may actually have had more specialized skills. Juan Francisco Archuleta, who had moved his family to Boulder in the 1930s, worked as a stonemason on the campus in the later 1940s.[45] The number of Latinos employed by the university had risen to 18 by 1965. Most were still unskilled workers, but the university now hired two female secretaries, two male Professors or Associate Professors, and a woman who described herself as a teacher there.[46]

Additional kinds of professional, technical, skilled, and administrative support work opened up during the 1950s and early 1960s. Some were created by the federal government. The Federal Aviation Administration established an air traffic control center in Longmont, which handled flights coming into, out of, and over the Denver airports. Don Archuleta worked as an air traffic controller starting in 1963; based in Longmont, he was also sent to Peru to train Latin American controllers.[47] By 1965 the FAA was hiring a few other Latinas/os, as was the National Bureau of Standards in Boulder.[48] These new installations contributed to the rising

---

[42] For health problems, see Ch. 6C below and Vol. II, Ch. 3B.
[43] "Occupations and Employers, Three Towns, 1965."
[44] "Occupations and Employers, Three Towns, 1946," and "Occupations and Employers, Three Towns, 1955."
[45] "Archuleta family history."
[46] "Occupations and Employers, Three Towns, 1965."
[47] Archuleta, Don, interview, 2009.
[48] "Occupations and Employers, Three Towns, 1965."

Illus. 5.2. Fabricio Martinez with his mail truck, Longmont, 1960s

number of Latino professionals (37) and technicians (7).

Some men entered types of work that had previously been closed to Latinos or were just emerging as communication, mass media, and transportation developed. Construction companies began to hire Latinos. After his return from the Korean War in the mid-1950s, Richard Tafoya worked as a cement finisher.[49] Oli Duncan's father learned how to do electrical work while in the coal mines and was later hired as an electrician by a construction company.[50] When Lloyd Martinez of Lafayette left mining, he became a welder and developed skills in metal work.[51] Phil Hernandez's father was a builder, but although he qualified for admission into the carpenters' union, he was blackballed by the Italian Americans who dominated that trade; after being injured and out of work for two years, he found a job as a custodian with the Boulder schools.[52] Railroads, which still hired 14 Latinos in 1946 and 5 in 1955, then dropped out of the picture, but other kinds of transport

[49] Tafoya, Mary Gonzales, interview, 2009.
[50] Conversation with Marjorie McIntosh, April 12, 2013.
[51] "Martinez, Lloyd and Sally (Salazar), biography."
[52] Conversation with Marjorie McIntosh, Feb. 6, 2013.

work increased: 4 men were truck drivers in 1955 and 16 in 1965.[53] In Longmont, Cliff Martinez was hired to handle a new, faster printing press at the *Longmont Times-Call*.[54] In the early 1940s, a considerable number of men and a few women were still working for New Deal, post-Depression programs: the WPA, CCC, or local governments.[55] By 1946, however, most of those special opportunities were gone. Some of the men who had formerly been employed by them went into the military.[56]

In a small but important step forward, one that benefited both their families and the economy of their communities, some Latinos began to run their own businesses. This pattern was to expand during the following decades. In the early 1940s, a few people were already demonstrating their entrepreneurial ability through income-generating activities operated from their own homes. In Boulder, the Saragosa family had a large house on the western edge of town, adjacent to the land on which they raised animals and grew food for sale.[57] They also rented out rooms, taking in boarders, mainly men. If their lodgers were not able to pay rent in cash, the Saragosas had them work in the vegetable gardens or orchards instead. E. E. Bernal, employed during the week at a coal mine, a processing mill, or in construction, had a weekend business too: a trash collection service.[58] Going around to people's houses with his truck, he emptied the ashes out of incinerators and took them and other waste to the dump. His enterprise was so successful that he spun off trash collection in certain neighborhoods to other Latinos, but under his general control. After Roy Maestas returned to Colorado in 1943 and took a job with Allied Chemical, working in a mill that processed gold brought down from the mountains, he too hauled trash on the weekends, assisted by his children.[59] In the 1930s and early 1940s, David Toledo had operated a little barber shop in Frederick to supplement his earnings as a miner; he continued that work after moving to Boulder in 1943.[60]

Larger businesses were still rare. Only four or five Latinos said

---

[53] "Occupations and Employers, Three Towns, 1946," "Occupations and Employers, Three Towns, 1955," and "Occupations and Employers, Three Towns, 1965."
[54] "New printing press."
[55] See Ch. 3C above.
[56] See section B below.
[57] Euvaldo Valdez, conversation with Marjorie McIntosh, July 23, 2013.
[58] Ibid. and Bernal, Mr. and Mrs. Emerenciano, interview, 1977.
[59] "Maestas, Pedro (Roy), Ruby, and Abe, biography." Roy was also sent to Mexico to train workers in a new mill there.
[60] Toledo, David, interview, c. 1978.

Illus. 5.3. José Esquibel with his dad,
Longmont, 1979

Illus. 5.4. Joe Esquibel, owner of
several pharmacies, 1989

they owned or managed a business other than farming in 1946, 1955, and 1965.[61] Hank Blazón recalled that the only Latino businesses in Longmont in the 1950s were George Martinez's barber shop and the auto body shops owned by Benny Rodriguez and later Casey Najera.[62] Benny, whose parents had come from Mexico in the late 1910s, set up his body shop in 1949, and by 1965 he was hiring four workers.[63] When interviewed in 1979, he spoke proudly of his successful business, for which his wife served as bookkeeper.

These early enterprises usually relied upon skills acquired as an employee. Tom Lopez of Lafayette learned to handle machinery while working in the Morrison and Lincoln mines in the later 1940s and early 1950s.[64] In 1956, he founded his own backhoe business and obtained the contract to install new sewer lines for the expanding town. José (later known as Joe) Esquibel, who had come from New Mexico with his parents as a young child, went into the military and then studied

---

[61] "Occupations and Employers, Three Towns, 1955" and "Occupations and Employers, Three Towns, 1965."

[62] Blazón, William ("Hank"), interview, 2013.

[63] Rodriguez, Benny, interview, 1979.

[64] Lopez, Thomas, interview, 1986. He was later elected to the Lafayette City Council and then became mayor.

pharmacy.[65] After working for several drug stores, he opened two pharmacies of his own in Longmont (first Mountain View, then Francis Street) as well as ones in Boulder and Denver.

One of the most important mid-century changes was the expansion of paid work for women. Whereas only 5-7% of the total Latino workforce in these towns as recorded in the *City Directories* had been female in 1926 and 1936, in 1946 one-eighth of the workers were women; in 1955, the fraction reached one-quarter, before dropping slightly in 1965.[66] Their participation was due in part to the movement of Latino families into towns. During the 1940s and early 1950s, Dora Bernal of Boulder did domestic work for other families and babysat; Lola Martinez worked as a household servant for well-off families on University Hill.[67] Other women in the Water + Goss Streets neighborhood took in laundry, and Teresa Alvarez and her older daughters operated a beauty shop behind their house.[68] While most of these income-generating activities were carried out within their own or other people's homes, some women were able to transfer their domestic skills into waged employment. Teresa Alvarez had worked in the kitchen at Mount St. Gertrude Academy in Boulder to pay for her daughters' tuition there, while Mary Martinez left the turkey plant in Longmont in favor of a job at a laundry.[69]

By the 1950s and 1960s, there were entirely new ways for Latinas to earn money, most of which required formal schooling. For the first time, they were breaking out of the lowest level of the occupational stratification system, which had been segregated by gender and race or ethnicity. Dolores Silva of Lafayette and Becky Ortega and Diana Arroyo of Boulder worked for NeoData, doing data entry.[70] Mary Martinez became a nurse's aide, then got her GED, and finally became the first Latina Licensed Practical Nurse in the county.[71] As of 1965, the *City Directories* show 99 Latinas working for pay outside the home, including

---

[65] Esquibel, Jose, interview, 1979, and see "Mountain View Pharmacy," "Opening of Francis Street Pharmacy," "Profile of Joe Esquibel," "Francis Street Pharmacy," and "Joe Esquibel inside his Francis Street Pharmacy."

[66] App. 3.3.

[67] Maestas, Virginia, interview, 1978; Vol. II, Illus. 1.7.

[68] "Martinez, Juan and Josephine; Marcella Diaz, biography," and Alvarez, Teresa, interview, 1976.

[69] Alvarez, Teresa, interview, 1977, and Martinez, Mary, interview, 1979.

[70] Silva, Dolores, interview, 2013; Phil Hernandez, email to Marjorie McIntosh, Jan. 13, 2015.

[71] Martinez, Mary, interview, 1979, Martinez, Mary, interview, 1988, and Vol. II, Ch. 6A.

secretaries (8), school teachers (5), clerks (5), nurses (4), and nurse's aides (3).[72] Although such positions took women away from the home and required them to work with men as well as other women, their duties could be regarded as extensions of familiar female roles. So long as they accepted male authority in the workplace and at home, and so long as the income they produced was used to supplement their husbands' earnings and contribute to the well-being of the family as a whole, these jobs do not appear to have caused conflict between spouses.

Some Latinas profited from employment in defense industries during and after World War II.[73] Lola Martinez of Boulder worked on an aircraft assembly line during the war, while Theresa Borrego Vigil took a job at the Rocky Mountain Arsenal after World War II.[74] She was on the assembly line for explosives, where employees "were required to wear gas masks, fire proof coveralls and to work under water when handling the numerous and various chemicals. They were also trained to identify the different gases by odor, a very dangerous assignment for all." Workers in these factories were not, however, predominantly female, and they did not develop the kind of independent "women's work culture" seen, for example, in citrus packing houses or canneries in California during the 1940s and 1950s.[75] Female production workers in Boulder County were instead employed in settings shaped by male Anglo values and behaviors.

Family tension could result from women's participation in well paid defense-related work. Oli Duncan believed that because women had taken jobs to help win the war and were earning their own incomes, they became less submissive to their husbands and other male relatives, causing problems within the home.[76] In the early 1940s, when her parents were living with her father's parents, her mother was becoming increasingly resentful of the expectation on the part of her father-in-law and husband that as men they would make all the decisions for the family.[77] One whole summer she worked in the beet fields to earn money for the down payment on a nice set of bedroom furniture, but when

---

[72] "Occupations and Employers, Three Towns, 1965."
[73] See, more generally, Escobedo, *From Coveralls to Zoot Suits*, chs. 3-4.
[74] See Vol. II, Illus.1.8, and "Vigil, Rudy and Theresa, biography."
[75] Matt Garcia, *A World of Its Own*, pp. 167-171, citing also Ruiz, *Cannery Women, Cannery Lives*, pp. 31-32.
[76] Duncan, "Some Notes."
[77] Ibid., and see "Olivas, Ralph and Rose, biographical account."

the fall came, her husband refused to continue the monthly payments because he saw no need for fancy things like that. Infuriated, she left her two children in the care of their grandmother and set off for California. There, with her brother's help, she found work in the Navy shipyards. But her husband, realizing how much he cared about her, picked up the children and joined her in California. For the rest of the war they both worked in the shipyards, enjoying a lively social life when not on the job. Dora Bernal moved to California in 1952 without her children in hopes of getting better employment than the domestic service she had been doing in Boulder.[78] She remained in California for eight years, finding work in several different towns and going to dances on the weekends with friends. Those cases were atypical, however. Most local families adapted to the new forms of female employment because they contributed to a higher standard of living for all their members.

Child labor was greatly reduced after 1940. The children of farming families still commonly worked alongside their parents, but now they began their employment at a later age and were required to fit their work around the edges of school: on weekends, in the summers, and perhaps in the late afternoons/early evenings. Mary Gonzales first met her future husband, Richard Tafoya, when she was 14 years old and they were both picking beans near Longmont.[79] Eleanor Montour, born in 1944, worked in the fields around Lafayette during the summers when she was in high school.[80] Secundino Herrera had an argument with a farmer who employed him near Longmont in the 1950s because the man wanted to pay Secundino less than agreed for the labor of one of his daughters because she was small in size.[81] Boys were not allowed to start mining until they were 16. For children living in towns, part-time work might be available. High school girls in Boulder sometimes found jobs in drug stores, dime stores, or movie theaters, and by the 1960s, at least an occasional Latino boy was hired to deliver newspapers.[82]

[78] Bernal, Dora, interview, 1978. When her husband divorced her a year later, the children chose to stay with their father in Boulder after a custody fight in court (Maestas, Virginia, interview, 2013).

[79] Tafoya, Mary Gonzales, interview, 2009.

[80] Montour, Eleanor, interview, 2013. She said it was hard not to be able to join in activities with other young people, because she and her siblings had to work. "At daylight, we were already in the car heading out to whatever field we were going to work at, and by the time we got home it was dark and we would take our baths and eat and go to bed and rest for the next day."

[81] Herrera, Secundino, interview, 1979.

[82] Alvarez, Teresa, interview, 1977, Maestas, Virginia, interview, 1978, and "Daily Times-Call newspaper paperboys."

B. Military Service in World War II, Korea, and Vietnam

Latinos have made a major contribution to our nation through their military service. In Colorado, Hispanics who had moved from northern New Mexico into the San Luis Valley volunteered for the Union army during the Civil War (1861-1865).[83] In the country as a whole, some Latinos fought in World War I (1914-1918), and their numbers soared in World War II (1939-1945) and the Korean War (1950-1953).[84] Many Latinos also went to Vietnam (main U.S. activity, 1965-1969). In addition to regular enlisted soldiers, members of the National Guard from several southwestern states, including many Latinos, were mobilized for active duty in the Caribbean or Pacific in several of the twentieth-century wars.

Although exact numbers are hard to obtain because Hispanics were initially not identified as such in the records, a higher fraction of all military personnel in the twentieth century was evidently Latino than was true for the general population. They were also courageous and effective fighters, as demonstrated by the disproportionate number of Latino soldiers who were awarded military honors and the number who were killed. During the full span of the Vietnam conflict, about 80,000 Latinos served in the U.S. armed forces. Although Latinas/os constituted only 4.5% of the country's total population at the time, they accounted for 19% of American casualties.[85]

Joining the military offered some practical benefits. Signing up could resolve the problem of poor employment opportunities at home and provided a chance for skilled training while in the service. Soldiers who had come as immigrants to the United States might be granted citizenship in thanks for their contribution to their new county.[86] The Servicemen's Readjustment Act of 1944, known commonly as the G.I. Bill, provided benefits to all veterans who had been on active duty for at least 90 days during the war years and been honorably discharged, even if they had not seen combat. These benefits included money for low-cost mortgages or to start a business; cash payments for tuition for vocational education

---

[83] White, *La Garita*, pp. 23-24. Nearly all other New Mexican Hispanics likewise supported the Union cause (Jaramillo, *Spanish Civilization and Culture*, p. 155).
[84] Miguel Gonzales, *Mexicanos*, pp. 163-168 and 214-215, and Acuña, *Occupied America*, pp. 168-9, 237-239, and 264-265.
[85] "Latinos in the military."
[86] Hamilton, *Footprints in the Sugar*, p. 329.

and high school; tuition plus living expenses for college or graduate school; and one year of unemployment compensation. Modified versions of the G.I. Bill applied to veterans of later wars as well, assisting millions of servicemen and women. In practice, however, this program proved less advantageous for returning soldiers of color than for whites, as they often had to work through local organizations that were racially restrictive, such as the underwriters for home loans.[87] At a national level, the G.I. Bill also encouraged the flight of millions of Anglos out of the cities into the suburbs and indirectly facilitated urban renewal, both of which had negative effects for many Latinas/os living in poverty.[88]

Boulder County's Latinas/os were generally proud to be defending their country. Although some soldiers were drafted, others enlisted voluntarily, as an act of patriotism. Their families were willing to let them go, though they feared for the soldiers' safety and dreaded receiving a telegram from the military.[89] The dozens of photos of men in uniform preserved by Latino families for decades after their service reflect the honor in which soldiers were held.[90] Most members of the armed forces were men, but starting with World War II, a few Latinas from Boulder County joined up. Women had to assume a more important place within their households when fathers or husbands were in the service. This gender destabilization presumably required some readjustment when the men returned to their families.

The importance of military service to Boulder County's Latinas/os is reflected in oral histories and family biographies. Many of the people who provided information about their families mentioned proudly that a father, uncles, brothers, or sons had been in one of the wars.[91] When

---

[87] "Race Matters." As illustrated there, a white veteran who was able to buy a house thanks to the G.I. Bill could use it later as collateral to borrow money to send his children to college; at his death, the house would pass to his heirs. Latinas/os or African Americans who did not meet the conditions of discriminatory local mortgage underwriters, even when money was available from the G.I. Bill, remained in rental housing and therefore found it much more difficult to pay for their children's college education and had nothing they could pass on to them. This situation is presented as an example of embedded racial/ethnic inequality.

[88] Acuña, *Occupied America*, pp. 277-278.

[89] For special prayers offered for the safe return of soldiers, see Vol. II, Ch. 5B.

[90] E.g., "Terry Aragon as soldier in Berlin, early 1960s (text)," "Victor David Romero in the Navy," "Fabricio Martinez in Germany, WWII," "Ray Vigil in military uniform," "Eddie Vigil in military uniform," "Paul Cortez in military uniform," and "Ted Aragon in military uniform."

[91] E.g., Bernal, Mr. and Mrs. Emerenciano, interview, 1977, Bernal, Dora, interview, 1978, Silva, Dolores, interview, 2013, and "Estrada, Cleo, autobiographical information."

Illus. 5.5. *Flavio (Floyd) Martinez in World War II uniform with parents*

Illus. 5.6. *Terry Aragon as soldier in Berlin, early 1960s*

Illus. 5.7. *Ronnie Quintana in military uniform*

Illus. 5.8. *Dan Pineda in military uniform*

Ted Archuleta of Longmont died at age 89, the eulogy delivered by his brother stressed Ted's patriotism.[92] He was studying at the University of Denver at the time of the Pearl Harbor attack in 1941 but immediately signed up for the Army Air Corps. Thanks to his good math skills and successful training as a bombardier, he was sent to England to fly B-17s over Germany. Oli Duncan wrote that one of her three uncles who fought in World War II regarded that service as "his greatest moment of glory"; he "reveled in his warriorhood" and asked to receive a veteran's funeral when he died many years later.[93] Her other uncles survived being prisoners of war (one in Europe and one in the Pacific) because they had learned as children how to live through hunger and physical hardship. One of Doris Gonzales's cousins was a prisoner of war in Japan for five years.[94]

We have some evidence about how many Latinos from Boulder County fought in World War II from the occupations given in *Polk's City Directories* for 1946.[95] The listing was made after some soldiers had already been demobilized, but even so, the figures are very high. In both Longmont and Lafayette, one-third of all Latino males for whom an occupation was provided in the *Directories* were currently in the military, as were about a quarter in Boulder. The total of 67 servicemen and women included 53 men in the Army, 11 men and 1 woman in the Navy, 1 man in the Air Corps, and 1 woman in the WAVE. A booklet that gives the names of 58 Latino soldiers from Lafayette who fought in World War II, in some cases with detailed information and a photo, indicates that these men were active in the European and Pacific Theaters of Operation and the South Pacific Liberation effort.[96] Nearly all were decorated with multiple medals for valor and sacrifice. In rank, however, none rose above sergeant.

Local Latinos fought in later wars too. The *City Directories* for 1955 show that 16 men from Lafayette were in uniform, 7 from Longmont, and 6 from Boulder.[97] By that time, however, most of the soldiers who fought in Korea had returned home, leaving only those who chose to

[92] "Archuleta, Ted, eulogy."
[93] Duncan, "Some Notes."
[94] Gonzales, Doris, interview, 2013.
[95] "Occupations and Employers, Three Towns, 1946."
[96] VFW, *Service Record Book*, passim.
[97] "Occupations and Employers, Three Towns, 1955," and see, e.g., "Local GI's sent to battlefield in Korea."

remain in the military beyond their minimum years of service. The *Directories'* listings of soldiers in subsequent years are almost certainly incomplete, probably because they excluded people who were not living in the community on a full-time basis, and we have only a few references from other sources.[98] In 1965, when the U.S. was starting its active involvement in Vietnam, three men and a woman from Longmont and three men from Boulder were listed as being in the military; by 1975, after the draft had ended, only a single Latino from Longmont and one from Boulder were said to be servicemen.[99]

Some Latino families furnished soldiers over several generations. John Martinez of Boulder served in Europe during World War II, working with radar and anti-aircraft artillery; his brother Victor was in a combat engineering battalion, reaching the rank of sergeant.[100] Tom, John's son, enlisted in 1969 after his graduation from Boulder High School and was assigned to a signal battalion in South Korea.[101] The Archuleta family likewise furnished three soldiers over two generations.

A few men made the military their career. Seferino Espinoza joined the Navy right after graduating from Boulder High School in 1955.[102] During his 23 years in service, he was twice sent to Vietnam as a Field Medic Corpsman and ended up as chief of a dental facility in California. Sergeant Felix Lopez of Longmont, who enlisted in the Marines at age 17 in 1952, was particularly dedicated.[103] During the next 18 years, he had one tour of duty in Korea and two in Vietnam, receiving the Silver Star for his valor and distinction. He then joined the Army for yet another round of service.

On the battlefield, soldiers obviously faced enormous dangers. It may have offered some comfort to the grieving family of Arthur F. Archuleta of Boulder, who was killed in action in 1944, when his remains were returned for reburial in Green Mountain Cemetery.[104] The first soldier from Lafayette to be killed in Vietnam was Charles E. (Johnny) Manzanares, who was shot in the chest while on a search and destroy

---

[98] E.g., "Quintana completes naval training."
[99] "Occupations and Employers, Three Towns, 1965"; "Occupations and Employers, Three Towns, 1975." The 1975 and perhaps the 1965 *Directories* evidently excluded soldiers who were living away from home at the time of the survey.
[100] "John Martinez, military service"; "Victor Martinez in the military."
[101] Tom left the military as a sergeant and later trained as an accountant.
[102] "Espinoza, Seferino Albert, biography."
[103] Newby, *Longmont Album*, p. 89, and "Sgt. Felix Lopez receiving Silver Star."
[104] "Arthur Archuleta buried as war hero" and "Archuleta family history," p. 13.

304ᵗʰ Sig Bn, Yongsan, South Korea   121ˢᵗ Signal Bn, Ft Riley, KS

Tom Martinez
Drafted in Apr 1969, Basic at Ft Ord, CA.
then on to Ft Gordon, GA for Signal School.
Stationed at Camp Long then Camp Coiner,
South Korea with the 304ᵗʰ Signal
Battalion. Reassigned to the 121ˢᵗ Signal
Battalion at Ft Riley, KS

SP4. MARTINEZ

Illus. 5.9. Tom Martinez in South Korea, 1970s

Arthur Archuleta, son of Juan Clofes Archuleta US
Army, drafted June 4, 1942 killed in action,
Aachen, Germany, October 20, 1944 Interred
Green Mountain Cemetery, Boulder, Colorado

Frank Ernest Archuleta, US Army, WWII enlisted
in 1944 paratrooper 11ᵗʰ Airborne South Pacific,
Philippines, Japan, Korean War, California, drill
instructor with an honorable discharge.
Deceased: July 26, 2011

Arthur (Archie) Fermin Archuleta, US Air Force:
Vietnam, enlisted in 1964, Jet mechanic,
Honorable discharge 1968

Illus. 5.10. Archuleta men in the military

mission in December, 1965.[105] Johnny had been in the army for two years but in Vietnam for only two months. Paul Rodriguez was the first Longmont soldier to die in Vietnam, on April 5, 1966, 12 days before his 20th birthday.[106] In 2013, Paul's buddy from their teenage years, Michael Bravo Lopez, headed a project to erect a memorial to Paul in Kensington Park.[107]

Even if soldiers survived, experiences in war often left lasting scars. When talking about her husband Richard's experiences as a Marine in Korea, Mary Gonzales Tafoya said, "It was terrible for him, and sometimes he would have flashbacks. He didn't like going to the Fourth of July fireworks. All the noise would unnerve him. Once we were at a party in Denver when a guy came in and yelled something in Korean. Richard immediately dove for cover behind the sofa."[108]

The armed forces were overtly segregated on racial grounds during World War II, and although Hispanics were in general classified as whites by the military, ethnic discrimination continued there as it did in civilian life. Jessie Velez Lehmann described the difficulties one of her brothers experienced after entering the army during World War II.[109] Especially while stationed in the South, he was called names and taunted by other soldiers because he was Mexican. Although normally he did not react violently, in one case he responded so furiously that he was sent to the guardhouse for punishment. Mary Gonzales Tafoya said that when Richard was in Korea, he was frequently in the midst of active fighting.[110] He believed that "Mexicans and Blacks were always on the front line because the brass seemed to think they were more expendable than the other guys."

For those who came through military service relatively unscathed, there might be positive features to their service. Members of the armed forces interacted with people from throughout the U.S. and were often stationed overseas. These experiences expanded the horizons of many Boulder County soldiers.[111] Robert Borrego described the impact of his time in the military, which started when he was 18 and having trouble finding work. "In 1951, with the Korean War going on and feeling pretty

[105] "Vietnam War."
[106] "Memorial to Latino soldier."
[107] "Longmont, film of places of historical importance."
[108] Tafoya, Mary Gonzales, interview, 2009.
[109] Lehmann, Jessie Velez, interview, 1978.
[110] Tafoya, Mary Gonzales, interview, 2009.
[111] E.g., "Gilbert Espinoza in Viet Nam."

Illus. 5.11. *Ted Aragon with Vietnamese children*

futile about leaving my mark on this planet (as if it was waiting), I joined and served nine months in a combat tank, Co. A on tank no. 34. Back to the states, then to Germany for eighteen months as a troop train commander. I got to see all of that country, learned to love it in a way and can see how it influenced the American way of life."[112]

Thanks largely to the G.I. Bill, the armed forces offered not only job training but also veterans' benefits in the form of educational opportunities. Al Cardenas learned to be a diesel mechanic in the navy during the Korean War, a skill he was able to use in his 20-year career at Rocky Flats.[113] After Abe Maestas left the Navy, he went to college on the G.I. Bill and became a high school teacher.[114] Don Archuleta was trained in communications while in the Navy, 1950 to 1954, and then studied at the University of Colorado before joining the Federal Aviation Administration.[115] Larry Rosales spent four years in the Air Force—one

[112] "Borrego, Robert Raymond, biography."
[113] Cardenas, Alfonso, interview, 2004, and see Ch. 6C below.
[114] Maestas, Virginia, interview, 1978.
[115] Archuleta, Don, interview, 2009.

of them in Vietnam—after signing up in 1966; when he returned, he studied computer programming in college and worked as a database specialist.[116]

Although in some parts of the country veterans' organizations like the VFW (Veterans of Foreign Wars) and the American Legion discriminated against returning soldiers of color, in Boulder County the local posts of the VFW provided a social community for many veterans and their families.[117] Career officer Sergeant Felix Lopez, after his final retirement from the military, became head of the VFW's Color Guard in Longmont.[118] Francisco ("Frank") Valenzuela was in the Air Force during the Korean War and later went into the merchant marines; before his death in 2014 he received a pin as a 55-year member of the Lafayette VFW.[119] The wives and widows of veterans could join the Auxiliary of their local VFW post. Mary Manzanares Garcia, who worked as a clerical translator for the Boulder Valley School District and Clinica Campesina, was president of the Lafayette VFW Auxiliary in 1971.[120] Angelina Casias, in her upper 60s and a widow for eight years, listed Lafayette's VFW Auxiliary as one of her main social activities in the late 1980s, together with the Senior Center and Immaculate Conception Church.[121]

A group created specifically for Latino veterans was the G.I. Forum, founded in Texas in 1948. In 1961, 80 Latinos met in Longmont to sign the organization's national charter and form a local chapter.[122] The Longmont association, which described itself as a "non-profit, charitable, veteran's family organization," helped men stay in touch with others who had been through similar military experiences and held activities for their families. Among the photos provided to the Longmont Hispanic Study in 1988 are several showing the ceremony when a young G.I. Forum Queen was crowned, accompanied by her escort and "court," a group of elegantly dressed male and female attendants.[123]

[116] "Rosales, Larry and Linda, biography."
[117] Because military activity in Vietnam was never officially termed a "war," soldiers who had fought there were at first ineligible for the VFW, but that was later corrected.
[118] Newby, *Longmont Album*, p. 89.
[119] "Valenzuela, Francisco, Obituary."
[120] "Andrew Gilbert Garcia and Mary M. Garcia."
[121] "Casias, Angelina and Raymond, biography."
[122] "Spanish speakers sign national charter." At the national level, the organization advocated for veterans, and in some parts of the Southwest it wielded considerable political power.
[123] "Angie Perez as GI Forum Queen," "A GI Forum Queen with her escort," "A GI Forum Queen with her escort and court," and "A GI Forum Queen and parents."

C. Challenging Racism, Increasing Inclusion, Searching for Identity

Overt forms of discrimination were still present in Boulder County during the 1940s and 1950s. Some businesses continued to display the racist signs put up during the period of Ku Klux Klan influence.[124] When Alex Gonzales went into a bar in Louisville, a few miles from Lafayette, and asked for a beer, the bartender said, "We only serve white people. 'White Trade Only,' that's what the sign says, see?"[125] Alex replied, "I'm as white as you are," to which the bartender responded, "Sorry, but I just work here and follow the manager's orders, and one of them is not to sell to you people." So Alex used his pocket knife to remove the sign from the window and said, "Now can you serve me?" But the bartender still refused. Another time, Alex was told at a pool hall with a "White Trade Only" sign that he could play because he "looked a little white." But when he learned that he could not bring in his friends, he cut down that sign too.

Even if a business did not display a written statement, Latinas/os might be excluded or given inferior service. That was particularly true in Longmont. Fabricio Martinez commented that if you tried to walk into some stores, "They'd meet you at the door and say, 'Sorry, we don't want your trade.' We were very, very intimidated."[126] A Latina who was a child in the late 1940s and early 1950s remembered having to enter a shoe store in Longmont through the alley, not the front door, and stay in the back of the building, not the section where Anglos were being served; her family had friends with darker complexions who had to drive to Berthoud to buy food since they could not get it in Longmont.[127] Longmont's movie theater let Latinas/os attend but seated them separately. When Virginia Maestas occasionally went to see a Mexican movie in the late 1940s and early 1950s, Anglos in the theater would call out, "Tamale Eaters!"[128] Racism showed up in other ways too. A Latina friend of Ester Quintana Matheson's was walking down a sidewalk in Longmont with her brother

---

[124] See Ch. 4B above.
[125] Gonzales, Alex, interview, c. 1987.
[126] *Longmont Times-Call*, Aug. 11, 2002, B1.
[127] As reported by Cherry Emerson in an email to Marjorie McIntosh, July 23, 2013.
[128] Maestas, Virginia, interview, 2013.

Illus. 5.12. *Discriminatory sign like the ones in Boulder County, from Lancaster, Ohio, 1938*

when they were in high school.[129] They met a group of white youths who told them to get out of their way. When her brother refused, they were both pushed off the sidewalk.

The decision about whether someone was a Latino was apparently based in large part on skin color. Oli Duncan's grandfather, who was fairly light complexioned and worked year-round on the Pace ranch, used to ignore the "White Trade Only" signs when he took his daughter shopping in Longmont in the early 1940s; he got away with it partly because he did not appear obviously Latino but also because of his strongly confident manner.[130] Doris Gonzales described an incident in 1947, when she was 19 and had taken the train from Boulder to Longmont to apply for a job.[131] She was too early for her interview, so she went into a little café near the depot, dressed in her good clothes. She sat down, but no one came to serve her. After a while she noticed that the waitress and the owner were "conferring in a little huddle," so she got up to ask why they had not waited on her. The waitress then brought her a glass of water

---

[129] Conversation with Marjorie McIntosh, April 4, 2013.
[130] "Olivas, Ralph and Rose, biographical account."
[131] Gonzales, Doris, interview, 2013.

and took her order. But as Doris was leaving, she turned back and saw a big sign in the window, "White Trade Only," that she had not noticed when she went in.

Racism in Colorado was by no means limited to Boulder County. The 1940s saw a new concern with intergroup relations, leading to several studies of how Mexicans and *Hispanos* were treated in the state.[132] Each of those projects found severe discrimination in jobs, housing, public health, social inclusion, and education, but although they made recommendations for change, prejudice continued to limit the options open to Latinas/os. In Denver, a task force created by liberal mayor Quigg Newton in 1947 to examine human relations in the city observed massive discrimination against Hispanics, as well as against African and Asian Americans.[133] That committee and its successors reported that people of color were sometimes denied admission to hospitals; realtors might refuse to show them houses; they were excluded from consideration for many kinds of employment; they were not served in some restaurants and had to go to the back entry of some stores; and the police often used greater physical force when dealing with minority people. In one example, "a Latino boy went to the back door of a well known local restaurant to inquire about a job. Police seized him, demanded to know what he was doing, and knocked out his two front teeth."[134] In another instance, a Latino man was sitting in a restaurant awaiting service. "Police arrived, attacked, and beat him with blackjacks. Several other Mexicans who tried to protest were taken to jail."

In Longmont, the most openly discriminatory of our three towns, racist signs were gradually removed between 1945 and 1955. Their disappearance was due largely to the anger of Latino veterans, bolstered by a surprising degree of support from the police, some of whom may have been former servicemen themselves. Latino soldiers, who had served their country and put their lives on the line in World War II and Korea, were outraged to come home only to find that they could not get served by local businesses. They may have been particularly resentful because the rhetoric during World War II had stressed that the county was pulling together to fight the enemy, that we are defending our

---

[132] Donato, *Mexicans and Hispanos*, pp. 57-63.

[133] Delgado and Stefancic, "Home-Grown Racism," pp. 747-748, citing Denver Commission on Human Relations, "A Report on Minorities in Denver, 1947," for the rest of this paragraph.

[134] Delgado and Stefancic, "Home-Grown Racism," p. 748, for this and below.

shared values. The "Americans All" campaign created the image of an inclusive nation with a common identity, not one where some people faced ongoing racial or ethnic discrimination.[135]

A graphic account of one of the local episodes that led to removal of Longmont's racist signs was given by Mary Gonzales Tafoya, daughter of Alex Panfilo Gonzales.

> Dad opened the City Café because they wouldn't serve him and [his brother or son] Albert at a restaurant. Albert served in World War II on the *USS South Dakota*. He was home, in uniform, and his leg was all burned from when his ship was attacked. Dad took him out for a hamburger. Everyone else in the place was getting served except Dad and Albert. Dad threw a fit. He knocked over a pie case, tore the "White Trade Only" signs off the window, and threatened bodily harm if they tried to serve anyone else. They called the cops. When Chief McPhillips got there, he agreed with Dad.[136]

As the result of that confrontation, Alex "decided that there needed to be a place in Longmont where Mexicans could go for a drink or to eat and not have to worry about being hassled or not getting served." He therefore approached the owner of the City Café, located at 333 Main Street, and was able to buy the restaurant in 1945.

Sonia Marquez's uncle had a similar experience when he came back from World War II. He went into a bar on Main Street, wearing his uniform, and asked for a beer.[137] When he was denied service, he refused to leave and they called the police. The police officer said, "This man just got done serving for you, for your freedom, for your country. You serve him a beer!"

The attack on discrimination occasionally assumed more organized form. Romolo Martinez was one of the founders of the Spanish-American Club in Longmont, a veterans' group evidently similar to the G.I. Forum.[138] One of the club's goals was to end exclusion of Latinos, especially from eating places. Its members once paraded as a group down Main Street, stopping at each place that displayed a "White Trade Only" sign. As Martinez later described the event, with some satisfaction, "They told the proprietors it made Spanish-Americans feel like dogs. And the signs

---

[135] Escobeda, *From Coveralls to Zoot Suits*, pp. 8-9. Government agencies were now willing to investigate charges of discrimination in defense industries.

[136] Tafoya, Mary Gonzales, interview, 2009, for this and below. Mary said that Albert was Alex's brother, but in his own interview Alex said Albert was his oldest son (Gonzales, Alex, c. 1987).

[137] Marquez, Sonia, interview, 2013.

[138] *They Came to Stay*, p. 159.

were removed." Frank Martinez was active in the Spanish-American Club too, helping to enforce accurate record-keeping for Latinas/os who worked in factories and getting equal pay for them.[139] It is disappointing that we have no further information about the Spanish-American Club.

Although some racist signs in Longmont were removed during the 1940s, certain businesses continued to refuse service to Latinas/os in the following decade, to their increasing resentment. When Secundino Herrera moved to Longmont in 1951,

> They had signs on grocery stores, barber shops, and stores like that that said, "White Trade Only." I don't know where they got the idea of a white race. They got to be color blind to call themselves white, because we're all a little bit on the shady side, or pinkish side, or dark. . . . The family tree of the human race, if the Bible doesn't misinform us, tells us we all came from Adam and Eve. So if we are all brothers, why in the heck don't they treat us like brothers, I'd like to know. This is disgusting.[140]

Hank Blazón had two uncles who fought in the Korean War. When they got back to Longmont, they went into a restaurant but were denied service.[141] They insisted and said they would not leave the place until they had been treated like the other customers: "Hey, we went to war, we went for our country, and we're not leaving here until we're served." The police were called, and eventually the veterans were allowed to order their food.

The willingness of the police to support fair treatment for Latino soldiers is unexpected, for some local police officers were racially biased. Mary Gonzales Tafoya remembered an incident that occurred in 1947, when she was about 12 years old and living on the edge of Longmont.

> My cousin, Kangy Sanchez, had a new bike. His sister Cleo and I decided to ride it into town to buy some candy. We rode down the path to town to this little store that used to be on Third Avenue. When we came out of the store, a police officer was there, standing by the bike.
>
> "Whose bike is this?" he wanted to know.
>
> We explained that it belonged to Kangy Sanchez and that we had borrowed it to ride to town.

[139] Ibid., p. 158.
[140] Herrera, Secundino, interview, c. 1987.
[141] Blazón, William ("Hank"), interview, 2013.

"No," he said. "You stole this bike. Mexicans don't have nice bikes like this."

He confiscated the bike. We had to walk home and tell our parents what happened. My dad was furious: at us for taking the bike without permission, and at the policeman for his prejudice, his assumption that we had stolen the bike. . . . It's a good thing Aunt Trinidad still had the receipt for buying the bike. With that proof of ownership, they went down and got the bike from the police station.[142]

The positive response of policemen to the claims of returning veterans was probably due to the Latinos' status as former soldiers: the officers may not have intended to enforce the rights of all Latinos to equal treatment. But once the signs had been torn down for some, the doors were opened for others as well. Racist attitudes continued in Longmont, but overt discrimination of this sort was gone by the end of the 1950s.

In Lafayette, inclusion of Latinas/os in local social activities was increasing by around 1955. This pattern was probably affected by the small size of the town (only 2,000-2,600 residents into the early 1960s), its mixed neighborhoods, and its relatively stable population, which meant that many adults had grown up with people from other backgrounds. The Boy Scouts integrated quite early: Louis Cortez became cub master of Cub Scout Pack 79 in 1956.[143] He was followed the next year by Jim Hutchison, who remained active as a troop leader (of Cubs, Scouts, and Explorers) for 30 years. Jim later recalled that in the mid-1950s, about half of the boys were Latino, with most of the others from Italian backgrounds, but ethnic or national status was never a concern within his troops.[144] Photos of Lafayette's Bluebird and Campfire Girl troops from 1962 and 1965 include girls with Latino names, though they were in the minority.[145] Among adults too, Latinas/os were moving into the public sphere. Lloyd Martinez was president of the Lafayette Days Association in 1963, and his wife Sally was active in the Parent Teacher Association and the Altar and Rosary Society of their parish church; the Martinezes helped to start the Latin American Education Foundation in 1960.[146]

---

[142] Tafoya, Mary Gonzales, interview, 2009.
[143] *Lafayette, Colorado*, T119.
[144] Conversation with Marjorie McIntosh, Jan. 7, 2014.
[145] Lafayette, *Colorado*, T117.
[146] "Martinez, Lloyd and Sally Salazar, biography."

Illus. 5.13. Sharon Martinez
(Stetson) as "Miss Princess" of the
City of Lafayette, 1958

Another sign of growing integration of Latinas/os into the fabric of Lafayette's life was the more frequent mention of their activities in the local paper. By the mid-1950s, the *Lafayette Leader* was reporting on the social engagements of established Latinas/os as it did for Anglos, though it generally identified them ethnically. On June 14, 1956, for example, the society page noted that Jake Espinoza and his wife, a Latino couple, had left for a trip to California.[147] The *Leader* also published short articles about Latino graduates from the high school in the 1950s and 1960s.[148] But even in Lafayette, some degree of prejudice remained. Latinas/os felt that they were treated less well than others when they reached junior and senior high school, and although Sharon Martinez (later Stetson) was chosen as "Miss Lafayette Princess" in 1958, she was soon sidelined from that position.[149]

Boulder became a somewhat more diverse and internationally-minded community in these decades. The change was due in part to returning

---

[147] "Latino couple leaves for visit to California."
[148] E.g., "Latino student graduates High School, 1956," "Latino student graduates High School, 1962," and "Latino students graduate High School, 1964, Pts. 1 and 2."
[149] For education see Vol. II, Ch. 6B; for Sharon, conversation with Marjorie McIntosh, Jan. 15, 2014.

veterans of color who came to study at the University of Colorado under the G.I. Bill. Although the *City Directory* for Boulder in 1946 shows only nine students with Spanish surnames living off-campus, not all of them necessarily veterans, we know that pressure for housing for returning soldiers was mounting.[150] In that year the City of Boulder built 20 quonset huts on land owned by the Boulder Valley School District, each with two apartments, specifically for veterans and their families. The new housing was located at 21st and Water Street (later Canyon Boulevard), adjacent to the existing Latino community along Water + Goss Streets.[151]

The number of Latino students at the university rose over the following decade. Many of the 56 students listed in the *City Directory* for 1955 were already married and may well have been veterans. In 1965, only 27 Latino students were named in Boulder: soldiers from the Korean War would already have graduated, but the influx of new G.I.s from Vietnam had not yet begun. The growing presence of Latino students between 1940 and 1965—especially of mature veterans who had been all over the world, undergone the challenges of warfare, and were now eager to get an education—broadened the diversity of the community as well as of the university.

The Board of Education of the Boulder Valley School District took a small step in the late 1950s toward what could be called multiculturalism: providing Spanish language instruction for children in the elementary grades. Although this plan may have made the few Latino students feel somewhat more welcome, the measure was intended primarily to help Anglo youngsters become better global citizens. In 1956, a committee of parents and teachers in Boulder began to push for foreign language teaching in elementary schools.[152] Pilot programs in a few schools in the next two years offered Spanish, French, and German, but on an optional basis, not during regular school hours, and only if parents paid extra for the instruction. In 1958 the committee recommended that foreign language instruction be instituted in all third grades in the district, and that only Spanish should be taught, as "the most useful for children of

---

[150] "Occupations and Employers, Three Towns, 1946."

[151] "Biographical sketch, Emma Gomez Martinez," Garcia, Ricardo and Anna, interview, 1977, and see Vol. II, Ch. 2B.

[152] Over the next two years, the *Boulder Daily Camera* ran many articles on this topic, including statements by educators about how valuable foreign language instruction was and that young children learned more easily: Feb. 16, March 5, April 23, 25, and 27, May 1, 3, 7, 10, and 11, June 3 and 7, Aug. 30, Sept. 3, 6, 25, and 27, Oct. 2, and Nov. 1 and 22, 1957, and Jan. 2, March 21, and May 13 and 19, 1958.

this region." The school board accepted that recommendation, agreeing that Spanish classes would be part of the regular curriculum and free.

In fall, 1958, "Specially trained teachers who speak Spanish fluently and with excellent accents" began to teach classes of 20 to 30 minutes per day during school time.[153] The Back-to-School section of the *Boulder Daily Camera* laid out the benefits of the new plan:

> Teaching of a foreign language for younger children was initiated because it is becoming increasingly evident that Americans need to know more languages than they do now, that children at an earlier age learn a foreign language more readily, and the cultural benefits of international understanding resulting from the knowledge of the languages of other peoples.[154]

In another form of internationalism, children in some Boulder elementary schools within the next few years were studying Mexico, talking about its geography, economic life, and foods.[155]

During the 1950s and early 1960s, at least a few younger members of Boulder County's second- and third-generation Hispanic families were trying to define themselves in positive terms with respect to both their own and Anglo cultures but finding it difficult to do so. We see the first signs of an emerging identity formulation among established families living in Boulder's Water + Goss Streets neighborhood and central Lafayette, but in later decades the conception spread more widely within the county. The terms used by young people to describe themselves and their culture in these years (Mexican American, *Mexicano*, Mexican) suggest that the distinction between people from Mexico and New Mexico as present among first-generation immigrants had been subsumed within a shared Hispanic/Latino identity.[156]

This definition of what it meant to be from a Spanish-speaking background included ongoing loyalty to many aspects of traditional Hispanic culture. Parents wanted their children to take pride in their heritage and sustain familiar social, cultural, and religious patterns. This was generally not a problem for young people when they were at home or with other Latinos: they enjoyed Mexican American parties and forms

---

[153] *Boulder Daily Camera*, Aug. 22, 1958.
[154] Aug. 25, 1958.
[155] "4th grade students prepare Mexican lunch."
[156] See, for example, "Maestas, Virginia, interview, 1978," who uses those labels to refer to herself despite the fact that her mother was from the San Luis Valley and had New Mexican roots.

of recreation, and they went to church with their parents or joined in whatever Catholic religious practices their families maintained at home.

But some adults and children were at times embarrassed, perhaps even ashamed, by the differences between their own culture and that of Anglos.[157] Housewives might hide their food when a white visitor came to the door, and Hispanic children often sat away from others during lunch at school so they could speak Spanish and it would not be obvious they were eating tortillas instead of sandwiches.[158] Such reactions raise the possibility that Hispanics had internalized some of the racist views of the society around them. As Gordon Allport pointed out, it is difficult for people of color to resist seeing themselves in negative terms through the eyes of the dominant society, and hard to withstand the pressure to assimilate.[159] In the case of these Boulder County Hispanics, discomfort about their culture was sometimes based upon painful personal experiences: being ridiculed about the kind of work their parents did or the food they ate, punished for speaking Spanish at school, or humiliated because their teachers assumed they were dirty and carried head lice.

At the same time, many parents in these settled urban families recognized and stressed to their children the importance of functioning well in settings dominated by Anglos. Some were making a deliberate effort to help their youngsters succeed within that world, insisting, for example, that they speak only English at home and encouraging them to graduate from high school.[160] A few paid for their children to take music lessons alongside their Anglo peers, they were happy to have youngsters play on sports teams and join clubs at school, and they allowed them to participate in social activities with same-sex Anglo friends.[161] These attitudes did indeed help the next generation to do well in the wider community. Many of the young people finished high school, some went on to college, and they were viable candidates for jobs that required them to interact comfortably with Anglos.

Although information about identity issues is limited in quantity and comes largely from retrospective accounts, the sources we have suggest that the inherent contradictions within a self-definition that

---

[157] Virginia Maestas said explicitly that when she was a young woman, there was no conception of a positive "Chicano" culture (interview, 1978).

[158] See Ch. 4B above and Vol. II, Chs. 3A and 6B.

[159] Allport, *The Nature of Prejudice*, e.g., pp. 142-162, esp. 150-152.

[160] For example, the Arroyo, Martinez, and Hernandez families in Boulder.

[161] See Vol. II, Ch. 4. In Boulder's schools, Latino children formed a tiny minority: only 3% of all K-12 students in 1955 had Spanish surnames (see Vol. II, Ch. 6C).

tried to accommodate participation in two different cultures hampered the efforts of some young people to establish a solid and affirming identity. Virginia Maestas highlighted the complexities when describing the situation of her Latino peers in the 1950s, when they were in their teens and early 20s.[162] Although she and her friends loved Mexican movies, music, and dancing, they did not have regular access to that culture. Instead they lived primarily within "the Boulder Anglo society, and so you became, as much as you could, part of that mainstream." Pressure to assimilate, to accept a form of Americanization that preached homogeneity, was strong. Many young Mexican Americans, Virginia said, were trying for something "better" than what they saw at home, "in terms of a better education, in terms of speaking without an accent, learning to speak the language, learning to write the language, learning to compete with the [Anglo] people." In an interview in 1978, Virginia commented at first that her friends had not really been embarrassed about their own background, that they had not consciously hidden their traditions and the *Mexicano* culture being practiced within their own families. But upon reflection, she changed her mind. If you wanted to get ahead, "you left behind that which you thought was not good enough." When you close the door, "you close the door on the traditions and the cultures also." The challenges faced by these young people in creating a positive identity were intensified by a generational contrast between them and their parents about how to relate to their Hispanic heritage.

Although Virginia felt personally that giving up one's own culture was a loss, she said she did not have any

> bitter feelings, frustrations as far as my parents were concerned for not bringing us up in a more *Mexicano* community. I guess I'm glad that I had the education that I did in Boulder in terms of learning to live with the Anglos and learning their ways and so forth. I have a choice of the two worlds, and many times I mingle them. . . . It's kind of neat to know that you can swing either way and know that you're just as much at home with one as you are with the other.[163]

But in fact she was not fully at home with the dominant culture: she reported that she would never have dated an Anglo boy, and even as a respected teacher in her 40s, she said she automatically mistrusted

---

[162] Maestas, Virginia, interview, 1978, which refers also to the song, "Chasing the Rainbow." Her family had settled in Boulder when she was ten, having previously been farmworkers who moved between local employers each year.

[163] Maestas, Virginia, interview, 1978.

Anglos until she came to know them well as individuals.

Internal tension resulting from the differences between Anglo and Hispanic expectations was articulated also by Eleanor Montour when describing her experiences growing up in Lafayette in the 1950s and early 1960s.[164] She was the daughter of Alicia Sanchez, a powerful woman who founded the Clinica Campesina and wanted her children to finish high school. Eleanor said that by junior high she had learned the survival skills that let her manage at school. She could handle discrimination at the hands of her teachers and exclusion from sleepovers and other social activities organized by Anglo students, though such treatment took an emotional toll. But she had an entirely distinct life outside school, going to Mexican dances and listening to Mexican music with her friends, most of whom had already left school to start earning money to help support their families. "So I was like two different people."

Further, although some degree of assimilation to Anglo society might be seen as desirable by parents and young people, it by no means ensured acceptance by that community. Virginia Maestas, unhappy at Casey Junior High in Boulder for both academic and social reasons, dropped out of school in 1951 at age 16, lied about her age, and went to work full-time: first at Kress's, a dime store, and later at the Flatirons Theater.[165] Although she performed her duties well, she experienced discrimination from customers in both places. At the theater, the assistant manager once questioned her ethnicity: "You're from Boulder, you don't sound like you're Mexican. You don't talk like people from Lafayette." When Dora Bernal, who had moved from Boulder to California in the 1950s, returned from Berkeley in the early 1960s, she found Boulder much less welcoming than its sister university town on the edge of a truly multi-ethnic city.[166]

In explaining why these efforts to create an ethnic identity that validated activity in both Hispanic and Anglo socio-cultural worlds began to surface among these particular Boulder County families in the 1950s and early 1960s, we can suggest several probable factors. The emerging self-definition seems to have rested upon a foundation of modest economic and residential security within towns. Most of the male heads of these households had made the transition from labor in the beet fields or coal mines to somewhat better urban employment, such as

---

[164] Montour, Eleanor, interview, 2013. For her mother and the Clinica, see Vol. II, Ch. 3B.
[165] Maestas, Virginia, interview, 2013.
[166] Bernal, Dora, interview, 1978.

carpentry, masonry, being a grounds man on the University campus, or working in a factory. In such jobs they interacted regularly with Anglos and learned their expectations. Their family income had been increased in many cases by women's earnings, and nearly all bought their own houses after they moved into town. They saw a high school or even a college education as a realistic way for their children to advance. Being perceived as respectable also mattered to them.

The need for a self-conception that accepted and even praised one's ability to navigate within two worlds was presumably intensified by growing contact between Hispanics and Anglos, not only at school and work but also in the neighborhood. Unlike the overwhelmingly Mexican-American *barrios* of many large cities, Boulder County's urban Hispanics lived in ethnically mixed though low-income neighborhoods.[167] Within them they dealt regularly with people from Italian or other European backgrounds and, in the case of Boulder's Water + Goss Streets neighborhood, with African Americans too. Women exchanged goods, and children grew up playing with friends from different cultures. (Dating between ethnic groups was, however, frowned upon, and marriage across ethnic lines was rare in this area until the 1970s.)

The identity that was becoming visible among at least a few families in Boulder County during the 1950s and early 1960s differed from what has been described among middle class Mexican Americans in regions with larger Hispanic populations and among people living in urban *barrios* during roughly the same period.[168] The leading Latino adults in Boulder and Lafayette at this time would have been defined as members of the upper working class, not as middle class, and they had not yet expressed a clear oppositional consciousness directed at institutionalized forms of racism. The associations they formed rarely fought for issues important to Latinas/os as a whole.[169] When, for example, Emma Gomez Martinez mobilized her neighbors, they acted on matters of concern to their own immediate racially- and ethnically-mixed sub-community.[170] Nor is there evidence that Boulder County's young people dressed and behaved in deliberately unconventional ways in order to display pride in their Mexican American culture.[171] Female

---

[167] See Vol. II, Ch. 2B.
[168] See Ch. 1B above.
[169] The only exception encountered in this period was Longmont's Spanish-American Club.
[170] See Ch. 6C below.

sexuality remained closely supervised by parents and was largely confined to traditionally acceptable forms. Living successfully within the Anglo-dominated system that surrounded them generally meant fitting in as much as possible in public settings while maintaining their ethnic identity in more private contexts.

By the mid-1960s, some Latinas/os in Boulder County were poised to take active part in the Chicano movement, whose concerns and activities were to dominate the local community for the next 15 years. Due to improved educational and employment opportunities, they were better able to bring their issues into public view. Some Latinos and a few Latinas were gaining experience and confidence through participation in the armed forces. Thanks in large part to veterans, the most overt forms of racism and exclusion had been removed. During the later 1960s and 1970s participation in the Chicano movement would encourage local people to define themselves in more culturally affirming and visible ways and to organize to confront systemic racism.

[171] See Ch. 1B above and Vol. II, Ch. 1A.

Chapter 6

Being Chicano, Migrant Workers, and New Jobs, 1966-1980

The period between 1966 and around 1980 was a time of turmoil and change throughout the United States. Reacting against the social and political conservatism of the post-World War II era, many groups began defining their own identities and demanding their full civil and human rights. Chicanos, African Americans, Native Americans, and Asian Americans pushed for an end to racist attitudes and policies and fought for a more equal and visible place in government, the law, the educational system, and other settings. Chicano leaders of *El Movimiento* tried to unite all people from Spanish-speaking backgrounds—regardless of their economic or educational level, national origins, and how long they had been in this country—into a powerful force that could wrest improvements from the hands of generally recalcitrant institutions dominated by Anglos. Puerto Rican nationalists wanted either statehood or independence. The women's movement rejected discrimination based on sex and promoted female empowerment. People living in poverty insisted that they deserved the same rights in hiring, education, and politics as did the wealthy. Some of these initiatives benefited from the "War on Poverty" instituted by President Lyndon Johnson in 1965, which offered financial support for local projects designed to lessen economic disparities and make the country more inclusive. The Vietnam War and a compulsory draft were increasingly unpopular, leading to huge nation-wide protests.

Some Boulder County people were active in the loosely-defined Chicano movement, although they did not always use that term in describing themselves. A central feature of local concern was establishing and celebrating what it meant to be "Chicano." As part of the effort to create ties among all Latinos, members of established families reached out to migrant workers. The self-awareness and confidence of some Chicanos was enhanced by a striking increase in job opportunities at middling and even upper levels. Projects operated by the federal government's Office of Economic Opportunity [OEO], the administrative wing of the "War on Poverty," drew many Latinas and Latinos into positions where they gained work experience, sometimes a formal education, and training in community organization. The federal government was thus important in this period as it had been during the "New Deal" era of the 1930s and early 1940s. Large employers like the Rocky Flats Nuclear Weapons Plant and the International Business Machines Corporation [IBM] offered semi-skilled manufacturing jobs and positions for Latino engineers and scientists, computer programmers, managers, accountants, and secretaries.

Expanding employment opportunities drew in new families who contributed to a marked rise in the Latino population. In the decade between 1965 and 1975, the number of Spanish-surnamed adults mentioned in *Polk's City Directories* for our three communities more than doubled (rising from a total of 1,219 to 2,542), with particularly rapid growth in Longmont and Boulder.[1] By 1980, the county's Latino population differed in significant ways from what it had been in 1966.

A. Creating An Inclusive Chicano Identity

During the later 1960s and 1970s, questions of cultural definition and identity came to the fore among Boulder County's Chicanos as they did elsewhere in the country.[2] Although such issues had been explored previously, they assumed new importance within the context of the push for Chicano self-realization and empowerment. Local Chicanas/os were now focusing on who they were and what it meant to come from a Spanish-speaking background. What was their ethnic and racial heritage, and what terms should they use to describe themselves? What economic, religious, and cultural contributions had their people made

[1] App. 1.2.

[2] For broader attempts to define what *Chicanismo* entailed and the often limited role for Chicanas within that movement, see Acuña, *Occupied America*, pp. 329-332, and Ernesto Chávez, "*¡Mi Raza Primero!*," pp. 5-7.

to the United States in the past, and what was their role today? Rather than trying to assimilate themselves to the dominant Anglo culture of the country and hiding their customs from public view, why did they not celebrate their traditions for everyone to see and appreciate?[3] Why were Latino children in the schools often neglected or—if they spoke Spanish—punished? Further, if there really was a shared identity among all Chicanas/os, did established local families not have an obligation to help newer arrivals and migrant workers, rather than distancing themselves from them?

Definitional words acquired new significance. In Boulder County, older ethnic descriptors like "Hispanic" or "Spanish-American" were discarded by some Chicanas/os, because those terms emphasized the European side of what was now coming to be acknowledged as a more complex racial and cultural mixture.[4] The terms "Mexican" or "Mexican American" were too specific to cover people from all national or state backgrounds. Those who called themselves "Chicanas/os" commonly used the word both to express pride in their own shared culture and to indicate their social and political activism. Some people did not want to be termed "Chicanos," a label which they saw as reflecting values that threatened the possibility of acculturation into the Anglo world and created a public perception that all Latinas/os were radicals. Even some local activists whom we might term "Chicanos" still referred to themselves as "Mexican Americans" or "Hispanics."

Patsy Cordova was a student at Longmont High School "when the *la raza* movement hit our town in about 1967, 1968. I remember all of a sudden there was a pride to being, the new word was 'Chicano.' It was a very political term and the movement was very politically minded. My parents were even shocked that I would have anything to do with it . . . though my mother is very political by nature."[5] That statement shows that Boulder County people were becoming aware of *la raza* concerns at least in general terms, and it illustrates a gap between young and potentially activist members of Latino households and their somewhat more conservative parents. The Chicano movement accentuated generational divisions within some Latino families.

A feature of this new Chicano self-awareness was an effort to document

---

[3] These attitudes helped to weaken the cultural embarrassment felt by some earlier Latinos: see Ch. 5C above.

[4] See Ch. 1A above.

[5] Cordova, Patsy, interview, c. 1987.

and celebrate the past. In 1976-7, two Boulder women, Jessie Velez Lehmann and Regina Vigil, together with Manuel Arcadia, a graduate student at the University of Colorado associated with KGNU Public Radio in Boulder, set up a project called "Boulder's Chicano Community: Where Is It?" Supported by a grant from the Colorado Humanities Program, the group wanted to preserve and publicize the stories of some established Boulder families.[6] Over the next 18 months, the project recorded 13 audio interviews, some in Spanish, and prepared two films. The first, "Los Inmigrantes," featured excerpts from videographed conversations with local people and showed them dancing in costumes to Mexican music; the second, "Boulder's Chicano Community," had still shots of photographs and other documents, with a voice-over narrative. Over the next few years, volunteers took "Los Inmigrantes" around to other communities in Colorado, encouraging Latinas/os there to record their own histories.

One of the motivations of the Boulder project was worry that local Latinas/os were trying to assimilate, including not teaching their children Spanish, rather than honoring and maintaining their own cultural heritage. Jessie Velez Lehmann criticized the tendency of some Boulder people to keep their heads down, to avoid being noticed by the Anglo community around them. She spoke about her fear that the Spanish language and meaningful customs were being lost.[7] That fear was justified. An example of the linguistic transition across three generations comes from the family of Maria Medina of Boulder, who was born in a Spanish-speaking community in New Mexico in 1891.[8] Although she had lived in Colorado for most of her life, she did not speak English at the time of her interview in 1978. Her children knew English and some Spanish, but her grandchildren could neither speak nor understand Spanish, so Maria was completely unable to communicate directly with them. Roy Maestas, another New Mexican, was born in 1909 and as a child moved with his parents to a Spanish-speaking area in southern

[6] "Boulder's Chicano Community, 1978 KGNU radio interview," and see Ch. 1B above. The project was co-sponsored by the Canyon Park Community Center, the Migrant Action Program, and the Women's Resource Center, all branches of the OEO (see section C below). Although Jessie, who had come to Boulder 15 years before, was the prime mover of the project, she generally described herself as a Mexican American, not as a Chicana (Lehmann, Jessie Velez, interview, 1978).
[7] Lehmann, Jessie Velez, interview, 1978.
[8] Medina, Maria, interview, c. 1978.
[9] Maestas, Roy, interview, 1978.

Illus. 6.1. Phil and Eleanor Hernandez in Mexican costumes, Boulder, 1948

Colorado.[9] He learned some English at school but had to drop out when he was 14 to go to work in the mines. In the next generation, after the family's move to Boulder, Roy's children already spoke English when they started school, and they saw no reason to maintain the older language. His grandchildren knew no Spanish when Roy was interviewed in 1978. When Phil Hernandez's parents dressed him and his sister in Mexican clothing for a special occasion when they were young, it had cultural meaning for older members of the family, but not for the children. In Longmont, however, use of Spanish remained more common, due in part to the ongoing arrival of new immigrants.[10]

Other Chicanos were meanwhile taking steps to make Latino culture more visible and hence more accepted and even respected by Anglos. They organized a Mexican Fiesta dinner, Cinco de Mayo festivities, and performances by Mexican dance groups, open to all.[11] Activists pressured the schools to become more supportive of Latino children, and they

[10] See, e.g., Ben Rodriguez's popular Spanish-language radio station in the 1950s: Vol. II, Illus. 4.7.

[11] E.g., "Mexican holiday planned," "2-year-old wears a Mexican costume," "Local woman demonstrates traditional South American dances," "Chicano Fiesta de la Gente planned," and "Los Aztecas celebrate Cinco de Mayo." In Boulder County, there is no indication that Cinco de Mayo festivals served as venues for incipient political activism, as they did in Corona, CA (Alamilla, *Making Lemonade*, pp. 153-159).

organized special conferences for young people in an effort to build an affirming identity.[12] In religious terms, most Chicanos did not abandon their Catholic faith, but some pushed the local churches to adopt a more liberal theology, hire Spanish-speaking priests, and offer the Mass in Spanish.[13]

Another concern was the economic, social, and cultural gaps among Boulder County's Latinos, which stood in the way of a shared Chicano identity. The distance between established families and newer arrivals, already visible in the 1950s, had become greater by the late 1960s and 1970s. Whereas many families who had come prior to 1940 had by this time found ways of navigating adequately within the Anglo-based community and some had attained middle class status, the newcomers— mainly from Mexico—generally spoke no English and lacked the skills (and sometimes the necessary immigration papers) to do anything other than manual labor. Most older Latino families in Longmont and Lafayette interacted rarely if at all with recent Mexican immigrants or migrant workers.

Tom Abila, who moved to Boulder's Water + Goss Streets neighborhood in 1947 when he was 13, distinguished sharply in a later interview between "originals" (meaning the town's older families, including himself), and newcomers.[14] He praised the earlier families and what they had achieved but spoke disparagingly about the "aliens" and "wetbacks" who had come into the U.S. illegally and were willing to work for lower wages. Indeed, immigrants without papers were always subject to exploitation by employers, who could offer exceptionally low wages and unsafe working conditions to people who had the threat of arrest and deportation hanging over their heads.[15] Divisions between different generations of immigrants were by no means unique to Boulder County or to Latinas/os. In many settings, the most recent arrivals are disliked by the previous wave of immigrants, who have generally assimilated to the new culture at least to some extent and do not want to be lumped in the minds of the dominant group with the poverty-stricken and more obviously foreign immigrants who have just come.

Separation along class-based lines was becoming even more pronounced during the 1970s. This stemmed largely from the arrival

[12] See Ch. 7A and "Mexican-American youth conference scheduled."
[13] See Vol. II, Ch. 5C.
[14] Abila, Tom, interview, 1978.
[15] For this situation at the turkey plant in Longmont, see section C below.

of well-educated Latinas/os from elsewhere in Colorado, other parts of the U.S., or Spain who were attracted by opportunities in businesses like IBM, the new federal research facilities in Boulder, or the University of Colorado.[16] These middle class newcomers were generally welcomed by local Latinas/os with college degrees and formed common Chicano pressure groups with them.[17] Many urban residents who had achieved success in what was still an Anglo dominated public environment adopted the affirming features of the ethnic identity first visible in Boulder during the 1950s and early 1960s, validating the ability to function effectively in Anglo contexts while maintaining some features of their Latino heritage at home and with friends.

Local activists now felt they needed to bring the challenges that confronted all Latinas/os to public attention. In doing so, they were assisted by the growing willingness of local papers to report on these concerns. At Boulder's Congregational Church in 1968, Phil Hernandez, a Boulder native who was then the head of United Mexican American Students at the university, talked about the problems faced by Mexican American school children; Lupe Salinas gave a presentation at the church the following year about housing problems.[18] The *Boulder Daily Camera* published a long and thoughtful report on the state of local Mexican Americans in 1973, and two years later the paper described their concerns about the police.[19] Dr. Floyd Martinez spoke to the *Camera* in 1978 about the need for funding for Longmont's Mental Health Center, which served many poor Latinas/os, criticizing the city for cutting its allocation.[20] Despite these efforts, however, the local Latino community remained segmented for the rest of the twentieth century, based upon such factors as how long people had lived in this area, country or state of origin, economic and educational level, marriage patterns and number of children, types of health care utilized, and how they defined themselves in ethnic or cultural terms.

[16] Acuña has suggested that the growth of a Chicano middle class in the U.S. during the 1970s was good in that "it gave Chicanos more of a voice in government and society." It was bad, however, in that these people "often developed social and economic interests differing from those of the working class," and they might be coopted by the mainstream ruling class (*Occupied America*, p. 339). For a more positive assessment, see Manuel Gonzales, *Mexicanos*, esp. pp. 181-193.

[17] Emma Peña-McCleave, conversation with Marjorie McIntosh, July 20, 2013.

[18] "Mexican-American school problems discussed"; "Mexican-American housing problems discussed."

[19] "Report on State of the Mexican-Americans," and "Police a major Chicano concern."

[20] "Latino doctor backs funding" and "Latino doctor criticizes decision."

B. Reaching Out to Migrant Workers

A particularly vulnerable group of Latinas/os were the migrant workers—many of them Mexican nationals—who throughout the second half of the twentieth century provided most of the labor for Boulder County's farms. Following the crops across the growing season, these people usually remained in the area only temporarily. Prior to around 1970, Anglo members of the community, established Latinas/os, and the press had generally turned a blind eye to the deplorable living and working conditions of the men and families who came into the county each summer. In July, 1968, the *Longmont Times-Call* printed an illustrated feature article about how migrant workers enjoyed moving around between jobs; the next day the paper described local farmers' dissatisfaction with their mobile employees.[21] In 1969, the paper reported disapprovingly about an attempt by migrant workers in Fort Lupton, a farming community 10 miles southeast of Longmont, to obtain better conditions.[22]

But in the early 1970s, some local Chicanos—joined by socially concerned Anglo allies—turned their attention to migrant workers. Their activities were assisted by several OEO programs created in the mid- to late 1960s. Part of their task was to document the problems faced by mobile agricultural laborers, problems that had plagued field workers since early in the century. The key issues were housing and working conditions. The accommodations provided by farmers for their migrant workers were rudimentary and often unsanitary. Large families might be housed in small wooden shacks with just two rooms and no indoor plumbing; they had to carry water from a nearby ditch or pump it from a well, and they used an outhouse. Others lived in "barracks," where each family had a single room for sleeping and as many as 20 families shared a single kitchen and a few toilets.[23]

Agricultural work required people to be out in the sun with no shelter from early morning until the evening, sometimes with a break during

---

[21] "Migrant workers love Colorado, life of travel"; "Farmers concerned about irresponsibility."

[22] The laborers had set up a protest camp at the end of the summer and refused to vacate it: "Migrants refuse to move," "Winter looking bleak for migrants," and "Fort Lupton migrant workers to leave camps."

[23] Housing for more settled agricultural workers was also poor: see Vol. II, Ch. 2A.

the hottest part of the day. Migrant children of all ages commonly went to the fields with their parents, as there was no place else for them to be. Some farmers were still providing only short-handled hoes, which forced workers to remain in stooped positions.[24] A photo in a little booklet prepared by migrant teens in Longmont in summer, 1977 shows two adults bent down over their short hoes, a toddler in the field with them, and a teenaged boy smiling broadly while holding a long-handled hoe.[25] Adelpha Sanchez, aged 13, who took the photo of her family, provided this text to go with it: "They can only use those little hoes. This man, their foreman, whatever you call him, sometimes when he wants to he gives one or two of them long hoes. My brother, I think he's showing that he got one today. You know, 'cause it's harder with the little hoes. With the big ones you can just be standing up and with the little ones you gotta be bent down all day." Migrant workers were not covered by insurance against injuries or ill health and could be fired if they were unable to carry out their jobs. Bob Rangel's father had to sign an insurance waiver when he was hired, as was common for migrants; when one of his arms was cut off in an accident at work, the farmer said he did not need him anymore, and the family had to move on.[26]

Local efforts to improve conditions for temporary farm employees started around 1970. Colorado Rural Legal Services was a statewide project of the OEO that provided free legal assistance to farm workers and acted on their collective behalf.[27] In 1970, a group in Boulder County called Farm Workers United, backed by Colorado Rural Legal Services, publicized the shocking housing and sanitary conditions in which some migrant workers and their families were living.[28] The next year the *Longmont Times-Call*, in a startling reversal of its previous reporting, published a sympathetic illustrated article about the difficulties of migrant life.[29] Over the next few years, public health officials ordered some of the farmers to clean up and modernize the housing they provided; in response a few simply refused to provide any housing at all, leaving their workers to find whatever accommodations they could. The City of Longmont began creating some public housing for migrants:

[24] See Ch. 5A and Illus. 5.1 above, and Murray, "Abolition of El Cortito."
[25] *Como Ellos Lo Ven*, pp. 12-13.
[26] Rangel, Bob, interview, 1979.
[27] For the OEO, see section C below.
[28] "Farm Workers United worried about migrant housing."
[29] "Hardship of migrant living."

Illus. 6.2. Migrant worker child outside house near Longmont, 1990

Casa Vista, succeeded by Casa Esperanza.[30] But a set of powerful photos taken in rural areas around Longmont in May, 1990 make clear that some accommodations for migrant workers and their families remained poor.[31]

Other efforts to improve conditions for migrants included a special Community Action Program set up for east Boulder County's farm workers in 1970, again under the auspices of the OEO.[32] The following year, a team of Latino and Anglo lawyers with Colorado Rural Legal Services and the Colorado Migrant Council, another OEO program, brought suit against a local farmer for maltreating his foreign workers, claiming he was running a forced labor camp.[33] Tivi Gauna, a staff member of the Colorado Migrant Council, noted that some farmers exploited their Mexican workers not only by giving them very bad housing but also by restricting their freedom.[34] "Some of the men who live in shacks for this

[30] "Longmont, film of places of historical importance," a video made in 2013, which also displays the only migrant worker barrack still in use.
[31] See also "Six children in doorway."
[32] "Better season planned for migrant workers."
[33] "Valley farmer charged with mistreating aliens," "New action filed in alien case," "Suit filed to improve migrant workers' lot," "Area farmer denies labor camp charges," and "A different kind of poor."
[34] Gauna, Tivi, interview, 1979.

Illus. 6.3. *Backyard of migrant worker housing near Longmont, 1990*

one farmer told me they weren't allowed to leave. The farmer wouldn't even take them to town to shop. They weren't allowed to have visitors. A lot of them complained about it. Most didn't say anything." Medical care also improved gradually.[35]

Another form of assistance to migrant workers and other needy families grew out of the work of Sister Carmen Ptacnik, a Daughter of Charity and native of Mexico who was assigned to Immaculate Conception Parish in Lafayette in 1970.[36] Through her work with poor people in the parish, she came to know many of the migrant families living around Lafayette and Erie who did not speak English. She began collecting food, clothing, and household goods for them, gradually expanding her activities and the number of volunteers who helped her. After she retired in 1976, her work was institutionalized in the Sister Carmen Community Center in Lafayette, which continues to provide clothing and food banks, a thrift shop, and classrooms.

Migrant workers' children and the educational challenges they faced received particular attention. These children might attend multiple

[35] See Vol. II, Ch. 3B.
[36] "Sister Carmen Community Center."

schools over the course of the growing season, and even if they remained on one farm all summer, they often left school early in the spring for planting and started late in the fall, after the harvest.[37] (The laws pertaining to work and schooling for children of migrant families were far less stringent than those for settled farm laborers.) Chicano activists and committed educators in the 1970s tried to persuade local schools to be flexible in responding to the needs of migrant children. A few schools created special programs for them, to help them stay caught up with their peers even as they moved between schools or attended for less than the full year. Esther Blazón was instrumental in setting up an English-as-a-Second-Language program for migrant children at Columbine Elementary in Longmont in 1974.[38] Summer programs were created for both younger children and teens.

The ability of migrant children to participate in such programs depended on how long their families remained in the area and hence was always at the mercy of the weather. A painful illustration comes at the back of a photo album prepared by a summer school in the St. Vrain District.[39] After a series of nicely labeled pictures showing children and teens engaged in a variety of interesting activities, the final page has no photos. Instead it contains two sticky notes with the following written on them:

> 1) Aug. 2, 1986.
>   Terrible hail storm destroys 75% of crops.
>   No jobs for workers. Guess we will just move on . . . .
> 2) Adiós, Amigos
>   Adiós, Colorado

In several summer projects during the later 1970s, young people from migrant families interviewed local Latinas/os, took photographs, wrote about their experiences, and produced little books.[40] Some of the pieces shed troubling light on the lives of these children. Paula Torrez, age 15, whose family was working the fields outside Longmont in the summer of 1978, said:

> We leave at around five thirty in the morning and we come back at around twelve and we sleep for around two hours. We go back at

---

[37] For examples, see "Sugar beets brought early Hispanics to Longmont."
[38] "Woman of purpose: Esther Blazon."
[39] "Migrant Summer School Program records."
[40] *El Aguila, Segunda Mirada,* and *Como Ellos Lo Ven.*

three and we come back at seven thirty. We get paid by the acre. We do the first hoeing and then the second hoeing. The first hoeing you take out every other sugar beet and the weeds, and the second hoeing you take out only the weeds. I started doing it when I was twelve.[41]

Adelpha Sanchez wrote in 1977:

We started hoeing the beets and pickles and cabbage and onions, and we're going to start picking them pretty soon. I'm not going to pick them 'cause my dad doesn't let me. He says that I should stay home and clean house and make supper 'cause my mom comes tired from work. So I do it. That way when she comes from work everything is ready.[42]

The teens who participated in these projects heard some inspirational stories. The group who talked with Benny Rodriguez in 1979 learned how he had worked his way up from washing cars at a Chevrolet dealership in Longmont to having his own body shop.[43] Nothing, he said, is more satisfying than being your own boss. Maria Velasquez, director of the program for Bilingual Teacher Aides at Aims Community College, talked about her childhood living in deep poverty with a single parent mom and ten siblings, all of whom did hand work in the fields as the family followed the crops in California.[44] Maria, who did not speak English as a child, was miserable in school and dropped out in seventh grade to start doing full-time farm work to help her family. After marrying at age 17 and having her children, she took a factory job but later went back to school, got her GED, and was hired as a Head Start teacher, leading to her current position. The girls who talked with Mary Martinez, a Licensed Practical Nurse at the Longmont hospital, and those who later videographed an interview with her were told about her work in the fields as a child, her determination to become a nurse, and her successful struggles as an adult to get the necessary training.[45]

Some of the young migrant workers were encouraged to become activists. Secundino Herrera, a former farm laborer who fought against injustice all through his life, said to the five young people who interviewed him in 1979,

---

[41] *Segunda Mirada*, p. 8.
[42] *Como Ellos Lo Ven*, p. 4.
[43] Rodriguez, Benny, interview, 1979.
[44] Velasquez, Maria, interview, 1979.
[45] Martinez, Mary, interviews, 1979 and 1988. See also Vol. II, Ch. 6A.

> I think migrants should be treated with kind of special attention, with more consideration. . . . They should live better, have transportation, medical assistance, everything, considering that human beings shouldn't live where they put the pigs and hogs, or in a chicken coop. Many farm employers humiliate migrant people. People don't have an appreciation for what we do.[46]

He encouraged the teens to stand up for their rights.

> Look, kids, at what we should be doing. Our people, especially Mexicans, the migrants—we should take the initiative steps to defend ourselves, so employers will know that we already know our rights, and that we have hearts in our bodies just like them, . . . and the mentality to understand, to react.

C. Empowerment through New Opportunities for Work

One factor in the ability of local Chicanos leaders to address the problems confronting their fellow Latinas/os was the opportunities for higher status employment and leadership training that emerged during the later 1960s and 1970s. Programs set up under the OEO were key, because they not only assisted Latinas/os, they employed them. In Boulder County, the ones that had the greatest impact were the Community Action Program, with its many sub-projects, and Head Start. Professional and technical positions also expanded greatly in the later 1960s and 1970s, as did well-paid manufacturing jobs.

The impact of OEO programs

OEO projects required that local people from among the communities being served should be appointed to their boards and hired as staff members wherever possible. Although these programs relied heavily on volunteers, since they had shoe-string budgets, their policies for hiring paid staff were flexible, designed to bring members of under-represented groups into active participation in dealing with poverty.[47] OEO employees were not required to have formal educational qualifications, and they received on-the-job training plus—in some cases—the time

---

[46] Herrera, Secundino, interview, 1979, for this and below.
[47] For people remodeling space for an OEO center in Longmont in the late 1960s, see "Horace Hernandez and other volunteers." For the relaxed style of these organizations, see "A Head Start strategy planning meeting."

and financial support with which to get their GED or even a college degree. The Latinas/os who worked with these programs also learned about community organizing, and they acquired the experience and confidence that helped them move into leadership roles in other areas too. An impressive number of Latino leaders in Colorado around 2000, women and men working in a variety of different fields, received their initial jobs and training through the OEO programs of the later 1960s and 1970s. The OEO was closed at the national level in 1981, largely for political reasons, but several of its programs were still functioning under different administrative systems in the 2010s.

Although OEO positions were open to both men and women, they had a particularly profound impact on Latinas, who had previously faced limited options for public involvement. The women who worked with these programs were there on their own, not as appendages of their husbands, and some gained considerable visibility. The fact that their marriages survived these transitions again indicates flexibility and adaptability in the relationships between spouses.

In the short run, OEO employees gained an income, interesting work outside the home, and a chance to contribute to the community. Virginia Alvarez grew up on farms around Longmont, where her parents, Mexican immigrants, had jobs.[48] At Longmont High School, she was too poor to join the clubs that made Anglo young people feel part of a group. But when the OEO was created, she was hired by the Community Action Program in a project for senior citizens. She worked mainly with Latinas/os, making them welcome, organizing lunches, and setting up activities, including little trips. She later described the satisfaction she had gained, as a woman in her 20s and 30s, from helping elderly people remain active and connected with others.

In some cases, OEO work led to further education and leadership roles. Esther Blazón was one of 14 surviving children of a father from Mexico and a mother from Texas.[49] Her parents were migrant farm workers, following the crops seasonally, so Esther lived and went to school in many different places while growing up. The family eventually

---

[48] Alvarez, Virginia, interview, 2013.

[49] Blazón, Esther, interview, 2013, and "Woman of purpose: Esther Blazon." In that interview, she credited her husband, Hank, for his support and encouragement even when some people in the community in the 1960s wondered why he was letting her get an education and start working. Noting that Hank was continuing his education too, Esther said that together they became role models for other Latino couples.

settled near Longmont. Esther married when she was in her junior year of high school and dropped out when the first of her three children was born. Her teachers did not encourage her to stay in school or return to it: they told her she was "not college material." As her children got a little older, however, she began feeling restless, wishing she could do more than just stay at home. So, with her husband's backing, she went back to Longmont High and took the necessary courses to graduate fully, rather than simply doing a GED. (She had to start over again in ninth grade, because the school district had lost her records.) She also began volunteering with Head Start, which her children attended. She was then offered a position as a Family Coordinator with Head Start, and while in that job, she met a man who administered scholarship programs at the University of Colorado. He encouraged her to try for a college degree, connecting her with a funding program for migrant workers' children and supporting her as she tackled university classes. After receiving her bachelor's degree from the University of Colorado, Esther worked as a bilingual teacher with the St. Vrain Schools and took part in El Comité, a Latino action group formed after two young men were shot by the Longmont police in 1980.[50] Later she went on to earn a master's degree in counseling from the University of Northern Colorado and worked for 25 years as a mental health specialist with Latino families.

The benefits of engagement with OEO programs were even more pronounced for Emma Gomez Martinez, another highly capable and energetic woman.[51] Emma's parents had moved from Aguilar, a Spanish-speaking community in the southern Colorado coal mining area, to Erie in 1929, and she and her five brothers and sisters all finished high school, an uncommon pattern in that generation. After graduation in the mid-1940s, Emma went to Boulder to find work, but there were few opportunities even for a well-educated young Latina: she was hired first by a laundry and then as a hotel maid. While in Boulder she met John Martinez, who had grown up in the town, joined the military in World War II, and recently returned; he was currently going to college, thanks to the G.I. Bill. Five years after their marriage in 1947, the couple settled

---

[50] See Ch. 7C below. For her graduation from the University of Colorado, see "Esther Blazón and family, 1974"; for her graduation from U.N.C., see "Esther Blazón and family, 1980"

[51] The account in this and the following paragraphs is based upon information in "Martinez, Emma Gomez, letter to her children," "Biographical sketch, Emma Gomez Martinez," and "Profile, Emma Martinez."

in the Water + Goss Streets neighborhood of Boulder.[52]

At first Emma was mainly occupied with raising their five children, but in the early 1960s she was asked by Ted Tedesco, the city manager of Boulder, to serve as an interpreter for Spanish-speakers who were moving into this area from other states. In 1965, Tedesco, impressed by her ability, asked her to join the board of the newly created OEO programs for Boulder County and to recruit other Latino members. Shortly thereafter, she was hired as a Neighborhood Aide and Counselor by the Community Action Program. Her initial charge was to examine the status of poor, Spanish-speaking families in the county; she documented many cases of discrimination in housing, employment, and education. Later Emma, assisted by a tiny staff and many volunteers, set up operation in three quonset huts—built originally for returning veterans at the university—in a little park alongside what was then called Water Street. Under her leadership, the Canyon Park Community Center ran programs for children, provided health information and services, and offered job training through its Manpower Program. Over the following years Emma was named as program coordinator, director of the Boulder Center projects, assistant director for the county-wide OEO, and—after her "retirement"—chair of the county OEO's Board of Directors.

Emma used her energy and talent on behalf of her neighborhood as well, mobilizing Latinas/os and others to take public action. She later described an incident after she and John had settled in the Water + Goss Streets region in the 1950s:

> A group of speculators had approached the city of Boulder to name this area that I'm speaking about as a ghetto, and they wanted to eliminate it. The reason that they wanted to eliminate the ghetto where these families resided was because Water Street was planned on being converted to Canyon Boulevard, and the property would become very expensive. Well, John and I started a petition and recruited many of our neighbors and we took it to the city that we were against this urban renewal plan because this is where we resided. It was our community.[53]

Their efforts were successful.

Emma went into action again in the late 1960s, when Water Street was being rebuilt as Canyon Boulevard, designed to let traffic move more quickly across town. As the concrete sidewalks were being poured,

[52] For this area, see Vol. II, Ch. 2B.
[53] Martinez, Emma Gomez, interview, 2013.

a group of parents noticed they were only 24 inches wide, not broad enough to allow children to walk along them safely when going to school. They came to Emma as a spokesperson for the community. Researching the construction plans, she found that the sidewalks were supposed to be wider, whereupon she wrote and circulated a petition among the neighbors and presented it to the construction manager and the City Council. After some discussion, the sidewalks were re-poured at their proper width. Emma also fought repeatedly to save the area around the quonset huts as a park, the only place with playground equipment for neighborhood children, and she organized the local community to do periodic cleanups and maintenance. Eventually the city of Boulder acquired the land, preserving what was for 40 years called Canyon Park.

Starting in the 1970s, Emma applied the leadership experience she had gained through OEO work to other organizations. She contributed to a rather amazingly long list of groups throughout Boulder County devoted to the well-being of people living in poverty or experiencing educational or legal challenges, especially children and young people.[54] A statement written in 2013 says that "During her service on these Boards and Commissions, Emma was often the lone voice for the poor and disenfranchised of our community." She and her husband also operated several successful Mexican restaurants, in Boulder and the Denver suburbs. It was a fitting recognition of her lifetime of involvement with the community that in 2013 Canyon Park was renamed the Emma Gomez Martinez Park.[55]

While Emma may have been exceptionally dedicated and forceful, she was by no means alone in the impact that OEO programs had upon her life. Some people were pulled into community service work by Emma herself. Virginia Maestas said that although she had volunteered occasionally with Head Start when her daughter was enrolled in the program, she had not considered a paying job with OEO, in part because she had not finished high school.[56] But Emma motivated her in two ways. Virginia was extremely impressed when Emma prepared her petition about the Canyon Boulevard sidewalks and took it door-to-door: that was "my first real contact in terms of what we could do as *Mexicanos* to

---

[54] "Biographical sketch, Emma Gomez Martinez," for this and below.

[55] "Request to rename park," "Canyon Park renamed in Emma Gomez Martinez's honor," "At dedication of Emma Gomez Martinez Park," and "Dedication of Emma Gomez Martinez Park."

[56] Maestas, Virginia, interview, 1978, for this and below.

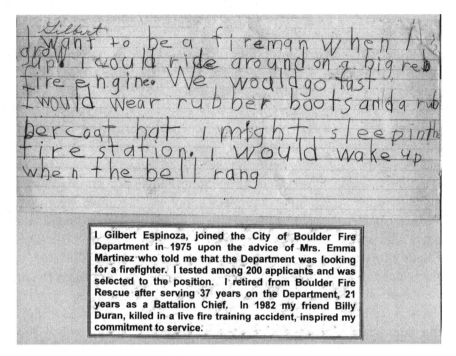

I Gilbert Espinoza, joined the City of Boulder Fire Department in 1975 upon the advice of Mrs. Emma Martinez who told me that the Department was looking for a firefighter. I tested among 200 applicants and was selected to the position. I retired from Boulder Fire Rescue after serving 37 years on the Department, 21 years as a Battalion Chief. In 1982 my friend Billy Duran, killed in a live fire training accident, inspired my commitment to service.

Illus. 6.4. Gilbert Espinoza's aspirations and career, 1955 and later

improve our plight." Emma later organized a conversation with Virginia and a few of her friends over coffee one day and gave them a pep talk about the programs OEO was operating, pointing out that part-time positions were available. Virginia first took a job as a substitute Head Start teacher and then moved to a regular position with an OEO program at a neighborhood center in Lafayette. She later obtained her GED and by 1978 was working as a bilingual aide in a public school kindergarten. At age 46 she began taking college classes; after receiving her bachelor's degree, she worked as an elementary school teacher.[57] When Doris Ogeda Gonzales was 19, she met Emma Martinez, who found jobs for her and "helped her climb the ladder."[58] Phil Hernandez's first job was with Head Start, an opening he heard about from Emma, who was his aunt.[59] She also encouraged Gilbert Espinoza, who had wanted to be a fireman

[57] Maestas, Virginia, interview, 2013.
[58] Gonzales, Doris, interview, 2013. For another example of Emma's influence, see Lehmann, Jessie Velez, interview, 1978.
[59] Phil spent his subsequent career as director of Equal Opportunity Employment programs for the University of Colorado and several divisions of Colorado's state government.

since he was a child, to apply for a position with the Fire Department, leading to his 37 years of service.

People were drawn into OEO programs through other kinds of personal contact as well. Ricardo Garcia and his wife Anna came to Boulder in 1970 so he could attend the university.[60] They lived at first in the quonset huts along Canyon Boulevard, which Ricardo described in his 1977 interview as "a very nice little *barrio* where people were friendly to each other." Later Ricardo helped to organize the group that applied for and received a $500,000 grant from the Federal Housing Administration to build the low-income residential complex known as Alvarado Village, sponsored by St. Thomas Aquinas Chapel at the university.[61] The Garcias' children were in Head Start, but Ricardo and Anna did not take active part until his sister sent Ruth Rodriguez to talk with them. Ruth, a Head Start teacher, stressed how important it was for Chicanos to be involved in their children's education. She encouraged them to join the Parent Advisory Council, because that group interviewed potential teachers and advised on the school's content and approach. Ricardo and Anna went onto the Council and later participated in the Follow Through program. He was then elected to the Boulder Human Relations Commission, where he worked on such issues as police harassment of Latinos, lack of recreation facilities, and attacks on Chicano students at the university by community people or the police. For the rest of his career, Richard promoted forms of teaching that meet the individual needs of all children, including bilingual approaches.[62]

The OEO's insistence that people who were assisted by their programs should also help to run them plus the lack of fixed criteria about educational level and previous experience thus enabled some highly competent people—especially women—to move into positions that served the community. People looking for similar jobs in the 2010s face far more restricted opportunities, based upon formal education, specialized training, and/or prior work. When one sees what valuable and often sustained contributions the OEO-trained people of the later 1960s and 1970s made to their communities, it seems unfortunate that the door has now been largely closed to people who lack rigidly defined qualifications.

[60] Garcia, Ricardo and Anna, interview, 1977, and Garcia, Richard, interview, 2013.
[61] For St. Thomas Aquinas, see Vol. II, Ch. 5C.
[62] In 2013, Richard was founder and director of the Colorado Statewide Parent Coalition and chair of the Board of Directors of The Community Foundation Serving Boulder County; see also Ch. 7B below.

Other types of expanding employment

Boulder County's Latinas/os gained additional authority and public legitimacy between 1965 and 1980 thanks to other kinds of new employment. These positions, which generally required at least a high school education, were filled by both local people and newcomers. The number of jobs for professionals and technical workers increased at Rocky Flats (which produced plutonium triggers for hydrogen bombs), the University of Colorado, the national research labs in Boulder, and the Federal Aviation Administration's air traffic control center in Longmont. Especially important was the large research and production plant founded between Longmont and Boulder by IBM.

These developments caused a substantial increase in the number of employees from Spanish-speaking backgrounds in Boulder County and the range of jobs they held. The 488 Spanish-surnamed workers whose occupations are listed in the three *City Directories* in 1965 had jumped to 903 in 1975, and the distribution of positions they held, by category of employment, had shifted markedly.[63] Whereas 31% of those employees in 1965 were unskilled laborers and another 20% were service workers, ten years later only 15% were laborers and 17% service workers. Instead, there was a rise in nearly all other classifications, with the exception of skilled craft workers. We will look here just at a few types of employment that had a particularly marked impact.

Although Rocky Flats had opened in 1952, production increased across the 1960s. Run initially by the Dow Chemical Company on behalf of the U.S. Atomic Energy Commission, Rocky Flats eventually employed thousands of semi-skilled or skilled workers from around the region, including some from Boulder County. At the time, jobs at the plant seemed to offer good opportunities: wages were high, and workers got good benefits. John S. Chavez, who worked at Rocky Flats for many years and was a union steward for the United Steelworkers, believed he was serving his country.

Initially there was some racial/ethnic discrimination in Rocky Flats' hiring. When Al Cardenas of Boulder applied for a job in the late 1950s, Dow Chemical's managers said that minority candidates were generally not qualified to do the work and could not pass the tests.[64] Out of some 1,200 employees, Al remembered that only nine were Hispanic and nine

---

[63] See App. 3.3.
[64] Cardenas, Alfonso, interview, 2004. Al did pass and was hired.

> John was being interviewed by a reporter for one of the T. V. stations in Denver. They wanted to know about the hazards of his job at Rocky Flats. He always defended what he was doing and said it wasn't any worse than being a police officer or fighting fires.
>
> Dad was a union steward for the United Steelworkers. He knew that there were a lot of criticisms regarding his work there. Rocky Flats employed many Hispanic men and women who like Dad were loyal American citizens and believed in what they were doing.

Illus. 6.5. John S. Chavez, Jr. at Rocky Flats, 1976

African American. Later, however, the number of Latinas/os increased. By 1975, at least 29 people from our three towns worked there.[65]

The drawback for employees at Rocky Flats was that many were exposed to massive amounts of radiation. They routinely handled ingots of uranium, their hands and faces were only a short distance away from the plutonium they were putting into the "buttons" that would become bomb triggers, and some worked with beryllium, which was particularly dangerous. The extent to which Dow Chemical and the Atomic Energy Commission were aware of the long-term risks to their employees is disputed, but some of the workers later died of radiation exposure, mainly berylliosis.[66]

Others workers, however, survived with no serious harm, especially if they were not employed inside the buildings that processed radioactive materials. When Frank Archuleta of Lafayette was drafted for the Korean War, having been a paratrooper in World War II, he was reassigned to

[65] "Occupations and Employers, Three Towns, 1975." For Polk's *City Directories*, see Ch. 3, note 62 above.
[66] See Vol. II, Ch. 3B.

Rocky Flats as a member of the Security Force; he remained there for the next 36 years, retiring as manager of the force.[67] John Martinez, Emma Gomez Martinez's husband, likewise worked at Rocky Flats for more than 30 years. Hank Blazón, Esther's husband, who had grown up on a farm near Longmont and had a certificate from an electronics school in Denver, did a four-year apprenticeship as a machinist at Rocky Flats.[68] Mounting concern about the danger and pollution caused by Rocky Flats, expressed through increasingly large protest marches (numbering as many as 15,000 people), a fine of $18.5 million imposed on the later operator of the plant for massive safety violations, and the ending of the Cold War all contributed to the decision to cease production in 1989.

Many more Latinas/os found jobs at the large manufacturing plant and research unit established by IBM in 1965. At its peak, in the later 1970s and 1980s, it had around 8,000 employees. Until 1971, IBM hired relatively few Latinas/os, and they were not promoted to higher positions.[69] But then a group of five employees, including Cookie Chavez (a graduate of the University of Colorado) filed a federal discrimination suit against IBM for lack of advancement opportunities. At about the same time, Joe Martinez joined IBM's Human Resources office.

In 1972, the company began a deliberate program of aggressive affirmative action recruitment for both professional/technical employees and manufacturing workers. It made jobs in the manufacturing division attractive to Latinos, African Americans, and Native Americans by providing higher wages and more extensive benefits than were normally available, and it allowed people who came in at an entry level to move up, including into management. For its research division, IBM cultivated young computer programmers, engineers, and skilled technicians from among the growing number of Latino students graduating from the University of Colorado and other institutions. It sent agents to talk with students of color in other states, especially Texas and California, and it hired people from foreign countries, including Spain. Claude Lamory, a Latino in Human Resources, brought in people of color as accountants

---

[67] "Archuleta, Frank and Cora, biography." He was also a Lt. Colonel in the Colorado National Guard.

[68] Blazón, William ("Hank"), interview, 2013.

[69] This paragraph and the next report information from Emma Peña-McCleave (based upon her own work experience at IBM, that of her husband, and recent discussions with other former employees), as described in a conversation with Marjorie McIntosh, July 30, 2013. For the IBM plant in 2013, when it had many fewer employees, see "Longmont, film of places of historical importance."

and lower-level managers.[70] By 1975, IBM was hiring 71 Spanish-surnamed people from our three towns, making it the largest single employer among those listed in the *City Directories*.[71] Many of these employees lived in nearby Longmont and became part of the Chicano activist group there.

Several people interviewed by the BCLHP had been long-time IBM employees. In 1974, Hank Blazón went from Rocky Flats to IBM, where he received further training in machine maintenance and took engineering courses.[72] Later he worked in the research labs, and when the company closed the manufacturing division, he re-trained to do computer work and scheduling. Heriberto ("Beto") Moreno was born in Ciudad Juarez, Mexico but was brought across the border by his grandparents as a child.[73] Becoming a U.S. citizen when he was 18, Moreno studied mechanical engineering at the University of Texas at El Paso. When he graduated in 1974, he was recruited by IBM and remained there until his retirement. He and his wife Marta (also from El Paso) settled in Longmont, where they were to be founding members of El Comité in 1980.[74] Augustine Eliseo Cordova, who had been active in the Chicano student movement at the University of Colorado in the mid-1970s, was invited to IBM as a software engineer in 1977.[75] He too remained with the firm until he retired.

Because of the new working opportunities, the number of Latino professionals, paraprofessionals, and technicians increased greatly in this period. In our three towns, the *City Directories* list only 37 professional people with Spanish surnames in 1965 but 101 in 1975; in 1965 there were 12 paraprofessionals and technicians but 60 in 1975.[76] In the latter year, the University of Colorado in Boulder employed 67 Latinas/os, 29 of them in faculty, counseling, or administrative positions; another 74 Latinas/os worked for the Boulder Valley or St. Vrain Valley public schools, 29 of them as teachers. The federal government's labs in Boulder, including the National Center for Atmospheric Research and the National Oceanic and Atmospheric Administration, employed 16 more. Additional positions were provided by municipal governments,

[70] Augustine Eliseo Cordova, conversations with Marjorie McIntosh, July 17, 2013.
[71] "Occupations and Employers, Three Towns, 1975."
[72] Blazón, William ("Hank"), interview, 2013.
[73] Moreno, Heriberto ("Beto"), interview, 2013.
[74] See Ch. 7C below.
[75] Cordova, Augustine E., interview, 2013, and see Ch. 7B below.
[76] App. 3.3. For below, see "Occupations and Employers, Three Towns, 1975."

which together hired 48 Latinas/os; 18 people worked as laboratory, electronic, or medical technicians or draftsmen.

Other jobs were opening up too. By 1975, unskilled Latino workers were employed not only in construction (39) and food processing firms (34), but also by Slack Horner Foundries (35) and Red Dale Coach's manufacturing division (20).[77] Only eight people said they owned businesses when asked by *City Directory* representatives about their employment, but nineteen were managers and seventeen worked in sales. Miguel Medina moved to Longmont in the late 1960s and set up his music shop, Casa Medina, which became a cultural center for local Latinas/os.[78]

Several earlier types of work were still present in 1975.[79] Great Western Sugar employed five Latinas/os in its processing plant and seven in its agricultural research center. Strikingly, however, not a single other person described himself as a farm laborer. (Because migrant workers were not permanent residents, they were not included in the *City Directories*.) Rather surprisingly, 24 men said they were coal miners. Since few mines were still producing coal, some of them were probably doing clean-up and maintaining security for ones that had closed.

Longmont Turkey Processors, which hired 13 male and 4 female Latino laborers and 2 supervisors in 1975, continued to provide an unpleasant and high-risk working environment. Lucia Villagran's husband, who had been a field worker in New Mexico, came to Longmont in 1967 because a relative of his who was already employed at the plant found him a job.[80] Lucia soon began to work there too. Although she enjoyed the regularity and sociability of the job, including the picnics in Roosevelt Park for employees, the work was dangerous. Her husband was injured when a hose broke loose and hit him, and she herself fell onto the cement floor and hurt her knee after tripping over a hose. She was sent first to the factory's nurse, who told her to get back to work; when her family protested to the manager a few days later because she was unable to walk, he agreed to have her see a doctor. She had to use a cane for three months, and the company denied her benefits from then on. When a neighbor cut his finger badly while on the job, his family had to hire an attorney to force the company to pay his medical bills.

[77] "Occupations and Employers, Three Towns, 1975."
[78] Medina, Miguel, interview, 2013, and see Vol. II, Ch. 4B.
[79] "Occupations and Employers, Three Towns, 1975."
[80] Villagran, Lucia and Lily, interview, 2013, for this paragraph.

Illus. 6.6. Turkey processing at the
Longmont plant, 1960s

As part of a summer program for migrant worker teens in 1979, several of the young people interviewed one of the managers of the turkey plant.[81] After taking them on a tour of the facility, he said that it offered good employment for temporary workers, since the factory needed extra employees during the summer. Although he admitted that conditions in the plant were cold and damp, as was necessary when working with meat products, he emphasized the training given to employees and noted that most of the accidents were minor—just cuts and falls. He mentioned also that the workers were unionized.

To balance that account, the teens wanted to hear from an employee of the turkey plant. They decided to interview Manuel Rodriguez, the 19-year-old brother of one of them, who was at the plant for a second summer.[82] He had started working that year in a freezer unit, but when he quit because the work was so cold, he was rehired to load the turkeys "from the trailer-trucks onto the hooks which move them slowly to their deaths, upside down." Manuel complained about many aspects of how employees were treated. They were paid by contract (their pay based on how much work they did), and the amount they received was too little. Working conditions were terrible. When he developed eye and

[81] Bine, Tom, interview, 1979.
[82] Rodriguez, Manuel, interview, 1979.

lung problems from the dirt, dust, and feathers, the company said at first it would send him to a doctor but then refused. Further, the plant was frequently raided by officials of the U.S. Immigration and Naturalization Service, who each time took away 15 or 20 Mexican employees who lacked formal papers. Because so many of the workers were "illegals," they could not protest against how they were treated. The union was so weak that Manuel did not even bother to join it.

Latinas continued their movement into the labor force in the later 1960s and 1970s. In 1975, 200 were reported by the *City Directories* as employed outside the home, as compared with 99 a decade earlier.[83] As before, they constituted somewhat under a quarter of all Latinas/os whose occupations we know, but the nature of their employment had continued to move up, away from the earlier preponderance of domestic service workers. Because more women were now graduating from high school and some were going to college, they qualified for a much wider range of jobs. Whereas in 1955, 65% of the women whose occupations are known in these three towns were service workers, unskilled laborers, or "helpers"/"employees," by 1975 that figure had dropped to 44%. In Boulder, 24% of the 90 Latinas listed held professional positions in 1975; 16% were paraprofessionals, technicians, or administrative support/ sales workers; and another 16% were machine operators. Some novel kinds of work for women had appeared. Starting around 1970, Becky Archuleta Ortega became a technical specialist for Ball Corporation Aerospace Systems in Boulder; her job was to check over the designs for the thermal blankets that covered space satellites, supervise their construction, and go to the launch sites to fit them into place or carry out repairs.[84]

The percentage of women within the total known Latino/Latina workforce was by no means the same in all three towns. Only 8% of Lafayette's workers as recorded by the *City Directories* were female, unlike the 21% in Longmont and the 31% in Boulder. That suggests that family patterns in Lafayette had remained fairly traditional, with the great majority of women working exclusively within the home and perhaps experiencing stronger male dominance. Lafayette's Latino community had received relatively little new immigration in the previous decades, and the older families may have preserved earlier economic and social

---

[83] App. 3.3, "Occupations and Employers, Three Towns, 1965," and "Occupations and Employers, Three Towns, 1975."
[84] "Archuleta family history."

ways. Longmont had many new arrivals, both middle class families and poor households in which women had to take paid employment to help make ends meet. The more highly educated and economically secure families in Boulder—older residents and newcomers alike—had apparently moved to the pattern of higher status female labor found among many local Anglo families as well.

In some families that had been in this area for several generations, an underlying change that facilitated Latinas' ability to take demanding jobs outside the home was what appears to have been a marked decline in the birthrate.[85] We do not have quantified evidence, but personal narratives suggest that whereas many immigrants to Boulder County prior to 1940 had very large families (8 to 10 children were common), the size dropped thereafter. By 1980, Latinas with a high school or college education seem to have had about the same number of children as their Anglo peers, though new immigrants generally had larger families.

By the end of the 1970s, leaders from Spanish-speaking backgrounds in Boulder County had created a Chicano identity for themselves and others. They were proud of their ethnic and cultural heritage and celebrated it publicly. They felt an obligation to articulate the challenges facing those who had not enjoyed the same opportunities, and they attempted to correct some of the problems faced by migrant workers. Although Latino educators created special educational initiatives for Spanish-speaking children and those from migrant families, such programs lasted for no more than a generation or two. By the 2010s, bilingual classrooms and activities for migrant worker children had been severely reduced in the Boulder Valley and St. Vrain Valley Schools Districts, even though the ongoing arrival of new immigrants and temporary field workers created a constant demand. Several of the people most heavily involved with the Boulder County Latino History Project had started their educational work in the 1970s and were bitterly disappointed that opportunities for Latino children had been cut back so sharply. The reductions derived in part from budgetary problems in the school districts, but they were promoted by some School Board members who believed that all Latino children should be put immediately into regular English-only classrooms.

The middle class newcomers who settled in Boulder County in the later 1960s and 1970s joined with local people who had attained

[85] See Vol. II, Ch. 1A.

comparable levels of academic and/or occupational success in forming a pool of natural leaders. But local Chicano activists were not drawn only from those families. Some factory workers, craftsmen, housewives, and others were equally committed to change, and they worked effectively with more highly educated Latinas/os in trying to bring it about. In Lafayette and Longmont, only 8% - 11% of the Latinas/os whose occupations are known in 1975 worked as professionals, para-professionals, and technicians, as contrasted with 34% in Boulder.[86] Yet as we shall see, Chicano activism was strong in all three communities.

---

[86] "Summary, Occupational Analysis, Longmont, 1926-1975," "Summary, Occupational Analysis, Lafayette, 1926-1975," and "Summary, Occupational Analysis, Boulder, 1926-1975."

Chapter 7

Chicano Civil Rights Activism in the Later 1960s and 1970s

During the period of civil rights activism, Chicano leaders in Boulder County formed organizations and took public action. Refusing to be treated as second-class citizens and calling attention to forms of institutionalized racism, these residents demanded correction for problems that limited options for Latino adults and children and subjected them to unequal treatment. As was true for many Chicano activists throughout the country, they found school boards, municipal governments, and other institutions of power maddeningly unresponsive.[1] Their ability to force change was, however, constrained by their moderate stance. Their organizations did not organize mass protests or affiliate with more radical groups, such as Corky Gonzales's Crusade for Justice, based in Denver, or even with the United Mexican American Students (UMAS) at the University of Colorado.[2] Although some young people in Boulder, especially at the university, were prepared to use militant tactics, the men and women who ran the associations of local Chicanos chose to use peaceful means in their attempt to bring about improvements for their people.

In the late 1960s and 1970s, the activities of Chicano students on the University of Colorado's Boulder campus became part of the county's broader history. Not only were there many more Spanish-surnamed

---

[1] For Chicano activism in Colorado more generally, see "La Raza de Colorado: El Movimiento."

[2] For various representations of this controversial leader and organization, see Ernesto Vigil, "Rodolfo Gonzales," John Chávez, *The Lost Land*, pp. 141-144, and Acuña, *Occupied America*, pp. 308-309.

students, their forceful stance and participation in national protest movements had an impact on the surrounding community. At the end of the 1960s the university set up a special program to recruit intelligent young Latinas/os who did not meet admissions criteria based the types of high school classes taken or grades received but showed promise. Hundreds of these students came to the campus, where—influenced by the wider civil rights movements of the period—they formed organizations of their own. UMAS was the main Chicano student group in Boulder, demanding changes from the university and becoming increasingly militant as its demands were refused or ignored. In addition to taking over several campus buildings, the students orchestrated mass protests, marches through the community, and boycotts of local stores in response to national issues. In 1974, six young people—most of them currently or previously active in UMAS—were killed in two car bombings. It is still not clear how the bombings occurred, but "Los Seis de Boulder" became symbols of the Chicano cause.

This disrupted period ended in 1980 with the shooting of two young unarmed Latinos by an Anglo police officer in Longmont. The response of the Latino community is an admirable example of determination to work for long-term change. Rather than resorting to violence, Latinas/os pulled together and formed an organization called El Comité to present its concerns about the police to city officials. Because little progress was being made, Latino leaders asked the U.S. Department of Justice to send in a mediator. The resulting recommendations, which were implicitly critical of the police, gave El Comité a recognized position as the representative of Latino residents.

A. Political Action by Boulder County Residents

During the late 1960s and 1970s, Chicano activists from local families drew public attention to forms of discrimination and worked to eliminate them. This meant abandoning any attempt to live quietly and respectably, without attracting notice from the Anglo community. When Emma Gomez Martinez was interviewed in 2013, she described the previous attitude toward racist practices and why it was hard for people to stand up against them. Until the mid-1960s,

Spanish-speaking people were very quiet about all these problems. You heard about them when families got together at weddings or parties or something, and they discussed it within themselves, but I never remember anyone saying, "Well, we must do something about it." And we didn't get any advice from those in power to change the discrimination and lack of employment, lack of education, and looking for work. Those were things that were discussed privately, in homes. I understood that they were embarrassed because, once you feel this discrimination, it kind of scorches your soul. It's not too hard to understand, but it keeps people down. You don't have the courage to voice it and get out and do something about it.[3]

Starting in the later 1960s, however, some Boulder County Latinas/os displayed new assertiveness and organization. Although many families, especially those with labor union connections, had traditionally been Democrats, very few people had even considered running for office. In 1969, however, two men were elected or appointed to their communities' town councils, the first Latinos to join those groups.[4] Thomas Lopez was elected to Lafayette's council, continuing until 1975; in his last two years there, he served as mayor of the town.[5] Ben Rodriguez was appointed as a council member in Longmont in December, 1969 to fill a vacated position for one of the wards. Two years later he was elected to that seat, which he held until 1979. These men did not campaign specifically as Latinos, but they demonstrated that Latinos could indeed hold political office. In another sign of change, Longmont in 1975 held its first election that provided ballots in Spanish as well as English.[6] The entry into politics of a few Boulder County Latinas/os was paralleled in Denver and at the state level by the rise of Latino leaders like Richard T. Castro and Federico Peña.[7]

More important in terms of improving the lives of local Latinas/os as a whole were the various associations created in the late 1960s and 1970s to address current problems within the community. Local Chicano leaders were now determined to make their voices heard, to speak out on behalf of their people. Displaying oppositional consciousness as they analyzed and confronted the forms of institutionalized racism

[3] Martinez, Emma Gomez, interview, 2013.
[4] "Latino elected officials," for this and below.
[5] Lopez, Thomas, interview, 1986.
[6] "First bilingual election in Longmont."
[7] No references were found here to Viva Kennedy clubs, popular in the 1960s, which encouraged some Latinos elsewhere to become politically active.

that restricted Latino lives, they banded together to push for change in such areas as the failure of the school system to provide an appropriate education for Latino children, police misconduct, and the shortage of Latinas/os in government positions. They demanded equal access to good housing, ending what had been some degree of de facto residential segregation.[8]

The local Chicano fight against racism gained some of its strength from people whose education, employment, and assurance gave their voices extra weight. Many of the key figures were working in OEO organizations and/or had college degrees. Yet Latinos cooperated effectively across the socio-economic range, and members of older families allied with newly arrived ones. Women were active members of those groups, but there is no evidence of a separate feminist movement among town-based Latinas, no attempt to create a distinctively Chicana identity or organizations.[9] At the University of Colorado, by contrast, progressive feminist Chicanas were campaigning for greater visibility for women and their issues within the emerging field of Chicana/o Studies and for more Chicana faculty members and students.

We know about the activity of these community organizations thanks to newspaper accounts and the preservation of some of their own records, rare among small local groups. Their efforts warrant close attention, for they illustrate grass-roots civil rights work in action. Yet the limited results achieved by these associations highlight the challenge faced by many other civil rights organizations in the country at the time: how could they force conservative leaders and institutions to accept and implement new policies and allocate funds in ways that would benefit under-represented groups if the only weapons they were prepared to use were presenting factual evidence and logical arguments?

Putting pressure on the schools

Boulder County's Chicano parents and community leaders pushed the public schools to make changes that would improve the quality of education for Latino children. Their efforts were in keeping with two Supreme Court decisions that identified Mexican Americans as "a

---

[8] See Vol. II, Ch. 2B.

[9] This contrasts with militant Chicana activism in Texas and California (Ruiz, *From Out of the Shadows*, pp. 99-126, and Salas, *Soldaderas*, chs. 6-7). A few local women did participate in a Chicana conference at the university (Chacon, Susie, interview, 1977). For Chicana students' involvement in UMAS at the university, see setion B below.

distinct class" or "an identifiable ethnic-minority group."[10] These rulings allowed Latinas/os to demand an end to segregation or discrimination in the schools based upon their ethnicity. In Boulder County, Chicano educational activists confronted considerable resistance to change among the Anglos who filled the School Boards and among some teachers and parents. The improvements Chicanos proposed and the opposition they faced sound painfully similar to efforts being made by people of color and multicultural educators in many parts of the U.S. in the 2010s to broaden the curriculum and staff of schools and become more responsive to the needs of every child.

In the early 1970s, local Chicano activists had a set of interrelated educational goals. They wanted bilingual education, so Spanish-speaking children would not be ashamed but could instead begin their schooling in a language they knew while at the same time acquiring competence in English. They argued further that all children would profit from an inclusive, multicultural curriculum, one that offered a better preparation for life in a diverse society. More Latino teachers would provide valuable role models for children and increase job opportunities. Better advising for Latino students and more practical training courses would lessen dropouts, while increased scholarship money for post-secondary education would provide an incentive for staying in school.

We know most about what happened in Longmont, a town still heavily dominated by conservative Anglo families in social and political terms. Newspaper accounts describe the interactions between a group that initially called itself "Los Chicanos para la Justicia" and the Board of Education of the St. Vrain Valley Public Schools across ten months in 1971. The *Boulder Daily Camera* noted on February 11 that parents in Longmont were calling for a Chicano advisory committee to address such issues as the lack of teachers who were able to relate to Chicano students and inadequate counseling programs for Latinas/os and low-income children, resulting in a high dropout rate.[11] On March 3, the *Longmont Times-Call* reported that Los Chicanos had presented a list of demands to the Board of Education at a previous meeting.[12] Their demands (they were not merely called "requests") included the following: that a committee be appointed to improve educational

---

[10] *Hernandez v. Texas* (1954) and *Cisneros v. Corpus Christi ISD* (1970), as discussed in Donato and Hanson, "Legally White, Socially 'Mexican.'"
[11] "Chicano Advisory Groups criticize district."
[12] "Chicanos win bid for school advisory role."

opportunities for Spanish-surnamed students; that students be allowed to celebrate Mexican Independence Day; that a Chicano Studies program be instituted in the schools; that the dress code be abolished; and that busing in east Longmont (where many Latino families lived) be investigated for inequities.

Thirty representatives of Los Chicanos met for three hours with school board members on March 3 to go over those demands.[13] The Chicanos came from a wide spectrum within the Latino community. The report of the meeting gives a clear impression that by its end the school board and administrators had decided they needed to do <u>something</u> to appease angry Chicanos. The easiest way to do that, without giving up any real authority, was to agree to the creation of a seven-member Mexican-American advisory committee to work with two district administrators. John Martinez, speaking for Los Chicanos, stressed that the most pressing duty before the new committee would be to recruit and hire Mexican-American teachers. Superintendent John Stephens, when asked for exact statistics, said that 6 of the 504 teachers in the district had Spanish surnames; among students, however, around 1,100 of the total enrollment of 10,900 had Spanish names. School board members and administrators noted the difficulty they had experienced in finding Mexican-American teachers interested in working in the St. Vrain district. While they said they looked forward to having help from the advisory committee in recruitment, they were unwilling to let the committee have any power in hiring.

The school board agreed to none of Los Chicanos' other demands.[14] The group had argued that discrimination was "not open and blatant, it's more subtle." It took such forms as advising Chicano students that their test scores indicated they should go into vocational training, not college prep courses, and it appeared in "the Anglo orientation of subject matter and activities." When pushed about a Chicano Studies program, including a class on Chicano history or sociology, the assistant superintendent for instruction said that steps had already been taken through the introduction of a class on minority literature. "He admitted, however, that the course was not taught by minority teachers, which met with some group disapproval." Los Chicanos also objected to the suggestion that mini-courses on Chicano history might be offered on a pass-fail basis. "Isn't this still a form of invidious discrimination?" one

---

[13] Ibid, for this paragraph.
[14] Ibid.

member of the group asked. The organization attacked the district's dress code as discriminatory, for it prohibited girls from wearing blue jeans to school. "How many of our girls can afford pantsuits?"

Two months later, the newly created advisory body, which now called itself the "Chicano Citizens Committee," delivered a five-point statement at a meeting of the Board of Education.[15] After Ben Romero, chairman of the committee, described their proposals for improving relations between Chicanos and the board, Angelo Velasquez expressed concern that the group was being "used" by the district. Why, he asked, "is it our duty to do all the work in planning a Chicano Studies curriculum? We'll aid, but as far as taking the initiative . . . ." He also pointed out that fewer Chicanos had graduated from Longmont High School in 1971 than in the previous year. But pressure from the committee may have contributed to the decision to hire two Latinos (a counselor and an earth science teacher) among the nine new staff members offered contracts at that meeting.

By early November of 1971, the group, which the school board henceforth termed the "Chicano Advisory Committee," had submitted a specific budgetary proposal.[16] The plan, which was described in the newspaper beneath the misleadingly optimistic headline, "Chicanos Winning Bid for Special Study Fund," asked for a total of $61,000. The budget covered in-service training for teachers, a full-time staff member to deal with Chicano issues in the schools, and three human relations staff members to serve as the connection between schools and the Chicano community. The group also requested a study to determine why the dropout rate for Chicano students was so high and monthly reports outlining efforts to recruit Chicano teachers. An article in the *Longmont Times-Call* on November 5 reported that the president of the school board said in an interview that although the full amount would probably not be appropriated, there was a real possibility that some of the request would be funded. Angelo Velasquez pressed school officials to accept the recommendations. "You have demonstrated your good faith so far, but right now this can go either way. The insensitivity of individual teachers in the system is your biggest problem. I think much of this can be corrected with a human relations staff and an effective high-level Chicano administrator."

[15] "Chicanos outline school aims" for this paragraph.
[16] "Chicanos winning bid for $61,000" for this paragraph. One suspects the board had insisted upon this name for the group, to emphasize that it had only an advisory role.

The hopes of the Chicano Advisory Committee were dashed at the school board meeting on November 10.[17] The board allocated only $4,500 and for only one part of the proposal: a modest program of in-service training. At the meeting Julius Beauprez, a successful Anglo farmer, argued that money should not be allocated to Chicano issues unless the same was done for all other "immigrant groups." When Beauprez objected to changing American history books to accommodate minorities, L. B. Adams, a member of the school board, responded, "Histories of this country have never really reflected the history of the Southwest. These folks [Latinos] are Americans, but we have never recognized that in our history books. They have made tremendous religious and cultural contributions that have been ignored for hundreds of years." But he ended weakly: "I wouldn't mind seeing a little about their culture in our schools."

Chicano committee members were frustrated by the decision. Esther Blazón said, "I'm very disappointed in the board's action tonight. Granting $4,500 of this proposal is nothing but tokenism." She stressed that at a bare minimum, the district should hire someone with the specific job of dealing with in-service activities and other Chicano issues. Because people on the Chicano Advisory Committee had other jobs during the day, they did not have the time to develop a successful program on their own. The committee's spokesman said they would continue to push for hiring a full-time Latino administrator. Several years later, after further complaints and proposals from the Latino community, the St. Vrain board hired Esther Blazón as director of bilingual/bicultural education for the district. By 1975, she was not only working within the schools but also writing forceful editorials for the local papers on behalf of educational inclusivity.[18]

Chicano educational activists were organizing in Boulder and Lafayette too, where the schools were part of the Boulder Valley School District. In Boulder, a District Minority Review Committee requested and then demanded in 1971 that the schools introduce a multi-ethnic emphasis within the curriculum, remove stereotypes based on race and ethnicity from teaching materials, and eliminate other kinds of bias.[19] The committee's growing frustration with the lack of response to their

[17] "Board grants part ($4,500) of Chicano request" for this paragraph and the next.
[18] E.g., "Why bilingual, bicultural education?"
[19] "Education articles," *Boulder Daily Camera*, e.g., Feb. 14 and 17, May 10 and 20, June 14, and Aug. 10, 1971. See also Ch. 5C above.

demands led to what the newspaper described as a "heated" meeting with the school board in March, 1972.[20]

Chicano parents were better organized in Lafayette, where as early as 1969 a Latina had been elected as head of the PTA.[21] In 1971, they called for more Latino teachers, arguing that they and their children could not communicate with teachers and counselors who were unable to speak their language.[22] In May, 1972, 150 Latino students from Lafayette's elementary and junior/senior high schools, with their parents, participated in a protest march to demand that a Chicano be named as assistant principal of the new high school (Centaurus), which was to open that fall.[23] That march, apparently the only large protest organized by the local Latino community in this period, did not achieve its desired result: an Anglo was appointed as assistant principal. A new group then formed, Concerned Chicanos of Lafayette, headed by Tony Montour, to keep fighting for change.

Chicano efforts to introduce change in the schools met with strong opposition from some Anglos. An example is an unsigned, typed letter sent by "A Citizen of Lafayette" to "Mr. Tony Montour and his Committee."[24] The letter begins,

> Will you pause for a moment and consider your opportunities and privileges you have in your own community within this great land of ours? For years there has been no discrimination in our town or within our schools. Stop and think of our Chicano athletes and student leaders. Everyone had school spirit which netted a great school. Now suddenly because of some outside element who is influencing you, you are ready to throw away your self respect and all reason.

The author, who says he or she becomes "irate when you begin on our schools," comments that if their group can recruit "qualified teachers for Hispano Culture and other areas, great. . . . But if you think education is going to lessen its requirements so unqualified individuals can teach,

---

[20] Ibid., March 21, 1972.

[21] "Mrs. Tony Garcia heads PTA."

[22] "Education articles," *Boulder Daily Camera*, e.g., July 20 and 26, 1971.

[23] Ibid., May 5, 1972. For below, see ibid., Aug. 15, 1972.

[24] Valdez Papers, MABCU file. The letter is undated but was probably sent later in 1972, when Montour was leading the Concerned Chicanos. He was highly visible at about that time, as he was also running for City Council (Tony Montour, conversation with Marjorie McIntosh, July 29, 2013).

you are wrong." The letter goes on to defend Anglo teachers, who "are not biased, because their job is to teach if the student has an open mind," and it attacked special scholarships for Chicano students at the University of Colorado. Mr. Montour's Committee might carry more weight if it "engulfed all of your race within Lafayette, . . . but there are many of your good people who are just as 'Fed Up' as the rest of us." The letter ends with a threatening paragraph that echoes the repatriation movement of the 1930s: "There are buses, planes and trains leaving for Mexico every day, if you don't like it here. We are not sitting by quietly. Clean up your minds and thoughts and get back to becoming a community with pride and respect for yourself and your culture."[25] Although that letter expressed particularly hostile views, some degree of racism on the part of many Anglos, including school board members, certainly underlay the resistance faced by Chicano educational activists.

Mexican Americans of Boulder County United

An association founded in 1971 that called itself MABCU [Mexican Americans of Boulder County United] had broader concerns and adopted somewhat more assertive tactics.[26] The name was significant in several respects. It indicated that its members came from throughout the county, rather than being focused on a single town, and the term "United" echoed the titles used by more militant groups within the Chicano movement. Yet the group chose to call itself by the older designation of "Mexican American," and most of its leading figures were college graduates who owned their homes and held responsible jobs, often in education or social services. The group included some newcomers to Boulder County, but many of its members were from established local families.

MABCU grew out of "casual conversations between several members of the Chicano community" about local problems early in 1971, leading to a realization that something needed to be done.[27] Its founders had been trying since the late 1960s to reach out to other groups or institutions, including the University of Colorado, in hopes of working collaboratively to improve conditions for all Latinas/os.[28] When they received no response or at least no action as the result of these efforts,

[25] Valdez Papers, MABCU file.
[26] "Mexican-American group formed for County."
[27] Valdez Papers, CU Archives, MABCU file, App. I to "Abstract, Financial Aid Project, and Constitution, MABCU," for this paragraph and the next.
[28] Euvaldo Valdez, conversation with Marjorie McIntosh, July 23, 2013.

they decided to set up their own organization.

Five issues troubled MABCU's founders. The first was that "Many Chicano residents of Boulder proper were professionals and as such had a tendency to be unaware about 'grass roots' situations affecting all Chicanos." That was related to a lack of unity between local Chicanos in other respects too—"a truly sad situation"—with gaps especially between students and residents, professionals and laborers, and residents of the various towns. Another concern was that Boulder County's Chicano community "lacked visibility and due recognition from political, social, governmental and civic agencies." Chicano organizations elsewhere in Colorado likewise overlooked people in this area because their numbers were relatively small. Because MABCU expected that more Chicanos would be arriving here as higher education and jobs expanded, it was particularly important to develop and maintain a united front.

After several preliminary meetings, the founders drafted a constitution that was approved by the general membership—numbering around 40—in early March, 1971.[29] The group elected its first set of officers. The chairman was Euvaldo Valdez, who had recently moved from New Mexico and was coordinator of community services for the Boulder Valley School District; Phillip Martinez, principal of Burke Elementary School in Boulder, was vice chairman; Emily Chavez, a counselor for Boulder County Planned Parenthood, was secretary; and Art Valdez, director of the Neighborhood Youth Corps of Boulder County (an OEO program), was treasurer. MABCU defined its initial priorities, those requiring immediate attention, as education, human relations, housing, employment, and increased cultural identification and awareness.

Detailed minutes of the monthly meetings of MABCU held over the next few years document the activities of the organization.[30] The group invited guests and speakers, including Mayor Robert Knecht of Boulder (who described the formation of MABCU as "a grand idea"), several Chicano members of the state House of Representatives, an officer of the Boulder County Democratic Party, and Len Avila of the United Farm Workers Organizing Committee. When Lalo Delgado, Executive Director of the Colorado Migrant Council, an activist group supported by the OEO, spoke to MABCU, he equated Mexican Americans with prisoners, confined geographically and by the many problems facing them; he

[29] Valdez Papers, MABCU file, "Constitution."
[30] Valdez Papers, MABCU file, minutes.

reminded his listeners that "regardless of your education, 'prestige,' position, you as a Chicano are never higher than the lowest Mexican." Samuel Herrera of the Migrant Action Program (MAP) at the University of Colorado suggested that MABCU and other Chicano organizations in the community join with them in one super-association. Although MABCU decided to contribute $25 to MAP, it did not affiliate with the group. Hesitation stemmed in part from concern that MAP's extremist reputation might deter local Latinas/os from joining MABCU.[31]

MABCU put its concerns into practice. It pushed for the hiring of Latinas/os in public positions, followed events on the university campus with interest, and supported efforts to make changes in the local schools that would benefit Chicano and other minority students.[32] The group's activities during the first year of its existence were summarized in a report prepared in March, 1972. It emphasized that a major accomplishment was that "more of us got to know each other better and realized that though we are "diverse in sentiment we can be united in purpose."[33]

MABCU also provided scholarships for people pursuing practical training. It had found that although there were various sources of financial aid to help minority students attend colleges and universities, no such funds were available for "economically disadvantaged persons enrolling in vocational and/or trade schools" within the county, many of whom were working adults.[34] MABCU's grants were generally small, ranging from $60 to $370, and given for a single term. Between April and September of 1972, for example, it gave 11 awards totaling $2,265 to people studying auto mechanics, body and fender work, welding, educational media, office occupations, licensed practical nursing, and cosmetology.[35] Most of the recipients, all of whom had Spanish surnames, were studying at the Vo-Tech Center of the Boulder Valley School District, but one was at St. Vrain Valley's Career Development Center and two at Wheatridge Beauty College.

To generate funds for these grants, MABCU submitted applications to multiple sources.[36] IBM awarded money through its Manager of

---

[31] Valdez Papers, MABCU file, minutes, October 27, 1971 and Euvaldo Valdez, conversation with Marjorie McIntosh, July 23, 2013.

[32] Valdez Papers, MABCU file, minutes, Nov. 30, 1971, and loose correspondence.

[33] Valdez Papers, MABCU file, annual report, 1971-2.

[34] Valdez Papers, MABCU file, Abstract, Financial Aid Project.

[35] Valdez Papers, MABCU file, Progress Report, Financial Aid Fund.

[36] Valdez Papers, MABCU file, financial aid papers.

Communications, Mile High United Way provided $2,520 through its Special Needs Fund, and the Social Action Fund of St. Thomas Aquinas Chapel in Boulder, which served the university community, contributed $168.[37] Larger and more elaborate applications for $10,680, submitted to the Campaign for Human Development of the United States Catholic Conference in 1972 and 1973, were not funded.

MABCU was ready to confront the police over harassment and excessive use of force. In 1971, the organization represented a group of Longmont youths in claiming maltreatment by Boulder County sheriff's officers and Boulder city policemen. On July 12, Euvaldo Valdez, as chairman of MABCU, wrote to Brad Leach, the Boulder County sheriff, about an incident that had occurred in Boulder early in the morning of June 13.[38] A sheriff's deputy on routine patrol in the area around 34th Street and Valmont stopped to investigate a car, driven by David Duran, which had apparently run into a ditch. While the officer was looking around, nine friends of Duran's who had been attending a party at a nearby apartment showed up, whereupon the deputy called other units from the Boulder police and Colorado State Patrol to the scene. A fight ensued. In his letter to Leach, Valdez said that MABCU was trying to determine "the extent of this confrontation" and asked the sheriff to make available to them the official reports of the incident and set up an appointment to discuss the matter. "Let me assure you that the intent and extent of involvement by our organization is not to conduct a 'witch hunt'. We are sincerely concerned and will cooperate with you to clarify the matter as expediently as possible. I hope that you will also cooperate with us."

In the following week, eight young Chicanos who were present at the altercation on June 13 recorded formal legal affidavits before a Notary Public, describing what they had seen and done.[39] They claimed that "a fat cop" had sprayed mace into David Duran's face when he attempted to flee. After handcuffing Duran, that officer and others had beaten him, including while he was lying on the ground, before dragging him into a sheriff's car and taking him to jail. Two other young people, they alleged,

---

[37] Carlos Lucero, an electrical engineer at IBM who was active in MABCU, may have arranged that contribution. For St. Thomas Aquinas, see Vol. II, Ch. 5C.

[38] Valdez Papers, MABCU file, police papers. This episode came on top of several conflicts between the police and young Latinos the previous year ("Chicanos throw rocks at Boulder policeman" and "Disturbance on Hill results in arrest").

[39] Valdez Papers, MABCU file, unlabeled file folder.

were spread-eagled on the side of a sheriff's car and made to stand there for 15 minutes, hit with a nightstick if they moved. Others, including women, were hit with clubs on their necks or legs when they protested or tried to help their friends. The nine participants other than the driver were then pushed into a car belonging to one of them and told to drive away from the scene.

MABCU brought this incident to the attention of the Boulder Human Relations Commission. At a meeting on July 21, Joe Lucero on behalf of MABCU and Ken Sterne, the Boulder city manager's administrative assistant for human relations, presented a report about the incident.[40] The Commission concluded that the officers had "used force which appeared . . . to be unwarranted, unnecessary and irresponsible in the circumstances, especially the force used upon the driver of the car and the use of a night stick in striking one of the youths." Norton Steuben, chair of the Commission and a professor of law at the university, wrote to MABCU that his group was "dismayed and deeply disturbed by the unnecessary use of force toward members of the Mexican-American community by various police officers." He outlined the steps the Commission had taken to ensure that the police, sheriff, and city manager would carry out a proper investigation and to see that such incidents did not occur in the future.

The City of Boulder also responded to MABCU's complaint. On July 28, Ted Tedesco, the city manager, reported to Valdez that he had reviewed with Donald Vendel, Boulder's Chief of Police, the file prepared in response to the allegations.[41] "We have both concluded that it appeared that two of our City patrolmen seemed to use excessive force in the circumstances surrounding the incident." After summarizing the City's policy on the use of force, Tedesco said that those two officers "have received appropriate and effective disciplinary action." He also reminded Valdez of his proposal that MABCU work with Ken Sterne to develop a training program to be used by all city departments.

After a long delay, Sheriff Leach wrote to Valdez on August 19, taking a different stance. He said he "could not see where accusations of excessive force should be directed to officers of his department."[42] To the contrary, he felt "it was a must to commend Lt. Hull for his cool-

---

[40] Valdez Papers, MABCU file, police papers.
[41] Ibid.
[42] Ibid.

headedness at the scene and who, with the assistance of other citizens of the area, contained and disbursed other citizens with calmness and reason." Leach agreed to attend the MABCU meeting on August 31 but failed to appear.

The matter did not end there, for MABCU had helped to arrange for two attorneys from the statewide Chicano civil rights organization El Centro Legal to investigate the case. On August 5, Edwin Lobato and Reyes Martinez (who was to be killed in one of the car bombings in 1974) sent to Valdez a summary and analysis of "the police brutality investigation we have been working on this summer," together with recommended steps to be taken.[43] They said that on July 7 they had been requested by Mrs. Eleanor Cruz, director of the Boulder Community Action Center (another OEO program), to look into the incident and meet with some of the young people involved, as well as with representatives of MABCU and Ken Sterne. That meeting led to a request that Lobato and Martinez conduct a full investigation. Sterne asked them, however, to exhaust administrative remedies within the relevant units first, initiating legal action only if those initial efforts proved unsatisfactory. The two lawyers arranged for the young participants to give formal affidavits, and they held additional meetings with city officials, police officers, and Sheriff Leach. Leach, who claimed that he had not yet been fully apprised of the situation, agreed to look into the matter and report his findings.

Lobato and Martinez concluded that "the results of the investigation and administrative remedies have been most unsatisfactory. As of yet, Mr. Leach has not responded to the complaint submitted on behalf of the Chicano youth by the Mexican-American United Organization. It is rather unfortunate for the residents of Boulder County that the Sheriff's Office has manifested such indifference and lack of co-operation and non-responsiveness to the needs and demands of the Chicano Community."[44] They noted also that the "appropriate and effective disciplinary action" taken against two officers of the Boulder City Police Department as reported by Mr. Tedesco was "less than adequate compensation for the physical injury and degrading insult sustained by the youths as a result of the officers' misconduct." They stressed that the treatment of "David Duran, who suffered extreme bodily injury, illegal incarceration for a period of several days, and subsequent non-judicial dispatch to California

[43] Valdez Papers, MABCU file, police papers, Lobato/Martinez report.
[44] Ibid.

by his probation officer," is "especially indicative of the shortcomings of the Boulder County law enforcement agencies."

Lobato and Martinez also criticized Ken Sterne. Sterne had "privately sought our trust and co-operation" in resolving the matter and said he wanted to establish a rapport with the Chicano community. They therefore agreed to work with him, "despite the centuries-old Anglo tradition of deceiving the Chicano people with empty promises. Much to our chagrin, our trust and cooperation was misplaced and abused once again. Mr. Sterne is but another example of a limp and incompetent liaison."[45]

The two attorneys made some specific recommendations. (1) They should be authorized to initiate judicial proceedings, filing a civil complaint without further delay. (2) Mr. Sterne should be removed from his position, and a Chicano, screened and selected by MABCU, be named in his place. (3) The practices and procedures of the Boulder Sheriff's office should be subjected to an intensive investigation by a Citizen Review Board composed of members from all ethnic groups in Boulder County. (4) More stringent measures should be taken against the officers involved in the incident and their superiors, and those actions should be made known to the general public. (5) MABCU should call a press conference and report to the media the results of this investigation.[46] MABCU's records do not indicate if those recommendations were implemented in full, but a later note says the incident was "resolved in favor of the kids."

That episode—and Sheriff Leach's failure to respond to it—had political repercussions as well. On August 15, Paul Hagen, a member of the Boulder County Democratic Party's Executive Committee and the Colorado Democratic Party's Equal Rights Commission, wrote to Leach.[47] After reviewing the meetings that had been held with the sheriff and the lack of any answer or investigation, Hagen made a pointed comment: "As a fellow Democrat, . . . I would ask your urgent consideration in lieu of the possibility of seriously alienating the Mexican American community, all of whom voted for you in the last election." He also reminded Leach that the Republican County Commissioners were attempting to discredit his work. "The conclusions are obvious."

MABCU became embroiled in another incident involving the police a

[45] Ibid.
[46] Ibid.
[47] Valdez Papers, MABCU file, police papers.

few months later. The group's challenge of the Lafayette City Manager's decision to take strong precautionary measures at the time of a public address by Rodolpho ("Corky") Gonzales links local events to the wider history of *El Movimiento*. On the evening of August 20, 1971, Gonzales, a Chicano activist and poet who headed the increasingly militant Crusade for Justice based in Denver, gave a speech at Lafayette High School. We do not know who organized the event, but it indicates that at least some Boulder County Chicanos were interested in what Gonzales was advocating. The local police had received a tip-off from an informer in Denver that Gonzales was going to promote violence in his speech. Lafayette therefore called in extra police units from surrounding towns, the county sheriff, and the state police. The local police also evacuated the adjacent elementary school and set up a riot control center there. A witness remembers seeing police cars from all over the region streaming bumper-to-bumper into Lafayette and a helicopter circling overhead, though whether the latter belonged to law enforcement or the press is not clear.[48] At the event itself, the police mounted an extensive presence within the auditorium, which the largely Latino audience found intimidating. No march or disruption grew out of Gonzales's speech, and he may never have intended such an outcome.

MABCU sent a letter of protest to Richard Flewelling, Lafayette's city manager, referring, among other charges, to a police helicopter hovering over the town that evening. Demanding a formal apology from the city of Lafayette, the group forwarded copies of its complaint to the governor, the county commissioners, a city councilman, the chairman of the Police Investigation Commission, the Colorado Civil Rights Commission, and the head of the Boulder chapter of the American Civil Liberties Union.

Their allegations elicited several replies. A. W. De Novellis, a Lafayette councilman, wrote to the MABCU members who had signed the letter, saying that he was at the event in question and their charges were exaggerated.[49] "Lafayette did, for the protection of all people concerned, take the usual precautionary measures deemed necessary, but did not by any means go to the lengths as you outlined in your letter." After stating his sympathy for Mexican Americans in many situations, he said he did not support all the issues raised by groups representing them. "There are many good points brought about by the work of Mr Gonzales, but again

---

[48] Eleanor Montour, conversation with Marjorie McIntosh, July 29, 2013.
[49] Valdez Papers, MABCU file, Lafayette papers.

there are a few which I term as radical and unnecessary to the cause of the Mexican people." De Novellis stated that he was willing to negotiate but "not tolerate demands, no matter which group presents them." He ended more diplomatically: "Although I do not deem a public apology is warranted as you demanded, I will sincerely say I regret tremendously the mis-understanding which arose from the Gonzales incident."

City Manager Flewelling sent a more hostile response. He began, "I would certainly advise each of you who signed the letter to be certain of your facts before sending any further communications of this type to any public official."[50] He said that the city of Lafayette, "acting upon information received from Denver intelligence," had requested neighboring agencies to provide help if needed. The City had indeed obtained permission to use a nearby elementary school, but no weapons, gas, or any other riot control equipment were placed there. No police helicopter was present over the city that evening, nor was any order issued by a public official requesting the closing of a Lafayette school or business on that occasion. Mr. Flewelling concluded,

> No public official can ignore a legitimate warning from another law enforcement agency in this era of national internal strife. Our preparation was mild and simply involved an alert and nothing else. The citizens of Lafayette, of all races, deserve protection of the highest order we can provide; we will continue to offer this protection in a logical, restrained fashion. I would hope that if further letters are forthcoming from your group, that they are written more responsibly, with greater attention to fact and less false indignation. It is you who owe the apology to the citizens of Lafayette for composition of this heresay document.

He copied his letter to all those who received MABCU's complaint.

Two months later, John Murphy, the chairman of the Boulder chapter of the American Civil Liberties Union, wrote to Mr. Flewelling, saying that MABCU had asked his group to look into the incident in Lafayette.[51] Their investigation was not complete, but he presented some tentative conclusions. "On the one hand, it seems unreasonable, and provocative of trouble, for the police and city officials to have used such extreme measures in reaction to a mere rumor. Further, one group in the population, the Mexican Americans, were singled out as dangerous,

[50] Ibid.
[51] Ibid.

and therefore justifiably felt harassed and intimidated. Further the situation that was created was hardly conducive to free assembly and to free speech (Mr. Gonzales's talk)." But, Mr. Murphy noted, MABCU "seem to have exaggerated somewhat their account of what happened on 20 August." He concluded, "The A.C.L.U. is very much concerned with problems of this sort, and will be keeping an eye on future events."

Over the next few years, MABCU's energy waned. Its limited success in trying to force change led some of its members to question whether a confrontational approach was the best way to achieve real improvement for Latinas/os.

The Boulder Council of LULAC

Another local organization, founded in 1973, had similar goals to MABCU and a partially overlapping membership but a different structure and method of operating. This was the Boulder County Council of LULAC, the League of United Latin American Citizens. LULAC was a nation-wide association composed largely of middle class Latinas/os.[52] In a notice sent out from the national headquarters sometime in the 1970s, LULAC reported that it had been founded in Texas in 1927 with several goals: the preservation of Latin culture; and better educational and employment opportunities, housing, health services, and economic development ventures for "Latin Americans of Mexican-American, South American or Caribbean descent.[53] Around 1974, LULAC had local councils in 33 states, with more than 256,000 members.

The Latinos who formed Boulder County's Council felt that being part of a national organization would offer some benefits.[54] They hoped also to draw in new members who had worried that MABCU was too aggressive. Avoiding direct conflict, Boulder's LULAC chapter was prepared to work with elected officials and institutions like the police, believing that discussion and cooperation were most likely to achieve lasting change. A more conciliatory attitude was further strengthened by the car bombings of 1974. Few local Chicanos supported violence, and the death of "Los Seis de Boulder" reinforced a sense that pushing too hard could be not just counterproductive but also dangerous.

---

[52] Acuña, *Occupied America*, pp. 183-184 and 223-224, and Manuel Gonzales, *Mexicanos*, pp. 181-184.
[53] Valdez Papers, LULAC file, "League of United Latin American Citizens," mimeographed notice, undated but 1973-4.
[54] Euvaldo Valdez, conversation with Marjorie McIntosh, July 23, 2013.

One concern of the local LULAC Council was what its members perceived as the racist attitudes of the Boulder Police Department. After helping in 1974 to arrange for the retirement of Chief Donald Vendel, due to his unwillingness to respond to Chicano concerns, LULAC took part in selecting his successor, John Barber, and then worked closely with him. On Sept. 30, 1975, for example, Philip Hernandez, an active member of LULAC, wrote to Barber reminding him that at a recent meeting, the group had "made a commitment to lend assistance to your department in recruiting Chicano applicants for the Police Department."[55] Barber had also asked LULAC to call to his attention any individuals who submitted an application to the city, saying he would "make every effort to see that they at least were interviewed." Hernandez's letter listed three Mexican Americans who had applied for positions with the Police Department within the past few months. He commented that the police department and LULAC shared the goal of hiring people with the potential to become good police officers, but in addition LULAC wanted to help the police "to establish credibility in the Mexican American community." He ended by saying that those goals "are by no means mutually exclusive. Let's work together."

By 1977, when its records become fuller, Boulder's LULAC Council was well organized and carrying out an ambitious array of activities. At a meeting on March 15, the 11 members present (out of 24 in the full group) elected new officers and then moved through an agenda that included contacts with other LULAC units, a decision to participate in its National Scholarship Program, and the possibility of hiring a paid staff member.[56] The group passed a resolution supporting a conference to be held in April at the University of Colorado on "La Chicana," for which several Boulder women active in LULAC served as co-organizers or panelists.[57] A big project sponsored by the council was to take 100 low-income Latino children to a Denver Bears baseball game on a Saturday in April.[58]

LULAC also raised money for college scholarships for Latino students,

---

[55] Valdez Papers, LULAC file, carbon copy of letter.

[56] Valdez Papers, LULAC file, minutes. Those elected were Ralph Chacon, President; Armando Gingras, Vice-President; Terry Aragon, Secretary; Euvaldo Valdez, Treasurer.

[57] Valdez Papers, LULAC file, flyer and mimeographed program. Susie Chacon, a business owner in Boulder, remembered the Chicana Conference of 1977 as a breakthrough, for it was organized on campus but included women from the community too (Chacon, Susie, interview, 1977).

[58] Valdez Papers, LULAC file, mimeographed flyer and newspaper clipping.

screened applicants, and awarded funds. Their recipients came from a different pool of people than those who had received MABCU's awards for vocational or trade schools. People chosen in August, 1978 included two recent graduates of Boulder or Erie High Schools who planned to attend the University of Northern Colorado to study education; two graduates of Fairview or Centaurus High School who planned to major in business at the University of Colorado or the University of Northern Colorado; one nursing student at the University of Colorado Medical School; and one doctoral student at the University of Colorado.[59] Additional students were assisted in the following years.[60]

In one of the newspaper articles that announced these scholarships, LULAC was described as "a community service organization of citizens of Hispanic background." That conservative wording reflects the shift in emphasis that distinguished LULAC's activities in the later 1970s from MABCU's work in the early 1970s. Although MABCU and the LULAC Council continued to meet into the 1980s, the fire of both movements had dimmed. Their leaders felt that although they had achieved some gains for Latinas/os, they were expending a good deal of energy with modest results.

B. Chicano Students at CU-Boulder, Organizations, and "Los Seis de Boulder"

Whereas the University of Colorado has appeared only in passing in earlier parts of this book, activities on campus became part of the general history of Boulder County's Latinas/os during the later 1960s and 1970s. Prior to that time, the few Latinos who attended the university, starting in the 1890s, came almost entirely from land-owning families in southern Colorado or northern New Mexico.[61] Most of these *ricos* identified with Anglo students on campus, not with the even smaller number of African or Asian Americans. But that situation changed quite dramatically at the end of the 1960s, due largely to the Migrant Action Program [MAP] run by the university and the federally funded Educational Opportunity Program [EOP]. The new Chicano students were active not only on campus but also in the town, as they tried to raise awareness of wider causes.

[59] Valdez Papers, LULAC file, copies of letters and press releases.
[60] Valdez Papers, LULAC file, newspaper clippings.
[61] Hays, "A Quiet Campaign of Education."

MAP and the arrival of new Chicano students

The Migrant Action Program was an experiment created around 1967 by Howard Higman and Bob Turner, faculty members at the University of Colorado.[62] Influenced by the philosophy of the OEO programs, they believed that many talented Latino children in Colorado who came from poor families and had gone to mediocre schools, especially the children of farm workers, could succeed in higher education if unnecessarily rigid admissions requirements were modified and if they received sufficient financial aid and good advising. MAP's organizers went out to recruit students, working initially with agricultural families in the San Luis Valley. The population of the Valley was overwhelmingly rural, and it had a low standard of living and very poor schools; few Latinas/os had finished high school. Soon MAP extended its program to students from other rural areas and to disadvantaged Latinas/os from urban communities, particularly Denver. MAP's representatives told prospective students that they could be accepted into the university without the usual requirements and would be given financial aid. Once on campus, they were supposed to receive extra academic and personal support. These recruitment efforts were highly successful. Between 1967 and 1969, the number of Latino students at Boulder rose from no more than 100 to about 500; by the summer of 1972, the program had recruited 950 students from throughout the state, though they did not all enroll.[63] The project was funded primarily by the EOP.

The students who arrived in Boulder through MAP and EOP had very different backgrounds than earlier Latinos. They were visually and socially different from their Anglo classmates at the university, and many of them hung together for support in an unwelcoming academic, economic, and cultural world that was unlike what they had previously known. A moving story about her acceptance and arrival at the university thanks to MAP was told by Cleo Jaramillo Estrada, who was a counselor in the multi-cultural advising center at the University of Colorado at Boulder in 2013, as she had been for many years.[64] Cleo grew up in Center, a small community in the San Luis Valley dominated by large

---

[62] Garcia, Richard, interview, 2013.

[63] Hernandez, Philip, interview, 2013; "UMAS y MEChA." Very few of these students show up in the *City Directory* listings, as they generally lived on campus.

[64] Estrada, Cleopatra, interview, 2013, and "Estrada, Cleo, autobiographical information" for this and the following paragraphs.

commercial farms owned by Anglos. Her grandparents had moved up from northern New Mexico, and her father was employed by the lumberyard, a good job by local standards. Her mother worked in the fields, as did Cleo and all of her seven siblings when they were not actually in school. They thinned and weeded lettuce in the spring and summer, hoed potatoes, and dug them up in the fall. In her interview, Cleo choked up when describing how, after an exhausting day of pulling up potatoes, when the children's backs ached so much they cried, her mother (whose back ached too) would give them all backrubs before she started cooking dinner for the family.

Cleo did very well in high school and hoped that one day she might be able to save up enough money to go to Adams State College, though no teacher or counselor at her school ever suggested that she could go to college. Adams State was in Alamosa, a town about 30 miles from Center where Cleo's family went once at the end of every summer to buy new shoes for the children to wear to school. In August, 1969, however, a few months after her high school graduation, Cleo was approached while working in the fields by her aunt Jenny Sanchez, a community organizer for an OEO program in Center. Jenny had heard that the University of Colorado had started a program of special scholarships for the children of farm workers and had nominated Cleo; she had just been notified that Cleo was accepted. "You are going to college," she announced, to Cleo's total surprise. In preparation, Cleo, who knew how to sew, made herself several dresses of the kind she had seen college girls in Alamosa wearing.

A few weeks later Jenny took Cleo to Boulder, where she registered and became a member of what was known on campus as MAP-EOP. Cleo was amazed at how undemanding her life as a university student was. She did not have to perform any physical work: all she was expected to do now was read, which she loved. "I started taking classes, and I thought, 'Man, this is so easy! If people even knew how hard it is to go from row to row [in the fields] all day long, but here you get to read a book." She called her mom with the astonishing news that she had maid service: Mexican women came into her dormitory room to sweep the floor, dust her dresser, and take the sheets. "Who knew that Boulder existed, and that people were treated like kings and queens here?"

Cleo experienced a different kind of culture shock when meeting Chicano students from other backgrounds. When she arrived on campus she was told that as her work-study job, she would be the secretary to a student group called UMAS. Cleo knew nothing about UMAS, so she put on one of her new dresses and walked over to its office. When she opened the door, petite Cleo found several "really big girls from Denver" wearing military fatigues staring at her! "They were kind of rough and tough, and they were scary!" One of them said, "Why're you wearing that cute little pink dress for?" Later they became good friends, and she was able to tell them, "'You guys scared the h--- out of me!' But way down deep inside they were just as scared as I was. Just that they were from Denver and I'm from the Valley. And they didn't speak Spanish, and they were kind of intimidated by my speaking Spanish." Gradually Cleo found that she could express her own opinions effectively, even though she came from a rural community, and that people paid attention to her suggestions and arguments.

Other MAP students entered the university in different ways. Ricardo Garcia had grown up in Monte Vista in the San Luis Valley but dropped out of high school.[65] His brother-in-law was one of the first people to come to the University of Colorado thanks to MAP, in 1968, and he kept telling Ricardo, who was married and working in Denver, to apply. When Ricardo finally submitted an application to MAP, he was accepted, provided that he get his GED first; he took a 5-hour exam and passed. He and his wife moved to Boulder, and he entered CU in the fall of 1970. Augustine Eliseo Cordova, who was likewise from the Valley and had not finished high school, was involved with activist groups there and in New Mexico and California for several years before he came to visit a brother in Boulder, learned about MAP, and applied to the university.[66]

MAP and EOP later affected some young Latinas/os living in the town of Boulder. The town's Latino residents had traditionally been sharply divided from the university, even though the Water + Goss Streets neighborhood where many of them lived lay just at the base of University Hill. Latino parents in Boulder generally wanted their children to go through middle school and ideally high school, but even bright students were not expected to go further. Boulder High School rarely placed Latino children into the college-preparatory track or advised them to continue into higher education.[67] Latinas/os might <u>work</u> for the university (often in unskilled jobs), but they did not <u>study</u> there. Virginia Maestas, who dropped out of school in the middle of ninth grade, remembered

---

[65] Garcia, Richard, interview, 2013; see also Ch. 6C above.
[66] Cordova, Augustine E., interview, 2013.
[67] See Vol. II, Ch. 6B.

looking wistfully up at the Hill in the early 1970s, knowing it was off-limits: college was for whites.[68] So it was a major change when diversity outreach programs on campus began to spill over into the surrounding community.

That impact is seen in the experience of Linda Arroyo-Holmstrom, who was raised in the Water + Goss Streets area. Her parents thought that finishing high school was important, and Boulder High had put her into a secretarial track.[69] But Linda's older sister Candy was dating a boy who worked for MAP on campus, and in 1972 he told Candy that she could apply to the university through that program and helped her to do so.[70] Linda decided that if her sister could go to CU-Boulder, so could she. After her acceptance into the university two years later, Linda took special MAP courses in the summer, to get her feet on the ground. From then on the program provided good advising and support but also close supervision. She lived at home, and once after she had been sick for several days, "Knock, knock, knock, somebody from the MAP program was at my door wanting to know why I wasn't in classes."

Some Latinas/os came to the university as mature students. Maria Dora Esquivel arrived in Boulder in 1972, together with her 16-year-old son David.[71] She became a leader in UMAS and after graduation continued to work on Chicano causes, building ties with the American Indian Movement, the rebels in Nicaragua, and the Communist Party. Esther Blazón, who finished high school only after her three children were born, graduated from CU in 1974, when her children were in elementary school.[72]

Student organizations

The new Chicano students at the university set up their own organizations, as was true on campuses throughout the Southwest.[73] UMAS was the first to form and initially the most active, but later other students formed a chapter of MEChA (*Movimiento Estudiantil Chicanos de*

[68] Conversation with Marjorie McIntosh, July 31, 2013.
[69] Arroyo-Holmstrom, Linda, interview, 2013.
[70] Candy studied in Mexico during her junior year and as a senior was a teaching assistant in an English class run for MAP students (Arroyo, Candace, interview, 1977).
[71] Young, David Atekpatzin, interview, 2013.
[72] "Esther Blazón and family, 1974," and see Ch. 6C above.
[73] For the Chicano student movement more generally and the role of the EOP, see Muñoz, *Youth, Identity, Power,* and Acuña, *Occupied America,* pp. 301-304, 310-313, and 341-345.

Aztlán), a national association. The groups at the University of Colorado had several goals: to provide a welcoming home and support for Chicano students; to put pressure on the university to make what they saw as necessary improvements; and to carry out educational activities and protests within the wider community. While the students agreed on the need to push for better treatment of Latinas/os, they did not agree on strategies: some supported the approach taken by Cesar Chavez and the farm workers in California, using strikes and peaceful mass protests, while other gravitated toward the more militant and occasionally violent approach of Corky Gonzales and the Crusade for Justice. *La Raza Unida* Party, founded in Texas in 1970 and later popular in Colorado too, opened the exciting possibility of a viable Chicano presence in politics.

Between 1969 and 1974, UMAS was very active at CU-Boulder.[74] The students demanded more scholarship funds for Latinas/os, better advising, more Chicano faculty members, and Chicano Studies courses. UMAS also organized protests against other kinds of racism—on campus and elsewhere—and against the Vietnam War. (For Chicano activists, the war was bad for two reasons: a disproportionate number of Latinos and other people of color were being drafted into the military and killed after being sent into high-risk settings; and the war was fought by what they regarded as a neo-colonial power against a nationalist movement organized by oppressed local people.)

Cleo Jaramillo became a committed member of UMAS, though she preferred not to give speeches but rather to make signs, bring food, and be sure people had the information they needed.[75] Shortly after arriving on campus she participated in the sit-in/take-over of the financial aid office to protest the shortage of scholarships for students of color and the late payment of the stipends on which many of these students relied; hundreds of other students were meanwhile demonstrating outside the building. After massive protests in 1972, the University expelled around 200 Chicano student activists. In spring, 1974, Cleo helped with UMAS's occupation of a building that housed all the university's affirmative action programs: MAP, the various other EOP units, and offices for UMAS, black students, Asian Americans, and Native Americans. The take-over, which caused no physical damage or harm to people but kept faculty and

---

[74] For film footage of Chicano student activism in Colorado, see "La Raza de Colorado: El Movimiento."

[75] Estrada, Cleopatra, interview, 2013.

staff members out of their offices, stemmed from UMAS's demands that the organization be allowed to handle its own finances and that the two administrators of the campus EOP be fired and replaced by people more responsive to the students' actual needs.

Augustine Eliseo Cordova, another active member of UMAS, focused on different projects: organizing boycotts, and providing music.[76] In their picketing, the students stood with signs outside stores in downtown Boulder and handed out literature explaining why people should refuse to shop there. They boycotted Safeway because the chain was selling lettuce and grapes, whereas the students were in solidarity with a lettuce workers' strike in Center and with Cesar Chavez and the grape workers' strike in California. They boycotted liquor stores, because they were selling California wines and Coors beer, the latter produced by a Colorado company that supported far right political causes and was thought to treat minority workers badly.

Augustine was also a musician, composing and writing songs, performing them with others, and taking part in the street theater events that UMAS students from Boulder presented on campuses all through the Southwest to raise public consciousness about Chicano issues. Two of his songs, "Yo Soy Chicano" and "Los Seis de Boulder," became anthems for the wider Chicano student movement.[77]

In these same years, student groups were agitating for change at Colorado State University in Fort Collins too. Edwina Salazar, later the director of Longmont's OUR Center for people living in poverty, was a student at Colorado State in 1968-1970, having previously worked in the defense industry in California.[78] She remembered that student radicals burned down the oldest building on campus, though she did not participate in that event, and she heard black civil rights leader Ralph Abernathy speak. Many protests and vigils were held on the campus: against the Vietnam War, when Martin Luther King was assassinated, and after the shooting of Kent State students in Ohio. Dr. Gregory Jaramillo, later the director of Salud Family Health Center in Longmont, was active

---

[76] Cordova, Augustine E., interview, 2013.
[77] Neither Cordova or the BCLHP could find old recordings of them, though a snippet from the latter was included in "La Raza de Colorado: El Movimiento." Augustine therefore kindly re-recorded his songs for the BCLHP, and they are now available on its website. For audios and English lyrics of the songs, see Sources, Pt. A below, under his name.
[78] Salazar, Edwina, interview, 2013.

Yo Soy Chicano
Words and Music by Augustine E. Cordova
©1977, 2014

Yo soy Chicano,
puro Chicano.
Si no les gusta,
pues a ver. . a ver. . a ver!
Tengo una historia,
llena de gloria.
Llevo en las venas,
la sangre de mi querer.

El nuevo mundo,
no me comprende.
Me llaman nombres,
otras cosas que no se.
Pero les digo,
cuidense amigos.
Porque el que no se cae hoy
ese cae manana.

Coro

Soy NUEVO Mexicano,
tambien soy de Tejas.
Soy de Arizona,
California. . . Colorado.
Soy campesino,
tambien vivo en las ciudades.
Por todo el mundo,
vivo y canto mi cancion.

Tengo enemigos,
y yo les digo.
Traigo la sangre bien caliente
no hagan pleito.
Yo soy Chicano,
puro Chicano.
Han de saber que vengo a ser,
si me hacen dano.

Yo soy Chicano,
puro Chicano.
No mido a nadie,
porque a mi me han de medir.
Desde el pasado,
me condenaron,
a ser esclavo pero no les consenti.

Illus. 7.1. Augustine E. Cordova, "Yo Soy Chicano," lyrics in Spanish

in UMAS and MEChA at Colorado State, where he was an undergraduate in the early 1970s.[79] Those groups supported the American Indian Movement, whose protest on the Pine Ridge reservation in South Dakota in 1973 developed into an armed standoff with U.S. Marshalls and the F.B.I. that lasted for 71 days and caused several deaths.

Former student activists at CU-Boulder looking back on the early 1970s highlighted the idealism and hope that permeated their organizations as they worked together toward important goals. Augustine Cordova noted that the members of UMAS had hot arguments about tactics.[80] But, he concluded,

> It was beautiful because we had community. There were so many of us there, and we had to fight for everything that we got, . . . but everybody was so involved and so together. . . . You didn't mind getting up on Saturday and going to a rally or a march or boycott . . . because it was community. You see your *compadres* over there and your friends, and some would bring food, and I was always there doing the music.

In an email about re-recording his two songs, Augustine wrote:

[79] Jaramillo, Gregory, interview, 2013.
[80] Cordova, Augustine E., interview, 2013.

It warms my heart to know you are using the music to portray the emotion of the times. We would sing at all gatherings. Marches, demonstrations, *teatro*. Music united us in a way that no other medium could. There were no disagreements when we were singing . . . we were one.[81]

Commenting also on how exciting the academic environment was (he was taking courses in history, geography, and sociology as well as computer science), Augustine concluded, "Boulder was an absolutely awesome experience. . . . For me, it doesn't get any better than that."[82]

Ricardo Garcia, who was selected as the student director of MAP in 1973, similarly recalled the energy and optimism of that period. "Man, it was such an exciting time when you go back and think about the Chicano Movement and all the different possibilities that could happen. The emotions that we all had for progress, for improvement and all of that."[83] He remembered the marches that UMAS organized down Broadway and the picketing and boycotts. When Corky Gonzales held a convention for *La Raza Unida* Party on the Boulder campus, the students hoped this was the beginning of a third party that would bring the concerns of Chicanos into public view. But Garcia also noted that "we were confronted with a lot of the racism and all the negative factors around trying to do a social movement in a pretty much all-white community where people didn't really understand."

Those negative factors were serious. The university and Boulder's police were alarmed by the degree of student militancy and organization. UMAS repeatedly presented demands to campus administrators, but the authorities generally refused even to meet with the students and certainly did not agree to the changes requested. In some cases, the university used force to break up protests—using its own police backed by city officers. Cleo remembered running across the campus, "and there would be tear gas thrown, and people would be screaming and yelling, and police were all over the place."[84] Chicano students were not the only ones upset, she said. "There was a lot of anger about everything, politically. Even the white students were angry, they called themselves anti-establishment. They were fighting against being pigeon-holed in

---

[81] Email sent to Marjorie McIntosh, March 14, 2014.
[82] Cordova, Augustine E., interview, 2013.
[83] He later used the English version of his first name: Garcia, Richard, interview, 2013.
[84] Estrada, Cleopatra, interview, 2013.

this 1950s model of just following the rules and being conservative." Cleo felt that in a longer perspective UMAS had forced the administration to examine its policies and procedures with respect to students of color and make gradual improvements.

Not all Latino students were part of or even necessarily in agreement with the aggressive stance of some Chicano militants. Phil Hernandez, who was the head of UMAS in the late 1960s, remembers walking into the office of the university's president, Joseph Smiley, and saying, "We want 2,000 Mexican American kids on campus next year, or you may not have a campus!"[85] Yet he later felt uncomfortable as UMAS became more radical, and he resented being treated with disrespect by some Chicano activists because he was too moderate. Susie Gomez Chacon, a mature student at CU in the 1970s who owned a restaurant in Boulder, thought that Latino students should not be pressured to join groups like MAP or UMAS.[86] She wanted to be able to pay her tuition and take whatever courses she chose, apparently not defining herself primarily as a Chicana.

The university's few Latino faculty members and even fewer low-level administrators were caught between intense Chicano students and the upper administration. Professors were commonly criticized vehemently by student groups if they did not back their demands, and administrators were accused of being sell-outs. Al Ramirez, hired by the university's Psychology Department as a beginning professor in 1971, later described the situation.[87] The university had suddenly accepted a large number of Latino students but was not prepared to deal with their self-definition as Chicanos or their demands and protests. The administration's refusal to negotiate intensified the conflict. Chicano professors found themselves in the middle, with no acceptable ground to stand on. Ramirez emphasized that the University of Colorado was a focal point for what became the wider Chicano movement of that period. Although people commonly stress Corky Gonzales and the strikes of high school students in Denver, Ramirez believed that it was in fact Boulder's Chicano student organizations that defined the key issues.

[85] Hernandez, Philip, interview, 2013, and conversation with Marjorie McIntosh, Sept. 25, 2013.
[86] Chacon, Susie, interview, 1977.
[87] Ramirez, Albert, interview, 2013, for this paragraph. See also his *Profe Files*, a slightly fictionalized account of the experiences of a Latino faculty member at the University of Colorado in the 1970s.

Los Seis de Boulder
Words and Music by Augustine E. Cordova
© 1974, 2014

Voy a cantar un corridor,
que. . . en Colorado paso.
Murieron Los Seis de Boulder,
dos noches en Mayo,
en Seteinta y Cuatro.

Era una noche ocupada,
cuando de pronto llego.
Ese bombaso hieloso,
como a las ocho,
tres vidas llevo.

Amenecio la manana,
alli en la sierra yo vi.
El alma de Neva Romero,
subiendo hacia el cielo,
sonriendo hasta el fin.

Coro
En este cielo de sierra,
de Colorado se ven.
Las almas de seis soldados,
seis fusilados,
seis hijos del bien.

Cuando se acabo la buya,
dos noches despues sucedio.
Murieron tres mas soldados,
tres mas fusilados,
Granados cayo.

Teran, Jacola, y Martinez,
Francisco Dougherty tambien.
Nunca seran olvidados,
siempre alabados,
soldados del bien.

La ley les dijo a la gente,
una mentira les dio.
Que murieron por su descuido,
que por su propio descuido,
la bomba exploto.
Coro

Illus. 7.2. Augustine E. Cordova, "Los Seis de Boulder," lyrics in Spanish

"Los Seis de Boulder"

On the night of May 27, 1974, 19 days into the UMAS take-over of the building on campus that housed the various minority programs, a bomb exploded in a car at Chautauqua Park on the edge of Boulder, killing three people.[88] Neva Romero, a 21-year-old junior at the university, was part of a coalition of students who had recently won election as heads of the University of Colorado's Associated Student Government; she was the first Latina to hold such office. Reyes Martinez, 26, a graduate of the university's Law School, was the attorney with El Centro Legal whom we have met before, and his girlfriend, Una Jaakola, 24, was a graduate of the university. Two nights later another car bomb went off in a parking lot in downtown Boulder. Those killed were Francisco Dougherty, 20, a Latino pre-med student from Texas, and two former UMAS leaders now working in the community (both also writers or artists): Heriberto Teran, 24, and Florencio Granado, 31. Antonio Alcantar, who was walking over to the car at the time, survived, though he lost a leg and was

[88] For this discussion, see "'Los Seis de Boulder' died in '74," "Los Seis de Boulder," Pts. I and II, KGNU radio, 2011, "Los Seis de Boulder" as aired nationally, 2011, and "Marchers Remember deaths of Los Seis." For Chautauqua Park in 2013, see "Boulder, film of places of historical importance."

severely burned. The Boulder police conducted a brief investigation and announced that the young people had been making bombs that exploded on them. Neva Romero, the report said, had been holding a bomb in her lap. The evidence taken by the police was then destroyed. A grand jury was later summoned to look into the bombings, but its findings were never announced and it produced no indictments.

Various explanations have been put forward about how and why the bombings occurred.[89] One theory suggests infiltration of the upper leadership of UMAS by the F.B.I.'s Counter Intelligence Program, whose charge was to weaken or destroy radical organizations. COINTELPRO, which is known to have had agents inside other activist groups in Colorado, may have placed representatives within UMAS as well, gathering information that allowed someone to plant bombs in or under the cars and thereby discredit the organization. Rapid destruction of the physical evidence by the police and the silence of the grand jury imply that information had been discovered that the government did not want made public. Some Chicano leaders believed that "Los Seis" were murdered as part of a conspiracy against their movement. A few people wondered if the bombs might have been planted by an opposing unit within the Chicano movement itself, such as a breakaway element of the Crusade for Justice.

It is conceivable that the young people had become so frustrated by the refusal of the authorities to accept their demands that they were indeed making bombs, but ones they planned to use against property, not people. Several bombs had gone off in Boulder during the previous three months, at night in empty but symbolic public buildings: the County Court House, the university's police station, and an elementary school where parents were demanding change. The perpetrators were never identified, though some people suspected the Weather Underground, an extreme left-wing group active in university towns throughout the county between 1971 and 1975 that placed bombs in various government buildings and banks elsewhere. Could Los Seis have been making bombs, perhaps encouraged to do so by COINTELPRO agents and using the deliberately defective material provided to them? Because the F.B.I. sometimes placed false information into the files of people it was tracking, we cannot trust the written evidence and will

[89] Even in 2013-14, "Los Seis" remained such a controversial topic among Latinos, with emotions still running so high, that several people who spoke with this author about what happened asked not to be named.

probably never be sure exactly what happened.[90] Nevertheless, to some Latinas/os then and now, "Los Seis" have been seen as martyrs.[91]

The deaths put a temporary damper on the Chicano student movement at the University of Colorado. Most UMAS students did not endorse physical violence.[92] They were frightened as well as angered by what had happened to people they liked and respected, especially because no one knew definitely how the explosions had occurred. UMAS continued to function, joined by MEChA, but its tactics became less directly confrontational. As was true in the local community, some student leaders decided that a certain degree of cooperation was more likely to yield long-term improvement for students of color, especially since some members of the university administration were now willing to work with them.

The contributions of CU-Boulder's Chicano student activists took two main forms. They did gradually persuade the university administration to make many of the changes they demanded. The campus had more Latino students and faculty members, a more diverse curriculum, and a somewhat more welcoming atmosphere in 1980 than it had in 1966. But of even greater importance is what leaders of MAP-EOP and UMAS gave to the state later in their lives. A remarkable number of them went into some kind of educational or community service work, in many cases becoming heads of their organizations. Their names appear in Colorado's political life too, led by Joe Garcia: he was active in UMAS as an undergraduate, went on to Harvard Law School, later became President of Colorado State University at Pueblo, and was elected Lieutenant Governor in 2010 and 2014. The long-term contributions of the Chicano student activists of the 1970s should be remembered and honored.

C. The Shootings in Longmont and Founding of El Comité, 1980

A tragic set of quick decisions by a rookie Anglo policeman led to the death of two young Latinos in Longmont in 1980. Late in the evening of August 14, an officer named John Davis stopped a car on Main Street

---

[90] E.g., the file of Leonard Peltier of the American Indian Movement.
[91] That view was the basis for a commemorative event held at Su Teatro in Denver in May, 2014, the 40th anniversary of the bombings.
[92] Augustine Cordova, conversation with Marjorie McIntosh, May 11, 2013.

for a minor infraction.[93] A second policeman, 22-year-old Glenn Herner, who had been in the force for only three months, was driving by at the time. When he heard the driver arguing with Davis, he pulled his car up behind Davis's. At that point, a Monte Carlo drove slowly past them, filled with young people who had left a wedding reception to get more ice for the party. The driver and three of the passengers were Latino. The other person in the front seat was an Anglo, who leaned out of the window and shouted at the policemen, "[Expletive] you, pigs!" Herner got in his car and set off after them, followed by Davis. When Herner stopped the Monte Carlo in a parking lot near 11th Avenue and Main Street, the driver offered his identification. Herner was only interested in the man who had shouted at him: "I want you with the big mouth," he said, pointing to the blond passenger. The latter got out of the car, but when he realized that Herner was going to issue him a ticket for harassment, he refused to show his ID and tried to leave the scene. Both Herner and Davis—who had now arrived—struggled to subdue him. The driver of the car and one of the other passengers left the scene.

But two of the men, both aged 21, stayed there to help their friend: Jeff "Beaver" Cordova, who had recently finished serving in the Army, and Juan Luis Garcia. In the fight that followed, Herner pulled his gun and shot Garcia in the chest, apparently because he thought the flashlight Garcia was holding was a weapon. Shortly afterwards, Davis fired a shot into the air, and Cordova began to run across Main Street. Herner, who did not see who fired the second shot, thought that Cordova had wounded Davis and was fleeing with his gun. He therefore took aim across the hood of his cruiser and shot Cordova in the back. Garcia died immediately, and Cordova died in the hospital a few hours later. Neither Cordova nor Garcia was armed.

The response of Longmont's Latino community to the shootings demonstrates how a tragic event can lead to constructive change. News of the deaths spread quickly in that town and the wider civil rights community. In the coming days local activists held meetings in the basement of St. John's Catholic Church and organized a candle-lit march, ending at city hall.[94] Large crowds attended the funerals of Cordova and

---

[93] The account in the next two paragraphs is based upon newspaper accounts and information from the inquest, hearing, and investigations that followed the shootings: "2 men shot by police," "100 protest in Longmont," "Inquest into shooting deaths," "Driver recalls night of shooting," and "One officer fired both bullets."

[94] "Sorrow, anger, hope fill meeting" and "Crowds bid farewell to victims."

Garcia. Emotions ran high among Anglos as well as Latinas/os. Tony Gomez was in junior high in Longmont at the time. He later recalled that shortly after the shootings he was "walking down the street and these white guys drove by and yelled at me, 'Too bad there weren't more of you f-----ing Mexicans killed.' That's what they said. They didn't scare me. I just went [middle-finger sign]."[95] Although some Anglo leaders rejected all criticism of the police and city officials, the events led to soul-searching among others. Even the normally conservative *Longmont Times-Call* published articles examining local biases against Latinos and deploring the city's lack of an affirmative action hiring policy.[96]

Latino community leaders attempting to deal with the situation formed a group that called itself "El Comité." El Comité immediately made three vital philosophical decisions, ones that shaped their actions over the coming months and years.[97] They committed themselves to using a non-emotional approach and rejecting violence; preventing militants from outside Longmont from inflaming the situation; and including a cross-section of the community in their work. Juan Luis Garcia's brother Frank went around Latino neighborhoods, encouraging people to use only peaceful forms of protest. El Comité's leaders turned down offers from outside groups (including the Crusade for Justice, the American Indian Movement, and the Communist Workers' Party) to come into Longmont to organize violent action. Tony Tafoya of El Comité responded to one of the groups, "If you burn down buildings, we'll be left with the ashes."

El Comité's efforts to interact constructively with Longmont's City Council and Police Department stemmed from its desire to establish long-term policies and procedures that would address a series of problems that had been building up over time and prevent similar tragedies from happening in the future. At the first negotiating session with city officials on August 17, just three days after the shooting, El Comité laid out its demands.[98] Charging that Longmont police officers commonly harassed Latinas/os, the group's list included a ride-along

---

[95] Gomez, Tony, interview, 2009.
[96] "Old friends, new faces," "Formal affirmative action plan lacking," and "Boulder 'affirmative action' aggressive."
[97] That approach was strongly recommended by one of El Comité's leaders, Tony Tafoya, then the Equal Opportunity Director for the National Oceanic and Atmospheric Administration in Boulder. The rest of this paragraph is from Tafoya's conversation with Marjorie McIntosh, Dec. 5, 2014.
[98] "El Comite presents list of demands."

program for civilians to go out with the police, a hotline for reporting incidents, and city-funded polygraphs (lie detector tests) for people who claimed they had been mistreated. The group asked also for an outside evaluation of the police and city administration and the appointment of a neutral person, hired by the city, to serve as an ongoing intermediary with the Latino community.

At the August 17 meeting, the city was represented by mayor Robert Askey, a councilman, the city manager, the city attorney, and Ed Camp, the Director of Public Safety, who was to be a strong ally of El Comité. Although some of the city's representatives said individually that certain of the demands could perhaps be met, they were unwilling to recommend to the City Council that they all be accepted. El Comité's chairman and vice chairman, Vic Vela and Dan Benavidez, accused the mayor and City Council of lack of good faith in refusing to negotiate with them directly.

To strengthen its bargaining position, El Comité defined itself more fully. By the end of August, its original officers had been joined by ten others, including teachers, government employees, an administrator with the Boulder County Youth Action Center, a secretary, and a restaurant owner.[99] Among them was Marta Moreno, described by the newspaper as "a housewife active in church and community activities." Due to its formal structure, the group was able to take a more unified and forceful stand.

But even with that change, El Comité lacked the power to compel Longmont to introduce the measures they sought. The group therefore turned to agencies of the U.S. government for help in persuading city officials to find out what had actually happened at the shootings, to get justice for those killed, and to develop better policies and procedures. During the two weeks after August 14, the *Times-Call* reported that first the U.S. Attorney General and then the F.B.I. had been asked to investigate the shootings.[100] Those inquiries apparently did not happen, but a different solution emerged through the U.S. Department of Justice [DOJ].

Within a few days after the shooting, the DOJ received more than 30 requests from Latino groups and individuals to send a representative to Longmont to act as a mediator.[101] The DOJ agreed, so that "tensions can

---

[99] "El Comite, City to focus on police-community relations." For Marta Moreno's role in church matters, see Vol. II, Ch. 5C.

[100] "U.S. Attorney General asked to investigate" and "FBI to investigate shootings."

[101] "FBI to investigate shootings."

be eased and the waters calmed." When Leo Cardenas, regional director of the Community Relations Service of the DOJ, arrived, he found that the Latino community had no faith in the goodwill of city officials or their commitment to introducing necessary changes. He learned also that the shootings came on top of a long series of lesser conflicts between the police and local Latinas/os, especially young people. He therefore sent Manuel Salinas and Art Montoya from his agency to attend and mediate all meetings between El Comité and the city or police.[102] Salinas said on August 26 that he would stay as long as both parties felt he was playing a meaningful part.

The DOJ's representatives remained in Longmont for another month. After extensive negotiations, a Document of Understanding was signed on September 23 between: (1) Robert Askey as mayor of the City of Longmont; (2) Vic Vela, Frank Garcia, and Dan Benavidez on behalf of El Comité; and (3) Manuel Salinas for the DOJ.[103] The agreement laid out the background to the tragedy and described the desire of all parties to foster "greater trust between the citizens of the Longmont Hispanic Community, the elected representatives and employees of the City, particularly those serving as police officers, and generally the entire populace of the City." It noted that the specific commitments it contained had been accepted by unanimous vote of the Longmont City Council. Those commitments were the same demands previously laid out by El Comité, though with provisions that allowed the city some degree of input and supervision. The agreement served its purpose of lessening tension and providing legitimate channels for reporting and addressing problems.

Thanks largely to El Comité's vigilance in responding quickly to potentially volatile situations, Longmont's Latinas/os kept the peace across the following year even at some difficult moments. Glenn Herner was tried for manslaughter in March, 1981. When he was acquitted, the Latino community was furious but again refused to resort to violence.[104] With the encouragement of other Latinas/os, El Comité set itself up as an ongoing association with three main purposes: to act as a

---

[102] "El Comite presents list of demands" and "El Comite, City to focus on police-community relations."

[103] "Document of understanding." This document was kindly made available to the BCLHP by Dan Benavidez. For his account of his own role after the shootings and his subsequent career in Longmont's government, see *For All the Wrong Reasons*, chs. 12-13.

[104] "Articles about Glenn Herner's acquittal."

negotiating body for Latino concerns; to improve the social, educational, and economic status of Latinas/os; and to facilitate communication and understanding between Latinos and non-Latinos.[105] The first anniversary of the shootings, in August, 1981, featured commemorations but no confrontations.[106] The *Times-Call* published an article describing El Comité's achievements and continued to report on the activities of the group in the following decades.[107]

Although some of the items to which the City of Longmont agreed in 1980 were no longer being honored as of the early 2010s, El Comité remained the town's leading Latino organization. In addition to providing practical assistance in the form of a food bank and helping people to find housing, it offered legal advice, ran citizenship classes, did voter registration, published monthly newsletters, and took over the Adult Education program when the St. Vrain Valley School District ran out of funds to support it. Its long serving head, Marta Moreno, was someone to whom Latinas/os knew they could turn for advice, whether they had been wrongly laid off from their job, lacked health insurance and could not obtain necessary medical care for their children, or had a teen-aged son who had been stopped by the police for a driving error and now faced deportation.

Although pressure for reforms by local Latinas/os did not end in 1980, its intensity died down and it commonly took somewhat different forms. Chicano leaders in Boulder County had taken important steps during the later 1960s and 1970s by creating a positive, socially engaged Chicano identity and working for better treatment for all Latinas/os. Chicano students at the University of Colorado had brought issues of national and local concern to the attention of local residents and had helped to make the university more diverse and welcoming to students and faculty of color. The shootings in Longmont and El Comité's response provide a model for how a tragic episode can be turned into an opportunity for lasting community improvement. Latinas/os of the early twenty-first century enjoy many of the benefits their predecessors worked so hard to achieve.

[105] "El Comite seeks permanent status," Tafoya, conversation with McIntosh, Dec. 5, 2014, and a PowerPoint presentation prepared by El Comité in May, 2002, which summarizes its history (kindly given to the BCLHP by Tony Tafoya).

[106] "Shooting anniversary passes without incident."

[107] "El Comite's first-year accomplishments," "*Longmont Times-Call* index entries, El Comite," and "*Longmont Times-Call* index entries, Marta Moreno." For El Comité's building in 2013, see "Longmont, film of places of historical importance."

Epilogue

Boulder County's Latinas/os in the Early 2010s

Before ending this historical account of Latinas/os in Boulder County, we will jump forward in time to look very briefly at immigration patterns after 1980 and present some quantitative information from the early 2010s. The number of Latinas/os in the county as a whole increased substantially in the decades around 2000. Whereas in 1990, they numbered 15,405 (6.8% of the total population), by 2010, there were 39,276 Latino residents, forming 13.3% of the total.[1] Much of that growth came from the arrival of newcomers. An assessment done in 2011 found that only 43% of local Latinas/os of all ages had been born in Colorado.[2] Another 21% had moved here from other U.S. states or territories, and 36% were foreign born. At that time, 50% of the county's Latino adults were native born U.S. citizens; 12% were naturalized citizens; and the remaining 38% were not citizens (some documented, some not).[3]

In the early 2010s, Boulder County's Latino community was not only larger, it was more complex. The divisions visible in the late 1960s and 1970s had become even more pronounced, with identifiable sub-groups based upon length of time in the U.S., country of origin, educational and economic status, religious and family patterns, and ethnic/cultural self-identification. Jorge de Santiago, director of El Centro AMISTAD, a non-profit organization in Boulder that works with recent immigrants, distinguished between three main groups of foreign-born Latinas/

---

[1] In 2000, 30,456 people constituted 10.5% of the total (for 1990, "Population Estimates Program, Population Division, U.S. Census Bureau"; for 2000 and 2010, "American FactFinder, U.S. Census Bureau").

[2] *Boulder County TRENDS 2013*, p. 39. Of Anglo residents, 33% had been born in Colorado.

[3] Calculated from *Boulder County TRENDS 2013*, p. 41.

os, depending primarily upon when they had arrived here.[4] The first consisted of immigrants who had been in Boulder County since at least the 1970s. These people, who sometime termed themselves "Chicanos" to separate themselves from newer arrivals, came mainly from Mexico but now thought of themselves as Americans. Well adapted to life in the U.S. and usually enjoying permanent resident status or citizenship, they differed little from Latino residents whose families had lived in this area for far longer. The second group had immigrated between around 1980 and 2000. Although some moved from Mexico, many came from other countries, especially El Salvador, Nicaragua, Guatemala, and Honduras, where war, violence, and political danger forced people to leave.[5] By 2013, Latinas/os in this category had generally learned how to function adequately in the American setting, their children received good educations, and some had become legal residents through the 1986 Amnesty Law.[6]

Very different were the lives of people in the third group, those who had been here for less than ten years. Although a few moved from Latin American countries to study or for personal reasons, bringing with them the necessary papers and some economic backing, most came from Mexico and arrived with no resources except their willingness to work. Often moving as family groups and lacking formal documentation, these immigrants lived in fear of being arrested and deported. They were hesitant to make use of government-provided social services or legal protection lest they be reported to Immigration and Customs Enforcement. Their children went to school, but the parents—who generally spoke little if any English—had an insecure existence, isolated in many respects from other local residents.

The three towns discussed in this book, which had such contrasting histories in the earlier twentieth century, continued to differ in 2010. Their widely divergent economic situations created dissimilar living and working environments for Latino families. If we use the median family income of all residents as a rough guide, Boulder emerges as by

---

[4] Conversation with Marjorie McIntosh, March 14, 2013, for this and the following paragraph.

[5] See, more generally, *Acuña, Occupied America*, pp. 354-356.

[6] The Immigration Reform and Control Act (IRCA) of 1986 made it illegal to hire undocumented immigrants and required employers to determine their workers' immigration status, but it also granted legal status to about 3,000,000 immigrants who lacked formal permission to live and work in this country.

far the wealthiest community ($113,700), though that average conceals pockets of real poverty.[7] Lafayette was next ($79,200), thanks to the construction of expensive new housing on the outskirts of town over the past 30 years. Longmont lagged behind ($58,000), due to more affordable housing and a heavier concentration of recent immigrants. The percentage of Latinas/os in the towns also varied considerably. According to the 2010 Census, in Longmont, 21,850 Latinas/os formed 25% of the total population; in Lafayette, 4,350 Latinas/os formed 17%; but in Boulder, 8,950 Latinas/os formed just 9%.[8] Because the Latino population included a higher proportion of children than did the Anglo community, they constituted somewhat larger percentages of the enrolment in the two school districts that serve Boulder County.[9]

Some analyses have compared Latinas/os here with other groups. Local Latinas/os were hardworking and comparatively well educated. In 2011, 72% of the county's Latinas/os aged 16 or over (whether documented or not) were engaged in the labor force, as compared to 70% for the total population.[10] They were also better educated than Latinas/os in Colorado as a whole or nationally. In 2011, 24% of local Latino adults had at least a bachelor's degree, well above the 13% found nationally.[11] But they lagged behind the figures of 58% with bachelor's degrees among the total population of Boulder County and 36% for all residents of Colorado. High dropout rates among Latino school children may suggest problems in the future. In 2012, only 67% of Latino children in the St. Vrain Valley School District graduated from high school within four years, as compared to 86% for Anglos; in the Boulder Valley School District, 78% of Latino students graduated as compared to 93% for Anglos.[12]

---

[7] App. 1.1. In Boulder, 14% of children lived in poverty; in Lafayette, 24%; and in Longmont, 18% (*Boulder County TRENDS 2013*, p. 57).

[8] *Boulder County TRENDS 2013*, p. 14.

[9] In fall, 2012, Latino students accounted for 17% of the total enrollment in the Boulder Valley District, which includes Boulder and Lafayette plus other towns; in the St. Vrain Valley District, including Longmont, Latinas/os formed 28% of the total (*Boulder County TRENDS 2013*, p. 87).

[10] *Boulder County TRENDS 2013*, p. 40. In 2010, the Pew Hispanic Trust estimated that 180,000 undocumented people were living in Colorado, of whom 108,000 (60%) were working, representing 5% of the state's total workforce but taking home less than 3% of the total earnings. Those 108,000 workers created 91,000 additional jobs that had not existed previously (*Boulder County TRENDS 2011*, p. 11).

[11] *Boulder County TRENDS 2013*, p. 40. For below, see ibid., p. 87.

Despite their high level of employment, Latinas/os were disadvantaged economically. The median household income for this county's Latinas/os in 2011 was only half of that for Anglos: $35,600 instead of $70,100.[13] Just 44% of them owned their homes, as opposed to renting, and that proportion was dropping.[14] Only 54% of Latinas/os had health insurance in 2011-12, as compared with 87% of Anglos.[15] Just 68% of Latinas/os ranked their health as good or excellent, as compared with 92% of Anglos.[16] A particularly troubling figure was that 35% of Latino children were living in poverty in 2011, as compared with just 14% for all children.[17]

Although overt discrimination—such as the threat of violence under the KKK and "White Trade Only" signs—had ended long ago, many Latinas/os still felt that they were not entirely welcome in the community and were not treated on an equal basis with Anglos. An assessment conducted in 2013 by the Latino Task Force of Boulder County, the follow-up to a similar study done in 2001, was based on questionnaire information from 386 Latino respondents plus some interviews and focus group discussions.[18] Participants drew attention to Latino contributions to the county, such as the rise in the proportion of respondents who owned their own business, up from 9.5% in 2001 to 14.4% in 2012.[19]

But the assessment also highlighted the need for improvement. Discrimination emerged as the third most common area of concern, following employment and education.[20] Fewer than one-quarter of the Latino questionnaire respondents felt that Boulder County was a good place for immigrants or racial/ethnic minorities.[21] Although

---

[12] Ibid., p. 23.

[13] Ibid., p. 59. The Latino income was also lower than the average of $40,800 for all Latinas/os in the U.S.

[14] *2013 Boulder County Latino Community Assessment*, p. 14, figures from the 2010 and 2000 U.S. Censuses.

[15] *Boulder County TRENDS 2013*, p. 88.

[16] Ibid., p. 46.

[17] Ibid., p. 89. The Latino figure had risen from 23% in 2000. The federal poverty guideline in 2011 was $22,350 for a family of four (ibid., inside front cover). Poverty was growing faster in Boulder County than for the U.S. as a whole (ibid., p. 57).

[18] *2013 Boulder County Latino Community Assessment; 2001 Latino Task Force of Boulder County Community Assessment.*

[19] *2013 Boulder County Latino Community Assessment*, p. 7.

[20] *Boulder County TRENDS 2013*, p. 40, and see *2013 Boulder County Latino Community Assessment*, pp. 11-16.

most respondents believed that progress in combatting racism was being made, a majority said they themselves had been discriminated against because they are Latino; they disagreed with the statement that Latinas/os are treated the same as everyone else within the community. In discussions, people referred to negative stereotypes and "subtle but painful" treatment based on the color of their skin, the way they spoke, or their ethnicity; they gave examples both of discrimination by individuals and of institutional practices that made them feel unwelcome or imposed barriers to full participation.[22] More than two-thirds of the respondents felt that the police were more likely to stop them because they were Latino.[23] Relationships with the criminal justice system were especially difficult for undocumented immigrants. Boulder County has work to do.

Whereas Latinas/os were barely visible in previous histories of Boulder County, this study makes clear that they helped to shape the nature of the community in many ways between 1900 and 1980. Their stories form an essential component of our knowledge of the past, as this chronological analysis has shown. The companion volume examines social and cultural aspects of local people's lives across that span and highlights the legacies left by earlier Latinas/os to people living in Boulder County in the early twenty-first century.[24]

This book adds to our understanding of the place of Latinas/os with respect to several topics of concern to American and Colorado historians more generally. They include migration, labor patterns, racism and discrimination, the impact of wars and veterans, and civil rights activity. Of the four interpretive questions explored in the study, three have been addressed directly in the present volume.[25] In considering the roles, experiences, and contributions of women, a subject discussed also in the other book, we have seen how their unpaid labor at home or in the fields formed a necessary part of their family's economic position,

---

[21] *2013 Boulder County Latino Community Assessment*, p. 16. For below, see ibid., pp. 15-16.

[22] *Boulder County TRENDS 2013*, p. 40.

[23] *2013 Boulder County Latino Community Assessment*, p. 15.

[24] McIntosh, *Latinos of Boulder County, Colorado, 1900-1980*, Vol. II, *Lives and Legacies*.

[25] The remaining theme, family relationships, is discussed primarily in Vol. II, Chs. 1, 3, 4A-B, and 5B.

supplementing their husband's earnings. We have noted their increasing role as paid workers in the public economy and their contributions to the community, such as participation in OEO organizations and civil rights activity.

Another issue is how patterns in Boulder County compared with those of communities that lay closer to the heart of the U.S.-Mexican borderlands or that contained large Latino populations. As will be pursued further in the second volume, the experiences of Boulder County's Latinas/os, living on the outer margin of the borderlands in towns dominated numerically, economically, and culturally by Anglos, differed in some key respects from those of people in more heavily Latino settings. In the 1940s and 1950s, Hispanics in Boulder County rarely formed organizations working for the betterment of all Spanish-speaking people, promoted by middle class, educated leaders. Such activity became common here only in the later 1960s and 1970s. The unwillingness of the leaders of community civil rights organizations in this setting to resort to militant tactics during the 1970s and in 1980 contrasted with the more radical approach of some Chicano groups elsewhere. Boulder County residents participated to a limited extent in a local Hispanic/Latino network. They had some cultural and religious contacts with people in Denver and agricultural Fort Lupton, especially during the first half of the twentieth century, and they interacted at least occasionally with groups based in Denver during the period of Chicano activism.[26]

A final question is how Latinos in Boulder County defined themselves, how they created an ethnic identity. We have observed the fluidity of terminology and described how a few young people from established families tried in the 1950s and early 1960s to formulate an identity that justified their efforts to succeed within an Anglo-dominated public world while at the same time continuing to value aspects of their Latino heritage. In that period, some Latinos felt embarrassed or even shamed by aspects of their own culture, rejections that the Chicano movement of the later 1960s and 1970s tried to overcome. Chicano activists delighted in their ethnicity and wanted to make their traditions visible. They worked to pull together the various elements of the Spanish-background community into a more unified group, one that could fight effectively against racism and discrimination and achieve reforms that

---

[26] For the former, see Vol. II, Chs. 4B and 5A.

would benefit all Latinos. But although they engaged at times with Hispanics/Latinos in other nearby communities, those ethnic ties did not outweigh a desire to create an accepted place within predominantly Anglo Boulder County.

As late as 2014, some highly visible and effective Latino leaders commented that when they were operating in the Anglo world, they had to submerge parts of who they really were. Even when they did, they commonly felt they were not fully respected or given credit for their accomplishments. Conversely, they were at times troubled personally or chastised by others for not maintaining their Latino heritage with sufficient commitment. We may hope that knowing more about the struggles and contributions of earlier Latinas/os to the county in which they live, information based upon sources produced and gathered by local people themselves, will help to strengthen Latinas/os' positive identity and their determination to gain full rights and recognition within the community.

Appendix 1.1

Total Population Figures, Three Towns and County, U.S. Census Data, 1900-2010

Year	Boulder (town)	Lafayette	Longmont	Boulder County
1900	6,150	970	2,201	21,544
1910	9,539	1,802	4,256	30,330
1920	11,066	1,815	5,843	31,861
1930	11,223	1,842	6,029	32,456
1940	12,958	2,062	7,406	37,438
1950	19,999	2,090	8,099	48,296
1960	37,718	2,612	11,489	74,254
1970	66,870	3,498	23,209	131,889
1980	76,685	9,014	42,942	189,625
1990	83,312	14,548	51,555	226,374
2000	94,673	23,197	71,093	271,651
2010	97,385	24,453	86,270	294,567

Median family income of all residents, 2009-2011			
$113,681	$79,212	$58,037	$70,572

Source: U.S. Censuses, 1900-2010

Appendix 1.2

Minimum Number of Latino-Surnamed Adults, Three Towns, 1900-1975

	Longmont		Lafayette		Boulder		Total	
	U.S. Census	City Directory	U.S. Census	City Directory	U.S. Census	City Directory	U.S. Census	City Directory
1900	0		0		4		4	
1904		2		0		6		8
1910	17		0		0		17	
1916		44		18		3		65
1920	83		25		2		110	
1926		58		17		8		83
1930	230		79		8		317	
1936		206		132		85		423
1940	249		91		36		376	
1946		206		184		127		517
1955		418		269		245		932
1965		465		337		417		1,219
1975		1,111		444		987		2,542

Appendix 1.2, continued

Minimum Number of Latino-Surnamed Adults, Three Towns, 1900-1975

<u>Notes and Sources</u>:   For the middle years of each decade through 1955, this table shows the number of adults (age 18 and up) with Latino surnames listed in *Polk's Boulder City Directory*. For 1965 and 1975, information comes from *Polk's Boulder* and *Longmont City Directories*. The count includes some college students.

For the years ending in -00 for Lafayette and Boulder between 1900 and 1940, the table shows the number of Latino adults living in Latino-surnamed households as listed in the U.S. Censuses. It is an under-count, as it does not include variant spellings of Latino surnames (from Ancestry.com; see "Information about Latino-Surnamed Households in U.S. Census Records for Lafayette" and "Information about Latino-Surnamed Households in U.S. Census Records for Boulder").

For the years ending in -00 for Longmont between 1900 and 1940, the table shows the number of all Latino-surnamed adults listed in the U.S. Census, regardless of the ethnicity of their household heads. It is a full count, based on detailed analysis of the Census returns by Rebecca Chavez ("Information about All Latinos in U.S. Census Records for Longmont").

Appendix 2.1

Birthplace of Latino Adults, Three Towns, U. S. Census Data, 1900-1940 *

Year	Longmont: full information				Boulder: partial information			
	1910	1920	1930	1940	1910	1920	1930	1940
No. of households with Latino-surnamed head	2	13	37	41	0	1	3	14
No. of households with any Latino residents	6	31	79	103				
Total no. of Latino adults recorded	17	82	232	250	0	2	6	28
Place of birth (if known)								
Men (age 18 +)								
Colorado	4	8	52	79		1	1	5
Mexico	5	30	50	22			2	4
New Mexico	1	1	31	33				3
Texas		1		5				1
Other U.S. state		2		3				1
Spain								
Total men listed	10	42	133	142	0	1	3	14
Women (age 18+)								
Colorado	4	13	48	63		1	1	6
Mexico	3	24	24	16			2	3
New Mexico		1	26	20				4
Other U.S. state		2	1	9				1
Total women	7	40	99	108	0	1	3	14

* No one with a Latino surname was listed in the 1900 Census records for Longmont or Lafayette; the Boulder Census recorded one unmarried man and one family.

Lafayette: partial information				Total			
1910	**1920**	**1930**	**1940**	**1910**	**1920**	**1930**	**1940**
0	13	29	40	2	27	69	95
0	22	56	76	17	106	294	354
	3	15	20	4 = 40%	12 = 22%	68 = 41%	104 = 54%
	6	9	7	5 = 50%	36 = 67%	61 = 37%	33 = 17%
		4	10	1 = 10%	1 = 2%	35 = 21%	46 =24%
			2		1 = 2%	2 = 1%	6 = 3%
					2 = 4%		4 = 2%
		2			2 = 4%		
0	11	30	37	10	54	166	193
	6	11	24	4 = 57%	20 = 38%	60 = 47%	93 = 58%
	3	5	5	3 = 43%	27 = 52%	31 = 24%	24 = 15%
	2	8	9		3 = 6%	34 = 27%	33 = 20%
		2	1		2 = 4%	3 = 3%	11 = 7%
0	11	26	39	7	52	128	161

Notes and Sources: See App. 1.2.

Appendix 2.2

Latino-Surnamed Children in School Censuses, Longmont, 1905-1964

	1905	1915	1925
Total number of children aged 6-21 enrolled			
Boys	715 = 49%	840 = 48%	1,164 = 52%
Girls	738	901	1,071
Total	1,453	1,741	2,235
Number of Latino-surnamed children aged 6-21			
Boys	2 = 20%	4 = 33%	25 = 47%
Girls	8	8	27
Total	10	12	52
Latino % of all children enrolled	0.7%	0.7%	2%
No. of Latino households with children in school	4	7	27
Birthplace of Latino-surnamed children	not given	not given	
Colorado			37 = 71%
New Mexico			11 = 21%
Elsewhere in the United States			
Texas			
California			
Wyoming			
Other U.S. state			3
U.S. but unspecified			
Total, elsewhere in the U.S.			3 = 6%
Mexico			
Unspecified			1 = 2%
Total			52

1935	1945	1955	1964
1,430 = 50%	1,162 = 51%	1,388 = 52%	2,930 = 51%
1,426	1,120	1,307	2,847
2,856	2,282	2,695	5,777
71 = 44%	111 = 49%	118 = 44%	282 = 51%
91	117	148	268
162	228	266	550
6%	10%	10%	10%
72	about 105	about 120	about 250
120 = 74	182 = 80%	208 = 78	439 = 80%
16 = 10%	29 = 13%	40 = 15%	65 =12 %
10	3	7	17
		2	7
2	4	1	10
3	9	4	10
		2	1
15 = 9%	16 = 7%	16 = 6%	45 = 8%
4 = 2%	1 = 0 %		1 = 0%
7 = 4%		2 = 1%	
162	228	266	550

Sources: "Latino-surnamed children in Longmont schools" for 1905-1935; later information from Census books, LM, St. Vrain Valley School District Records.

Appendix 2.3

Latino-Surnamed Children in School Censuses, Lafayette and Boulder, 1915-1955

	Lafayette				Boulder		
	1915	1925	1935	1944	1935	1944	1955
Total number of children aged 6-21 enrolled							
Boys	380 = 51%	438 = 52%	499 = 53%	435 = 50%	1,751 = 50%	1,861 = 51%	2,041 = 51%
Girls	368	399	450	433	1,731	1,822	1,964
Total	748	837	949	868	3,482	3,683	4,005
Number of Latino-surnamed children aged 6-21							
Boys	27 = 47%	50 = 49%	98 = 46%	130 = 48%	25 = 56%	48 = 46%	56 = 50%
Girls	30	53	115	142	20	56	55
Total	57	103	213	272	45	104	111
Latino % of all children enrolled	8%	12%	22%	31%	1%	3%	3%
No. of Latino households with children in school	21	24	33	65	19	40	47

Birthplace of Latino-surnamed children	Lafayette				Boulder		
	1915	1925	1935	1944	1935	1944	1955
children	not given						
Colorado		65 = 63%	195 = 92%	249 = 92%	38 = 84%	93 = 89%	109 = 98%
New Mexico		8 = 8%	11 = 5%	16 = 6%	7 = 16%		
Elsewhere in the United States							
Texas			4	2			
Wyoming		1	1	3			1
Other U.S. states		3	1			10	
U.S. but unspecified				2			
Total, elsewhere in the U.S.		4 = 4%	6 = 3%	7 = 3%	0	10 = 10%	
Mexico		7 = 7%	1			1 = 1%	1 = 1%
Spain		3 = 3%					
Unspecified		17 = 16%					
Total		104	213	272	45	104	111

Sources: "Latino-surnamed children in Lafayette schools, 1915, 1925, 1935, and 1944," and "Latino-surnamed children in Boulder schools, 1935, 1944, and 1955."

Note: Entries for Boulder were generally consolidated into one book per year, whereas those for Lafayette were entered into separate books by sub-district.

Appendix 2.4

Birthplace of Parents of Latino-Surnamed Children in School Censuses, Three Towns, 1925 and 1935

Birthplace of parents	Longmont 1925 fathers	mothers	Longmont 1935 fathers	mothers	Lafayette 1925 fathers	mothers	Lafayette 1935 fathers	mothers	Boulder 1935 fathers	mothers
Colorado	7 = 26%	14 = 52%	25 = 37%	30 = 45%						
New Mexico	5 = 19%	8 = 30%	20 = 30%	17 = 25%						
Other U.S. state	1 = 4%	1 = 4%	4 = 6%	4 = 6%						
Total U.S.	13 = 48%	23 = 85%	49 = 73%	51 = 76%	23 = 70%	23 = 70%	47 = 78%	51 = 85%	17 = 89%	17 = 89%
Mexico	13 = 48%	3 = 11%	18 = 27%	14 = 27%	9 = 27%	9 = 27%	13 = 22%	9 = 15%	2 = 11%	2 = 11%
Other/unspecified	1 = 4%	1 = 4%		2 = 3%	1 = 3%	1 = 3%				
Total number of parents with stated birthplaces	27	27	67	67	33	33	60	60	19	19

Sources: See Apps. 2.2 and 2.3.

Appendix 3.1

Birthplace of Latino-Surnamed Farm Workers and Coal Miners, Longmont and Lafayette, U.S. Census Data, 1920 to 1940

	1920			1930			1940		
	Sugar beet workers	General/ unspecified farm workers	Coal miners	Sugar beet workers	General/ unspecified farm workers	Coal miners	Sugar beet workers	General/ unspecified farm workers	Coal miners
Adult men (age 18 +)									
Colorado		3	1	22	15	10	5	23	15
Mexico	15	7	6	36	7	4	12	3	5
New Mexico				17	9	4	4	6	3
Other U. S. state		1				2	3	1	
Spain			2						
Total men	15	11	9	75	31	20	24	33	23
Adult women (age 18+)									
Colorado				5		1			
Mexico			1	2			1		
New Mexico				3	1				
Other U.S. state				1					
Total women			1	11	1	1	1		

<u>Sources</u>: See App. 1.2.

Appendix 3.2

Occupations, Three Towns, U.S. Census Data, 1900 to 1940

	Longmont (full info)				Lafayette (partial info)			Boulder (partial info)				
	1910	1920	1930	1940	1920	1930	1940	1900	1910	1920	1930	1940
No. of households with Latino-surnamed head	2	13	37	41	13	29	40	2	0	1	3	14
No. of households with any Latino residents listed	6	31	79	103								
	All workers of both sexes				Adult men (age 18 +)			Adult men (age 18 +)				
Lawyer (born in Spain)	1											
Agriculture												
Farmer/farm owner	1	3	5	2	1	2	1	1				
Contractor (for beet fields)		4					1					
Farm laborer												
In beet fields	4	13	131	25								
General/unspec/other		13	28	35		11	3					1
Sheep herder			1									
Teamster		1	1									
Mining and factory work												
Coal miner/coal worker		1	9	8	9	12	15				2	2
Coal mine supervisor				1								
Laborer, Sugar Factory		4	1									
Boss/foreman, Sugar Factory		3										

	Longmont (full info)				Lafayette (partial info)			Boulder (partial info)				
	1910	1920	1930	1940	1920	1930	1940	1900	1910	1920	1930	1940
Laborer; odd jobs/general	6	2	11	17								
Domestic services												
Domestic laborer	1		4	4								
Laundry worker	1	1	1									
Cook	3	3		1								
Nurse maid			1									
Other												
"Agent"										1		
Truck driver											1	1
Artist												1
Auto mech/motor engnr						1						1
Billiard hall operator			1									
Construction							2					
Railroad worker	1	2		1								
Lumber yard				2								
Linotype operater, newspaper				1								
Fireman				1								
Sales				1								
Government worker (some duplication with other categories)												
Roads/highways/streets				19			6					3
Water projects/pipelines				7								
Reforestation				3								
Bldg. construction/masonry				3								
Ditch work				2								
Parks				2								

Appendix 3.2, continued

Occupations, Three Towns, U.S. Census Data, 1900 to 1940

	Longmont (full info)				Lafayette (partial info)			Boulder (partial info)				
	1910	1920	1930	1940	1920	1930	1940	1900	1910	1920	1930	1940
City sanitarium				1								
Works Progress Administration												
City/county streets				3								
City government				1								
Golf course				1								
Plaster mixer				1								
Seamstress/sewing project				4								
Civilian Conservation Corps				3								
Total, government workers				49								
Retired							1					
Unemployed												3
Total, all workers (Longmont)	14	48	196	135								
Total, partial listing, adult male workers (Lafayette and Boulder)					10	26	30	1	0	1	3	12

	Longmont (full info)				Lafayette (partial info)			Boulder (partial info)				
	1910	1920	1930	1940	1920	1930	1940	1900	1910	1920	1930	1940
Adult women (age 18 +)												
Farm laborer: general/unspecified							1					1
Laundry/ironing services						1						
Cook/cook's helper					1							
Total, partial listing, adult female workers (Lafayette and Boulder)					1	1	1	0	0	0	0	1

Sources: See App. I.2, plus further information for Longmont (with thanks) from Rebecca Chavez, "Making Them Count," App. G.

Appendix 3.3

Summary, Occupational Analysis of Latino-Surnamed Adults, Three Towns Combined, *Polk's City Directories, 1926-1975*

	1926	1936	1946	1955	1965	1975
A. Officials and Managers	0	0	0	0	4 = 1%	9 = 1%
B. Professionals	0	0	2 = 1%	11 = 3%	37 = 8%	101 = 11%
C. Paraprofessionals	0	0	2 = 1%	0	5 = 1%	29 = 3%
D. Small Business Owners/ Managers	0	3 = 2%	4 = 2%	5 = 2%	7 = 1%	27 = 3%
E. Administrative Support/ Sales	1 = 5%	1 = 1%	4 = 2%	19 = 6%	28 = 6%	58 = 6%
F. Technicians	0	0	0	1 = 0%	7 = 1%	31 = 3%
G. Skilled Craft Workers	0	3 = 2%	7 = 3%	39 = 12%	74 = 15%	94 = 10%
H. Machine Operators	0	2 = 2%	4 = 2%	14 = 4%	45 = 9%	176 = 19%
I. Protective Service Workers/Military	0	0	67 = 27%	29 = 9%	9 = 2%	8 = 1%
J. Service Workers	2 = 10%	10 = 8%	28 = 11%	35 = 11%	97 = 20%	154 = 17%
K. Laborers and Helpers	17 = 81%	106 = 83%	128 = 52%	164 = 49%	153 = 31%	138 = 15%

	1926	1936	1946	1955	1965	1975
L. Others/Employees, type of work unspecified (probably unskilled laborers in most cases)	1 = 5%	3 = 2%	1 = 0%	15 = 5%	22 = 5%	78 = 9%
Total number of workers listed	21	128	246	332	488	903
No. and % of all workers who were female	1 = 5%	9 = 7%	33 = 13%	83 = 25%	99 = 21%	201 = 22%
Total number of students listed	1	24	16	60	63	247
No. of retired people listed					32	114

Sources: For breakdown by individual towns, see "Summary, Occupational Analysis of Latino-Surnamed Adults, Lafayette, 1926-1975," "Summary, Occupational Analysis of Latino-Surnamed Adults, Longmont, 1926-1975," and "Summary, Occupational Analysis of Latino-Surnamed Adults, Boulder, 1926-1975." Detailed information by year is given in "Occupations and Employers of Latino-Surnamed Adults, Three Towns, 1926, 1936, 1946, 1955, 1965, and 1975."

List of Illustrations, with Credits

All images listed below that have a reference number beginning with "BCLHP" are available online at the Boulder County Latino History website:

http://bocolatinohistory.colorado.edu/

Go to the Search page and type the BCLHP reference into the box labelled "Search by ID."

2.1. Espinoza family portrait, 1912, probably in northern New Mexico. Courtesy of Gilbert Espinoza. BCLHP-FP-089.

2.2. Engagement announcement, Pedro and Merenciana Chavez, aged 20 and 17 in 1911, probably northern New Mexico or southern Colorado. Courtesy of Mary Ellen Chavez. BCLHP-MKM-778.

2.3. Farm workers with mules, with adobe building in background, probably northern New Mexico or southern Colorado. Courtesy of El Comité de Longmont. BCLHP-LHS-495.

2.4. Large group at a traditional wedding, with musicians, probably northern New Mexico or southern Colorado. Courtesy of El Comité de Longmont. BCLHP-LHS-225.

2.5. Clefos and Apolonia Vigil, from northern New Mexico but living in Alamosa, Colorado, 1930s. Courtesy of Thomas Martinez. BCLHP-FP-141.

2.6. Covered wagon (with old car) like those used by Latino migrants, 1910s, in Nebraska. Courtesy of National Archives. Photo no. 30-N-9006. http://www.archives.gov/research/american-west/images/042.jpg

3.1. Vertical rows in a sugar beet field, Longmont, early 20th century. Courtesy of Longmont Museum. LM, 1973.109.328. http://longmont.pastperfectonline.com/photo/3BBD5DD2-B600-4481-807F-368260491136

3.2. Team of people with a horse-drawn digger, Longmont, 1900. Courtesy of Longmont Museum. LM, 1973.109.323. http://longmont.pastperfectonline.com/photo/1DC4B9BE-15B1-F14-8576-967829881472

3.3. Men topping sugar beets, Longmont, early 20th century. Courtesy of Longmont Museum. LM, 1973.109.318. http://longmont.pastperfectonline.com/photo/AACC468D-7AE6-40D6-AB81-377796659160

List of Maps

Sources

Explanations

BCLHP Collection, Carnegie Library. Materials collected by the Boulder County Latino History Project, 2013-2014. Deposited at Carnegie Branch Library for Local History, Boulder Public Library.

BCLHP references.[1] These provide the ID number for items accessible on the Boulder County Latino History website, bocolatinohistory.colorado.edu. Go to the Search page and type the BCLHP reference into the box labelled "Search by ID." In the online version of this book, all references are hyperlinked directly to the original source.

    If a given item contains multiple pages on the website, only the initial ID number is shown here; the following pages are linked to that one.

Carnegie Library. Carnegie Branch Library for Local History, Boulder Public Library.

LM. Longmont Museum.

LPL. Lafayette Public Library.

MROHP. Maria Rogers Oral History Program, Carnegie Branch Library for Local History, Boulder Public Library.

Valdez Papers. Materials preserved by Euvaldo Valdez concerning two organizations in the 1970s: Mexican Americans of Boulder County United (MABCU); and the Boulder County Council of the League of United Latin American Citizens (LULAC). University of Colorado at Boulder Archives, Norlin Library.

Information cited as from a conversation with Marjorie McIntosh on a stated date has been confirmed in writing and approved for use in this study by the authors of those statements.

All websites listed below were last accessed November 10-18, 2015.

---

[1] For entries with a BCLHP reference:

-- Items labelled as FP are family photographs loaned by community members and digitized by the BCLHP. The photographers are unknown unless specified.

-- Items labelled as LHS are photos loaned to the Longmont Hispanic Study in 1987-8 by a relative or descendent of the people shown. They were converted into slides by Oli Olivas Duncan for use in public presentations associated with the 1988 publication of *We, Too, Came to Stay: A History of the Longmont Hispanic Community*, which she edited. In 2014, the BCLHP was given permission to make digital copies of the slides, many of which showed unidentified people. The dates, locations, and photographers of these photos are unknown unless specified.

A. Sources about Boulder County Latinas/os

"2 men shot by police," *Longmont Times-Call*, Aug. 15, 1980. BCLHP-MKM-042.

"2-year-old wears a Mexican costume," *Boulder Daily Camera*, May 4, 1975. BCLHP-SCW-067.

"4th grade students prepare Mexican lunch," *Boulder Daily Camera*, Feb. 2, 1965. BCLHP-SCW-050.

"18 Mexican beet field picketers given jail terms," *Longmont Times-Call*, May 25, 1932. BCLHP-MKM-271.

"24 more agitators, mainly Mexicans, arrested," *Longmont Times-Call*, May 21, 1932. BCLHP-MKM-270.

"75 Mexicans quit country for Mexico," *Longmont Times-Call*, May 18, 1932. BCLHP-MKM-267.

"100 protest in Longmont," *Colorado Daily*, Nov. 19, 1980. BCLHP-MKM-039.

"300-400 Weld County Mexicans leaving," *Longmont Times-Call*, June 3, 1932. BCLHP-MKM-273.

"1,500 Mexicans loaded on trains in Denver," *Boulder Daily Camera*, May 18, 1932. BCLHP-MKM-274.

"8000 Colorado miners on strike," *Longmont Times-Call*, Sept. 23, 1935. BCLHP-MKM-260.

Abila, Mr. and Mrs. George. Oral history interview; Jessie Velez Lehmann, interviewer, 1978. Audio and transcript, MROHP. http://oralhistory.boulderlibrary.org/interview/oh0084.

Abila, Tom. Oral history interview; Jessie Velez Lehmann, interviewer, 1978. Audio and transcript, MROHP. http://oralhistory.boulderlibrary.org/interview/oh0085.

"All mines in Northern Colorado closed," *Longmont Times-Call*, Sept. 25, 1935. BCLHP-MKM-261.

Alvarez, Teresa. Oral history interview; Theresa Banfield and Regina Vigil, interviewers, 1976. Audio and transcript, MROHP. http://oralhistory.boulderlibrary.org/interview/oh0137.

Alvarez, Teresa. Oral history interview; Theresa Banfield and Regina Vigil, interviewers, 1977. Audio and transcript, MROHP. http://oralhistory.boulderlibrary.org/interview/oh0086.

"Alvarez, Virginia. Notes for her interview" by the BCLHP, July 13, 2013. BCLHP Collection, Carnegie Library. Not online.

Alvarez, Virginia. Oral history interview; Esther Blazón, interviewer, 2013. Video and transcript, MROHP. http://oralhistory.boulderlibrary.org/interview/oh1875.

"Andrew Gilbert Garcia and Mary Manzanares Garcia," biographical notes. Eleanor Montour, personal copy. BCLHP-FP-168.

"Angie Perez as GI Forum Queen," 1963-64. BCLHP-LHS-467.

Archuleta, Don. Oral history interview; Oli Olivas Duncan, interviewer, 2009. Draft transcript. BCLHP Collection, Carnegie Library. BCLHP-MKM-379.

"Archuleta family. Biography," in *Lafayette, Colorado*, F16. BCLHP-SCW-180.

"Archuleta family history." Prepared for Boulder Hispanic Families project, 2012. Becky Archuleta, personal copy. BCLHP-FP-232.

"Archuleta, Frank and Cora. Biography," in *Lafayette, Colorado*, F17. BCLHP-SCW-182.

"Archuleta, Ted. Eulogy" by his brother Jerry, 2009. BCLHP Collection, Carnegie Library. BCLHP-MKM-380.

"Archuleta/Ortega family information" sheets. Boulder Hispanic Families Project, 2012. BCLHP Collection, Carnegie Library. Not on line.

"Area farmer denies labor camp charges," *Longmont Times-Call*, PACE, Oct. 6, 1971. BCLHP-MKM-227.

"Arguello, Alfredo and Donaciana, and family. Biography." BCLHP Collection, Carnegie Library. BCLHP-MKM-381.

Arroyo (Arrollo), Candace. Oral history interview; Regina Vigil, interviewer, 1977. Audio and transcript, MROHP. http://oralhistory.boulderlibrary.org/interview/oh0087.

Arroyo, Patrick. Oral history interview; Robin Branstator, interviewer, 1989. Audio and summary, MROHP. http://oralhistory.boulderlibrary.org/interview/oh0426.

Arroyo-Holmstrom, Linda. Oral history interview; Euvaldo Valdez, interviewer, 2013. Video and transcript, MROHP. http://oralhistory.boulderlibrary.org/interview/oh1873.

"Arthur Archuleta buried as war hero." Unidentified newspaper clipping, 1946? Phil Hernandez, personal copy. BCLHP-FP-008.

"Articles about Glenn Herner's acquittal on manslaughter charge," p. 1, *Longmont Times-Call*, Mar. 29/29, 1981. BCLHP-MKM-237.

"At dedication of Emma Gomez Martinez Park," Oct. 11, 2013. Thomas Martinez, personal copy. BCLHP-FP-143.

"Beet dump" at Great Western Sugar factory, Longmont, 1900-1920. LM, 1973.109.320. http://longmont.pastperfectonline.com/photo/58DC4C62-4B17-43A0-8D01-300618509844.

"Beet growers disclaim responsibility for strike," *Longmont Times-Call*, May 19, 1932. BCLHP-MKM-268.

"Beet thinners get gold buttons," *Longmont Ledger*, Aug. 3, 1928. BCLHP-MKM-257.

"Beet workers protest," *Lafayette Leader*, May 20, 1932. BCLHP-MKM-280.

"Beets being irrigated," Longmont, 1900-1920. LM, B.059.057. http://longmont.pastperfectonline.com/photo/ED239CD7-9577-4C95-821A-268553973995.

"Beets outside Great Western Sugar Factory," Longmont, 1904-1906. LM, 1973.109.066. http://longmont.pastperfectonline.com/photo/5BB80578-6B54-4B27-9C20-051657526725.

Bernal, Dora. Oral history interview; Jessie Velez Lehmann, interviewer, 1978. Audio and English translation of Spanish interview, MROHP. http://oralhistory.boulderlibrary.org/interview/oh0079.

"Bernal, E. E. and Eva. Biography," written by Phil Hernandez in 2012, with photo. Tom Martinez, personal copy. BCLHP-FP-045.

Bernal, Mr. and Mrs. Emerenciano. Oral history interview; Jessie Velez Lehmann, interviewer, 1977. Audio and transcript, MROHP. http://oralhistory.boulderlibrary.org/interview/oh0081.

"Best beet thinners get gold buttons," *Longmont Ledger*, Aug. 5, 1927. BCLHP-MKM-256.

"Better season planned for migrant workers," *Longmont Times-Call*, May 29, 1970. BCLHP-MKM-209.

Bine, Tom, superintendent, Longmont Foods Turkey Plant. Interview; Olga Rodriguez and José Santana, interviewers, 1979. In *El Aguila*, pp. 14-18. BCLHP-MKM-626.

"Biographical sketch, Emma Gomez Martinez," written in 2012. Phil Hernandez, personal copy. BCLHP-MKM-455.

Blazón, Esther. Oral history interview; Linda Arroyo-Holmstrom, interviewer, 2013. Video and transcript, MROHP. http://oralhistory.boulderlibrary.org/interview/oh1879.

Blazón, William ("Hank"). Oral history interview; Jaime Rios, interviewer, 2013. Video and transcript, MROHP. http://oralhistory.boulderlibrary.org/interview/oh1877.

"Board grants part ($4,500) of Chicano request," *Longmont Times-Call*, Nov. 11, 1971. BCLHP-MKM-205.

"Borrego, Albert, and Elvinia ("Bea") Martinez Borrego. Biography." BCLHP Collection, Carnegie Library. BCLHP-MKM-382.

"Borrego, Andrew. Biography," in *Lafayette, Colorado*, F54. BCLHP-SCW-183.

"Borrego, Joseph Garfield. Biography," in *Lafayette, Colorado*, F55. BCLHP-SCW-184.

"Borrego, Robert Raymond. Biography," in *Lafayette, Colorado*, F56. BCLHP-SCW-185.

"Boulder 'affirmative action' aggressive," *Longmont Times-Call*, Aug. 30-31, 1980. BCLHP-MKM-217.

"Boulder County Commissioners' Resolution, 1932" (typed transcript). Boulder County Commissioners' Archives; Carmen Ramirez, personal copy. BCLHP-MKM-590.

"Boulder, film of places of historical importance" to Latinos, made in 2013. Linda Arroyo-Holmstrom and Phil Hernandez, narrators; Ana Gonzalez Dorta, videographer and editor. Produced for BCLHP. BCLHP-MKM-100.

"Boulder Klan fails to take action to give up Charter." *Boulder Daily Camera*, July 24, 1925. Carnegie Branch Library for Local History, Boulder Public Library. Not online.

"Boulder Ku Klux Klan rode thru streets," *Boulder Daily Camera*, Nov. 27, 1922. BCLHP-MKM-360.

"Boulder's Chicano Community, 1978 KGNU radio interview." Carnegie Branch Library for Local History, Boulder, OH 0201. BCLHP-MKM-049.

"Boulder's Chicano Community, 1979 film." Carnegie Branch Library for Local History, Boulder, DVD 978.863. BCLHP-MKM-047.

"Buildings at Industrial Mine," Louisville, 1900? LPL, LP03710. http://www.cityoflafayette.com/PhotoViewScreen.aspx?PID=385.

"Canyon Park renamed in Emma Gomez Martinez's honor," Boulder, 2013, p. 1. *Boulder Daily Camera*, Nov. 8, 2013. Tom Martinez, personal copy. BCLHP-FP-047.

Cardenas, Alfonso. Oral history interview; Dorothy D. Ciarlo, interviewer, 2004. Video and summary, MROHP. http://oralhistory.boulderlibrary.org/interview/oh1212.

Cardenas, Lou. Oral history interview; Oli Duncan, interviewer, c. 1987. In Duncan, ed., *We, Too, Came to Stay*, pp. 13-22. BCLHP-MKM-689.

"Cartoon: The KKK and Law Enforcement." *The Rocky Mountain American*, Vol. I, no. 2 (Feb. 13, 1925). BCLHP-MKM-375.

"Casias, Angelina and Raymond. Biography," in *Lafayette, Colorado*, F74. BCLHP-SCW-186.

"Causes of the Mexican trouble," p. 1, *Longmont Ledger*, June 30, 1916. BCLHP-MKM-194.

Chacon, Susie. Oral history interview; Regina Vigil, interviewer, 1977. Audio and transcript, MROHP. http://oralhistory.boulderlibrary.org/interview/oh0087.

"Chicano Advisory Groups criticize district," *Boulder Daily Camera*, Feb. 11, 1961. BCLHP-SCW-057.

"Chicano Fiesta de la Gente planned," *Boulder Daily Camera*, July 23, 1976. BCLHP-SCW-069.

"Chicanos outline school aims," *Longmont Times-Call*, May 27, 1971. BCLHP-MKM-213.

"Chicanos throw rocks at Boulder policeman," 1970. *Boulder Daily Camera*, May 3, 1970. BCLHP-SCW-093.

"Chicanos win bid for school advisory role," *Longmont Times-Call*, Mar. 23, 1971. BCLHP-MKM-203.

"Chicanos winning bid for $61,000 for Chicano Studies," *Longmont Times-Call*, Nov. 5, 1971. BCLHP-MKM-204.

The Coal and Metal Miners' Pocket Book, p. 1. Becky Archuleta, personal copy. BCLHP-FP-216.

"Coal miners' wage cuts denied," *Lafayette Leader*, May 27, 1932. BCLHP-MKM-281.

"Coal miners' wages cut," *Lafayette Leader*, May 20, 1932. BCLHP-MKM-279.

"The Columbine Incident." In *Lafayette, Colorado*, T39. BCLHP-SCW-165.

Como Ellos Lo Ven: Migrant Children Look at Life in Longmont. Ed. Judith Lessow Hurley, St. Vrain Valley Summer Migrant Education Program, Western Interstate Commission for Higher Education, 1977. Margaret Alfonso, personal copy. Excerpts in BCLHP Collection, Carnegie Library.

"Contract for Hand Labor for the season of 1928," Canuto Martinez. Phil Hernandez, personal copy. BCLHP-FP-036.

Cordero, Olga Melendez. Interview; Oli Duncan, interviewer, 2009. Rough draft transcript. BCLHP Collection, Carnegie Library. BCLHP-MKM-385.

Cordova, Augustine E. Oral history interview; Margaret Alfonso, interviewer, 2013. Video and transcript, MROHP. http://oralhistory.boulderlibrary.org/interview/oh1874.

Cordova, Augustine E., songwriter and performer. "Los Seis de Boulder." Written originally in 1974; re-recorded in 2014.
Performance of first half of song: BCLHP-MKM-395
Lyrics in Spanish: Illus. 7.2
Lyrics in English: BCLHP-MKM-397A and B

Cordova, Augustine E., songwriter and performer. "Yo Soy Chicano." Written originally in 1974?; re-recorded in 2014.
Performance of first half of song: BCLHP-MKM-392
Lyrics in Spanish: Illus. 7.1
Lyrics in English: BCLHP-MKM-394A and B

Cordova, Patsy. Oral history interview; Oli Duncan, interviewer, c. 1987. In Duncan, ed., *We, Too, Came to Stay*, pp. 23-25. BCLHP-MKM-696.

"Cortez, Jose Hilario ("J. H."), and Maria Sabina Maes Cortez. Draft biography." BCLHP Collection, Carnegie Library. BCLHP-MKM-383.

"County to deport 75 beet workers," *Boulder Daily Camera*, May 18, 1932. BCLHP-MKM-275.

"Cross burned on Flagstaff Mountain and lit up the plains far out," *Boulder Daily Camera*, May 21, 1924. Carnegie Branch Library for Local History, Boulder Public Library. Not online.

"Crowds bid farewell to victims," *Longmont Times-Call*, Aug. 20, 1980. BCLHP-MKM-233.

"Daily Times-Call newspaper paperboys," *Boulder Daily Camera*, Nov. 2, 1964. BCLHP-SCW-040.

"Dedication of Emma Gomez Martinez Park." *Boulder Daily Camera*, Oct. 11, 2013. Thomas Martinez, personal copy. BCLHP-FP-144.

"A different kind of poor," *Longmont Times-Call*, Oct. 15, 1971. BCLHP-MKM-228.

"Disturbance on Hill results in an arrest," *Boulder Daily Camera*, Sept. 10, 1970. BCLHP-SCW-098.

"Document of understanding," City of Longmont, El Comite, U.S. Dept. of Justice, 1980. Dan Benavidez, personal copy. BCLHP Collection, Carnegie Library. BCLHP-MKM-044.

"Driver recalls night of shooting," *Longmont Times-Call*, Aug. 18, 1980. BCLHP-MKM-230.

Duncan, Erminda "Oli" Olivas. Oral history interview; Philip Hernandez, interviewer, 2013. Video and transcript, MROHP. http://oralhistory.boulderlibrary.org/interview/oh1862.

Duncan, Oli Olivas. "Hispanic History of Longmont." Typescript of oral presentation, c. 1989, BCLHP Collection, Carnegie Library. Not online.

Duncan, Oli Olivas. "Some Notes Regarding Major Differences between Longmont (Bo. County) and the Chama Valley." Typescript, BCLHP Collection, Carnegie Library. BCLHP-MKM-405.

Duncan, Oli Olivas, ed. *We, Too, Came to Stay: A History of the Longmont Hispanic Community*. Privately published for the Longmont Hispanic Study, Longmont, [1988]. Individual interviews are available online, listed here under the person's name.

"Eddie Vigil in military uniform." BCLHP-LHS-296.

"Education articles," *Boulder Daily Camera*: Feb. 14 and 17, May 10 and 20, June 14, July 20 and 26, and Aug. 10, 1971; March 21, May 5, and Aug. 15, 1972. Not online.

El Aguila: The Eagle (written and illustrated by migrant teens), IDEAS,

Nederland, CO, 1979. BCLHP-MKM-612 through 654. Individual interviews are available online, listed here under the person's name. Margaret Alfonso, personal copy. BCLHP Collection, Carnegie Library.

"El Comite, City to focus on police-community relations," *Longmont Times-Call*, Aug. 26, 1980. BCLHP-MKM-236.

"El Comite presents list of demands to city," *Longmont Times-Call*, Aug. 28, 1980. BCLHP-MKM-214.

"El Comite seeks permanent status," *Longmont Daily Call*, Sept. 4, 1980. BCLHP-MKM-040.

"El Comite's first-year accomplishments," *Longmont Times-Call*, Aug. 15, 1981. BCLHP-MKM-263.

"Eracism: Exploring the roots of Boulder County Latinos," *Boulder Weekly*, Feb. 6-12, 2014, pp. 15-24. BCLHP-MKM-372.

"Espinoza, Seferino Albert. Biography." Gilbert Espinoza, personal copy. BCLHP-FP-094.

Esquibel, Jose. Interview; Rico Contrares, Carla Lovato, Hilda Nunez, and José Santana, interviewers, 1979. In *El Aguila*, pp. 24-27. BCLHP-MKM-637.

"Esther and Ann Blazón," 1949. Esther Blazón, personal copy. BCLHP-FP-020.

"Esther Blazón and family, 1974," at her undergraduate graduation from University of Colorado, Boulder. Esther Blazón, personal copy. BCLHP-FP-021.

"Esther Blazón and family, 1980," with her graduate degree from Univ. of Northern Colorado and son Bill's graduation from Longmont High School. Esther Blazón, personal copy. BCLHP-FP-022.

"Estrada, Cleo(patra). Autobiographical information." Typescript, BCLHP Collection, Carnegie Library. BCLHP-MKM-600.

Estrada, Cleopatra. Oral history interview; Monica Marquez, interviewer, 2013. Video and transcript, MROHP. http://oralhistory.boulderlibrary.org/interview/oh1883.

"Fabricio Martinez in Germany, WWII." LM, 1995.012.001. http://longmont.pastperfectonline.com/photo/65A14D72-EEF9-4833-9C32-563390145721.

"Farm work and coal mining make most jobs," *Longmont Daily Times*, July 24, 1931. BCLHP-MKM-258.

"Farm Workers United worried about migrant housing," *Longmont Times-Call*, Apr. 24, 1970. BCLHP-MKM-201.

"Farmers concerned about irresponsibility of migrant workers," *Longmont Times-Call*, July 3, 1968. BCLHP-MKM-196.

"FBI to investigate shootings," *Longmont Times-Call*, Aug. 26, 1980. BCLHP-MKM-235.

"First arrests in beet strike," *Longmont Times-Call*, May 18, 1932. BCLHP-MKM-266.

"First bilingual election in Longmont," *Longmont Times-Call*, Nov. 5, 1975. BCLHP-MKM-202.

"Formal affirmative action plan lacking," *Longmont Times-Call*, Aug. 30/31, 1980. BCLHP-MKM-216.

"Fort Lupton migrant workers to leave camps," *Longmont Times-Call*, Nov. 7, 1969. BCLHP-MKM-223.

"Francis Street Pharmacy," opened in 1983 by Joe Esquibel. Kathy Esquibel, personal copy. BCLHP-FP-012.

Gallegos, Reina. Oral history interview; Oli Duncan, interviewer, c. 1987. In Duncan, ed., *We, Too, Came to Stay*, pp. 27-29. BCLHP-MKM-698.

Garcia, Ricardo and Anna. Oral history interview; Pauline Romano, interviewer, 1977. Audio and summary, MROHP. http://oralhistory.boulderlibrary.org/interview/oh0088.

Garcia, Richard. Oral history interview; Philip Hernandez, interviewer, 2013. Video and transcript, MROHP. http://oralhistory.boulderlibrary.org/interview/oh1872.

Gauna, Tivi. Interview; Alex Gomez, interviewer, 1979. In *El Aguila*, pp. 12-13. BCLHP-MKM-624.

"A GI Forum Queen and parents." BCLHP-LHS-15H.

"A GI Forum Queen with her escort." BCLHP-LHS-14U.

"A GI Forum Queen, with her escort and court." BCLHP-LHS-15D.

"Gilbert Espinoza in Viet Nam," 1969. Gilbert Espinoza, personal copy. BCLHP-FP-084.

Gomez, Tony. Interview; Oli Duncan, interviewer, 2009. Draft transcript. BCLHP Collection, Carnegie Library. BCLHP-MKM-384.

Gonzales, Alex. Oral history interview; Oli Duncan, interviewer, c. 1987. In Duncan, ed., *We, Too, Came to Stay*, pp. 31-34. BCLHP-MKM-700.

Gonzales, Doris. Oral history interview; Jeff Dodge, interviewer, 2013. Audio and summary, MROHP. http://oralhistory.boulderlibrary.org/interview/oh1920.

"Hardship of migrant living," p. 1, *Longmont Times-Call*, PACE, Oct. 15, 1971. BCLHP-MKM-199.

"Harvesting peas," Longmont, 1900-1920. LM, 1990.036.012. http://longmont.pastperfectonline.com/photo/68425D0B-8DC0-462C-9094-023369147646.

"Harvesting sugar beets," Longmont, 1900-1920. LM, 1990.036.039.
http://longmont.pastperfectonline.com/photo/DDF82CA8-4210-418D-
AFBE-887319051479.

"A Head Start strategy planning meeting," 1968. Phil Hernandez, personal copy.
BCLHP-FP-031.

Hernandez, Philip. Oral history interview; Euvaldo Valdez, interviewer, 2013.
Video and transcript, MROHP.
http://oralhistory.boulderlibrary.org/interview/oh1857.

Herrera, Secundino. Interview; Maura Diaz, Rosa Garcia, Lorenzo Huerta, Hilda
Nunez, and Nati Santana, interviewers, 1979. In *El Aguila*, pp. 39-41.
BCLHP-MKM-652.

Herrera, Secundino. Oral history interview; Oli Duncan, interviewer, c. 1987. In
Duncan, ed., *We, Too, Came to Stay*, pp. 35-38. BCLHP-MKM-703.

"Historical hatred breeds contemporary contempt," *Boulder Weekly*, Oct. 2,
2014.
http://npaper-wehaa.com/boulder-weekly/2014/10/02/#?article=2346112.

"Homestead Record of Land Patent, 1862" (granted by Congress to Felesita
Baldizan on May 20). Tucumcari, New Mexico. Dixie Lee Aragon, personal
copy. BCLHP-FP-160.

"Homestead Record of Land Patent, 1915" (granted by Congress to Pedro
Uliberri de Aragon on July 20). Tucumcari, New Mexico. Dixie Lee Aragon,
personal copy. BCLHP-FP-161.

"Horace Hernandez and other volunteers" remodeling space for OEO Center in
Longmont, late 1960s? Phil Hernandez, personal copy. BCLHP-FP-007.

"Houses in camp, Industrial Mine." Louisville, 1905. LPL, LP03680.
http://www.cityoflafayette.com/PhotoViewScreen.aspx?PID=384.

"Information about All Latinos in U.S. Census Records for Longmont." Prepared
from copies of original U.S. Federal Census records by Rebecca Chavez.
1910, BCLHP-Cen-008
1920, BCLHP-Cen-009
1930, BCLHP-Cen-010
1940, BCLHP-Cen-011

"Information about Latino-Surnamed Households in U.S. Census Records for
Boulder," used through Ancestry.com. Prepared by volunteers with BCLHP.
1900, BCLHP-Cen-001
1920, BCLHP-Cen-002
1930, BCLHP-Cen-003
1940, BCLHP-Cen-004

"Information about Latino-Surnamed Households in U.S. Census Records for
Lafayette," used through Ancestry.com. Prepared by volunteers with BCLHP.
1920, BCLHP-Cen-005

1930, BCLHP-Cen-006
1940, BCLHP-Cen-007

"Inquest into shooting deaths," *Longmont Daily Call*, Sept. 4, 1980. BCLHP-MKM-041.

"Interior, Kuner-Empson factory," Longmont, 1946. LM, 1972.066.001. http://longmont.pastperfectonline.com/photo/EE987789-8DBD-48A3-B26B-054786675521.

"Interior of Longmont Foods turkey plant," 1960-70. LM, 1995.028.006. http://longmont.pastperfectonline.com/photo/D368035B-7468-4C34-8983-574989374860.

"Jacob Espinoza, Obituary," *Lafayette News*, Aug., 1977. BCLHP Collection, Carnegie Library. Not online.

"Jake Espinoza at 94," *Lafayette News*, May 13, 1976. BCLHP Collection, Carnegie Library. Not online.

Jaramillo, Gregory. Oral history interview; Philip Hernandez, interviewer, 2013. Video and transcript, MROHP. http://oralhistory.boulderlibrary.org/interview/oh1861.

"Joe Esquibel inside his Francis Street Pharmacy," 1989. Kathy Esquibel, personal copy. BCLHP-FP-014.

"John Martinez, military service," 1942-45. Tom Martinez, personal copy. BCLHP-FP-056.

"Josephine Roche speaks tonight," *Boulder Daily Camera*, May 24, 1932. BCLHP-MKM-276.

"KKK influence was strong here in the 1920s," *Longmont Times-Call*, Dec. 26, 1979. BCLHP-MKM-361.

"A KKK meeting in Boulder, 1920s, back of photo." History Colorado, photo #F37858. BCLHP-MKM-570.

"Klan had its heyday in county," *Longmont Times-Call*, Jan. 14, 1995. BCLHP-MKM-365.

"Kolorado Klaverns of the Ku Klux Klan," *University of Colorado Daily*, April 19, 1982. BCLHP-MKM-362.

"Ku Klux Klan ceremonial administered to Boulderites," *Boulder Daily Camera*, July 15, 1922. BCLHP-MKM-358.

"Ku Klux Klan controlled Longmont in 1920s," p. 1, *Longmont Daily Times-Call*, April 10-11, 1971. BCLHP-MKM-355.

"Ku Klux Klan in Lafayette." In *Lafayette, Colorado*, T38. BCLHP-MKM-353.

"Ku Klux Klan sends election instructions to Boulder County voters," *Boulder Daily Camera*, Nov. 1, 1924. BCLHP-MKM-354.

"Ku Klux Klan: the invisible empire in Boulder County," *Superior Historian*, vol. 6, no. 2 (Aug., 2009). BCLHP-MKM-368.

"Ku Klux Klan wielded much power in the 1920s," *Longmont Sunday Times-Call Magazine*, Nov. 1, 1987. BCLHP-MKM-363.

Lafayette, Colorado: Treeless Plain to Thriving City. Centennial History, 1889-1989 (ed. James D. Hutchison). Lafayette, CO: Lafayette Historical Society, 1990. Articles about Latino families and events are available online, listed here under the person's name or event's title.

"Lafayette Councilwoman Sharon Stetson." Sharon Stetson, personal copy. BCLHP-FP-199.

"Lafayette, film of places of historical importance" to Latinos, made in 2013. Eleanor Montour, narrator; Ana Gonzalez Dorta, videographer and editor. Produced for BCLHP. BCLHP-MKM-102.

"Lafayette's new swimming pool recalls 1934 incident," p. 1, *Longmont Times-Call*, Jan. 21, 1990. Sharon Stetson, personal copy. BCLHP-FP-188.

"Lafayette's 'white only' pool sparked 1934 lawsuit," *Boulder Daily Camera*, Apr. 10, 2011. Phil Hernandez, personal copy. BCLHP-FP-035.

"Latino couple leaves for visit to California," *Lafayette Leader*, June 14, 1956. BCLHP-SCW-125.

"Latino doctor backs funding of Mental Health Center," 1978, *Boulder Daily Camera*, Oct. 11, 1978. BCLHP-SCW-024.

"Latino doctor criticizes decision to cut funds," *Boulder Daily Camera*, Sept. 17, 1978. BCLHP-SCW-028.

"Latino elected officials," Boulder County's municipalities, 1960-2013. Compiled by the BCLHP from local records. BCLHP Collection, Carnegie Library. BCLHP-MKM-369.

"Latino student graduates High School, 1956," *Lafayette Leader*, June 14, 1956. BCLHP-SCW-126.

"Latino students graduate High School, 1962," *Lafayette Leader*, June 18, 1962. BCLHP-SCW-127.

"Latino students graduate High School, 1964," Pts. 1 and 2, *Lafayette Leader*, June 18, 1964. BCLHP-SCW-128 and 129.

"Latino-surnamed children in Boulder schools": names and other information. Compiled by BCLHP from annual School Census Books, Boulder Valley School District, Education Center.
1935, BCLHP-Sch-001
1944, BCLHP-Sch-002
1955, BCLHP-Sch-003

"Latino-surnamed children in Lafayette schools": names and other information. Compiled by BCLHP from annual School Census Books, Boulder

Valley School District, Education Center.
1915, BCLHP-Sch-004
1925, BCLHP-Sch-005
1935, BCLHP-Sch-006

"Latino-surnamed children in Longmont schools": names and other information. Compiled by BCLHP from annual School Census Books, LM, St. Vrain Valley School District Records.
1905, BCLHP-Sch-007
1915, BCLHP-Sch-008
1925, BCLHP-Sch-009
1935, BCLHP-Sch-010

"Latinos in the military," numbers and casualties, 1940s-1970s. Memorial Day special feature article, Houston Institute of Culture. Phil Hernandez, personal copy. BCLHP-FP-039.

"Law and Order." In *Lafayette, Colorado*, T27. BCLHP-SCW-164.

Lehmann, Jessie Velez. Oral history interview; Regina Vigil, interviewer, 1978. Audio and transcript, MROHP. http://oralhistory.boulderlibrary.org/interview/oh0089.

"Local GI's sent to battlefield in Korea," *Lafayette Leader*, Aug. 28, 1951. BCLHP-SCW-124.

"Local woman demonstrates traditional South American dances," *Boulder Daily Camera*, May 7, 1976. BCLHP-SCW-068.

"Longmont, film of places of historical importance" to Latinos, made in 2013. Esther Blazón, narrator; Ana Gonzalez Dorta, videographer and editor. Produced for BCLHP. BCLHP-MKM-101.

"*Longmont Times-Call* index entries, El Comite," 1980-2001. BCLHP-MKM-219.

"*Longmont Times-Call* index entries, Marta Moreno," 1980-2001. BCLHP-MKM-264.

"Lopez, Rich. Notes for his interview" by the BCLHP, July 12, 2013. BCLHP Collection, Carnegie Library. Not online.

Lopez, Thomas. Oral history interview; Fred Stones, interviewer, 1986. Transcript, LPL, oral history files, tape 1068. BCLHP-MKM-343.

"Los Aztecas celebrate Cinco de Mayo," *Boulder Daily Camera*, May 4, 1975. BCLHP-SCW-070.

"Los Inmigrantes," film showing interviews with Boulder Chicanos, 1979. Produced by Boulder's Chicano Community Project. Margaret Alfonso, personal copy. BCLHP-MKM-046.

"Los Seis de Boulder," as aired nationally. Sprouts radio broadcast by Irene Rodriguez, 2011. BCLHP-MKM-408.

"Los Seis de Boulder," Pts. I and II. KGNU radio broadcast by Irene Rodriguez, 2011. BCLHP-MKM-406 and 407.

"'Los Seis de Boulder' died in '74 car bombings." *Boulder Daily Camera*, May 15, 2009. http://www.dailycamera.com/ci_13121120.

"Madrigal family of Boulder. Biographies." Boulder Hispanic Families Project, 2012. BCLHP Collection, Carnegie Library. BCLHP-MKM-404.

"Maestas, Pedro (Roy), Ruby, and Abe. Biography." Boulder Hispanic Families Project, 2012. BCLHP Collection, Carnegie Library. BCLHP-MKM-370.

Maestas, Roy. Oral history interview; Jessie Velez Lehmann, interviewer, 1978. Audio and summary, MROHP. http://oralhistory.boulderlibrary.org/interview/oh0082.

Maestas, Virginia. Oral history interview; Regina Vigil, interviewer, 1978. Audio and transcript, MROHP. http://oralhistory.boulderlibrary.org/interview/oh0083.

Maestas, Virginia. Oral history interview; Jeff Dodge, interviewer, 2013. Audio and summary, MROHP. http://oralhistory.boulderlibrary.org/interview/oh1923.

"Mammoth Klan parade in Longmont," *The Rocky Mountain American*, Vol. I, no. 18 (June 9, 1925). BCLHP-MKM-377.

"Man killed during Immigration raid," *Noticias del Comité*, Vol. 2, No. 1 (June, 1982). BCLHP-MKM-452.

"Manzanares, David J. and Marguerite. Biography," in *Lafayette, Colorado*, F257. BCLHP-SCW-190.

"Marchers Remember deaths of Los Seis" de Boulder, *Boulder Daily Camera*, May 28, 1978. BCLHP-SCW-103.

Marquez, Sonia. Oral history interview; Esther Blazón, interviewer, 2013. Video and transcript, MROHP. http://oralhistory.boulderlibrary.org/interview/oh1885.

"Martinez, Canuto and Gregoria. Biography," written by Phil Hernandez in 2012. Tom Martinez, personal copy. BCLHP-FP-044.

"Martinez, Emma Gomez. Letter to Her Children." Tom Martinez, personal copy. BCLHP Collection, Carnegie Library. BCLHP-MKM-446.

Martinez, Emma Gomez. Oral history interview; Euvaldo Valdez, interviewer, 2013. Video and transcript, MROHP. http://oralhistory.boulderlibrary.org/interview/oh1893.

Martinez, Joe. Oral history interview; Rick Martinez, interviewer, 1977. Transcript, LPL, oral history files, with tape 1081. BCLHP-MKM-350.

"Martinez, Joseph and Pauline. Biography," in *Lafayette*, F261. BCLHP-SCW-193.

"Martinez, Juan and Josephine; Marcella Martinez Diaz. Biography." Boulder Hispanic Families Project, 2012. BCLHP Collection, Carnegie Library. BCLHP-MKM-371.

"Martinez, Lloyd and Sally (Salazar). Biography," in *Lafayette, Colorado*, F262. BCLHP-SCW-194.

Martinez, Mary. Interview; Becky Lovato, Olga Rodriguez, and Connie Saldivar, interviewers, 1979. In *El Aguila*, pp. 28-30. BCLHP-MKM-641.

Martinez, Mary. Oral history interview; interviewer unknown, 1988. Video and detailed summary, MROHP. http://oralhistory.boulderlibrary.org/interview/oh1912.

Martinez, Rick. Oral history interview, with other ex-miners; interviewer unknown, 1975. Audio and summary, MROHP. http://oralhistory.boulderlibrary.org/interview/oh0053.

Martinez, Sally, and other Pioneer Families. Oral history interview; Anne Dyni, interviewer, 1990. Audio and summary, MROHP. http://oralhistory.boulderlibrary.org/interview/oh0530.

"Martinez, Victoria Gerardo. Biography," in *Lafayette, Colorado*, F263. BCLHP-SCW-195.

"Mechanical beet harvester," Longmont, 1950. LM, 2005.033.050. http://longmont.pastperfectonline.com/photo/1F3F2EE1-C7F8-44A4-A4C5-201383763833.

Medina, Maria. Oral history interview; interviewer unknown, c. 1978. Audio and summary, MROHP. http://oralhistory.boulderlibrary.org/interview/oh0080.

Medina, Miguel. Oral history interview; Jaime Rios, interviewer, 2013. Video and transcript, MROHP. http://oralhistory.boulderlibrary.org/interview/oh1878.

"Memorial to Latino soldier killed in Vietnam," *Longmont Times-Call*, June 20, 2013. BCLHP-MKM-043.

"Men and women topping beets" by hand, Longmont, 1900. LM, 1973.109.329. http://longmont.pastperfectonline.com/photo/0D75A740-0BE9-4C78-8F21-324508530709.

"Men in interior of Eagle Mine," Lafayette, 1950? LPL, MF77. http://www.cityoflafayette.com/PhotoViewScreen.aspx?PID=365

"Men in interior of Vulcan Mine," Lafayette, 1910? LPL, LP02980. http://www.cityoflafayette.com/PhotoViewScreen.aspx?PID=390

"Mexican child drowns in ditch," *Longmont Ledger*, Oct. 11, 1929. BCLHP-MKM-191.

"Mexican deportation in the 1930s," by Emma Gomez Martinez, 2012. Tom Martinez, personal copy. BCLHP-FP-051.

"Mexican families deported at county's expense," *Boulder Daily Camera*, May 25, 1932. BCLHP-MKM-278.

"Mexican holiday planned," *Boulder Daily Camera*, Mar. 26, 1975. BCLHP-SCW-066.

"Mexican-American group formed for County," *Boulder Daily Camera*, Apr. 21, 1971. BCLHP-SCW-091.

"Mexican-American housing problems discussed at Congregational Church," *Boulder Daily Camera*, Feb. 24, 1969. BCLHP-SCW-079.

"Mexican-American school problems discussed in Congregational class," *Boulder Daily Camera*, Nov. 18, 1968. BCLHP-SCW-085.

"Mexican-American youth conference scheduled" (part 1), *Boulder Daily Camera*, May 6, 1969. BCLHP-SCW-081.

"Mexicans going south," *Longmont Ledger*, June 30, 1916. BCLHP-MKM-193.

"Migrant Summer School Program records." LM, St. Vrain School District Records, Box 8. Not online.

"Migrant workers love Colorado, life of travel," *Longmont Times-Call*, July 2, 1968. BCLHP-MKM-189.

"Migrants refuse to move," *Longmont Times-Call*, Oct. 17, 1969. BCLHP-MKM-220.

"Miners and tipple at State Mine," Lafayette, 1927. LPL, M990601. http://www.cityoflafayette.com/PhotoViewScreen.aspx?PID=500.

"Miners at Lehigh Mine," Lafayette/Erie, 1904? LPL, LP01110. http://www.cityoflafayette.com/PhotoViewScreen.aspx?PID=503.

"Miners at Puritan Mine" (National Fuel Co.), Erie, 1922. LPL, LP01120. http://www.cityoflafayette.com/PhotoViewScreen.aspx?PID=517.

"Miners at Standard Mine," Lafayette, 1909. Ed Tangen, photographer. LPL, LP02940. http://www.cityoflafayette.com/PhotoViewScreen.aspx?PID=621.

"Monarch Mine." In *Lafayette, Colorado*, T48. BCLHP-SCW-171.

Montour, Eleanor. Oral history interview; Euvaldo Valdez, interviewer, 2013. Video and transcript, MROHP. http://oralhistory.boulderlibrary.org/interview/oh1860.

"More than 50,000 donned hoods at Klan's height in state in 1920s," *Boulder Daily Camera*, Jan. 13, 1995. BCLHP-MKM-364.

Moreno, Heriberto ("Beto"). Oral history interview; Ray Rodriguez,

interviewer, 2013. Video and transcript, MROHP.
http://oralhistory.boulderlibrary.org/interview/oh1897.

"Mountain View Pharmacy," opened in 1971 by Joe Esquibel. Kathy Esquibel, personal copy. BCLHP-FP-015.

"Mrs. Tony Garcia Heads PTA," 1969-70, *Lafayette Leader*, Apr. 24, 1969. BCLHP-SCW-137.

"New action filed in alien case," *Longmont Times-Call*, Sept. 27, 1971. BCLHP-MKM-225.

"New printing press speeds production, 1964," *Boulder Daily Camera*, BCLHP-SCW-041.

"No benefits for strikers," *Longmont Times-Call*, May 17, 1932. BCLHP-MKM-265.

"Occupations and Employers of Latino-Surnamed Adults, Three Towns, 1926." Compiled by BCLHP from *Polk's City Directories*.
1926, BCLHP-Occ-001
1936, BCLHP-Occ-002
1946, BCLHP-Occ-003
1955, BCLHP-Occ-004
1965, BCLHP-Occ-005
1975, BCLHP-Occ-006

"Old friends, new faces," *Longmont Times-Call*, Aug. 28, 1980. BCLHP-MKM-215.

"Olivas, Ralph and Rose. Biographical account," p. 1, by their daughter, Oli Olivas Duncan, c. 1987. In Duncan, ed., *We, Too, Came to Stay*, pp. 39-44. BCLHP-MKM-706.

"One officer fired both bullets," *Longmont Times-Call*, Aug. 18, 1980. BCLHP-MKM-231.

"Opening of Francis Street Pharmacy," *Longmont Times-Call*, Aug., 1983. Kathy Esquibel, personal copy. BCLHP-FP-009.

"Ortega, John, family of. Biography," in *Lafayette, Colorado*, F332. BCLHP-SCW-201.

"Paul Cortez in military uniform." BCLHP-LHS-302.

Perez, Arthur. Oral history interview; Jaime Rios, interviewer, 2013. Video and transcript, MROHP.
http://oralhistory.boulderlibrary.org/interview/oh1882.

"Police a major Chicano concern," *Boulder Daily Camera*, May 6, 1975. BCLHP-SCW-107.

"Profile, Emma Martinez." *Boulder Daily Camera*, undated clipping, 1980s? Tom Martinez, personal copy. BCLHP-FP-046.

"Profile of pharmacist and business owner Joe Esquibel," *Longmont Times-Call*, Sept. 24-25, 1983. Kathy Esquibel, personal copy. BCLHP-FP-010.

"Quintana completes naval training in San Diego," *Boulder Daily Camera*, Dec. 12, 1963. BCLHP-SCW-038.

Ramirez, Albert. Oral history interview; Philip Hernandez, interviewer, 2013. Video and transcript, MROHP. http://oralhistory.boulderlibrary.org/interview/oh1899.

Rangel, Bob. Interview; Carla Lovato, Jose Santana, Marcus Medina, and Andrew Valencia, interviewers, 1979. In *El Aguila*, pp. 31-33. BCLHP-MKM-644.

"Ray Vigil in military uniform." BCLHP-LHS-016A.

"Relief units swamped by needy's calls," *Boulder Daily Camera*, May 25, 1932. BCLHP-MKM-277.

"Report on State of the Mexican-Americans in Boulder," *Boulder Daily Camera*, Jan. 28, 1973. BCLHP-SCW-156.

"Request to rename park after Emma Gomez Martinez," 2013. Philip Hernandez, personal copy. BCLHP Collection, Carnegie Library. BCLHP-MKM-351.

Rodriguez, Benny. Interview; Andrew Valencia, Maura Diaz, Alex Gomez, Lorenzo Huerta, and Theresa Zuniga, interviewers, 1979. In *El Aguila*, pp. 20-23. BCLHP-MKM-633.

Rodriguez, Manuel. Interview; Olga Rodriguez, interviewer, 1979. In *El Aguila*, pp. 18-19. BCLHP-MKM-631.

"Rosales, Henry and Alice. Biography," in *Lafayette, Colorado*, F374. BCLHP-SCW-203.

"Rosales, Larry and Linda. Biography," in *Lafayette, Colorado*, F375. BCLHP-SCW-204.

Salazar, Edwina. Oral history interview; Euvaldo Valdez, interviewer, 2013. Video and transcript, MROHP. http://oralhistory.boulderlibrary.org/interview/oh1854.

"Salazar, Jose Benito and Isabelle (Rivera). Biography," in *Lafayette, Colorado*, F379. BCLHP-SCW-206.

"Saragosa, Pete (originally Pedro Zaragoza). Property records" from the Boulder County Assessor's Office, copied by Leslie Ogeda. BCLHP Collection, Carnegie Library. Not online.

Segunda Mirada: Migrant Children Look at Life in Longmont. Ed. Judith Lessow-Hurley, St. Vrain Valley Summer Migrant Education Program, Western Interstate Commission for Higher Education, 1978. Margaret Alfonso, personal copy. Excerpts in BCLHP Collection, Carnegie Library.

"Sgt. Felix Lopez receiving Silver Star for gallantry, Longmont, 1968." LM, 1995.055.001.
http://longmont.pastperfectonline.com/photo/B98E50BF-EE18-48A1-9FD7-572333945163

"Sheriff saved prisoners from lynching, 1911," p. 1, *Boulder Daily Camera*, May 2, 2010. Phil Hernandez, personal copy. BCLHP-FP-003.

Silva, Dolores. Oral history interview; Margaret Alfonso, interviewer, 2013. Video and transcript, MROHP.
http://oralhistory.boulderlibrary.org/interview/oh1886.

"Simpson Mine, Erie/Lafayette, 1900?" LPL, LP02930.
http://www.cityoflafayette.com/PhotoViewScreen.aspx?PID=606.

"Simpson Mine, Erie/Lafayette, 1908." LPL, LP02860.
http://www.cityoflafayette.com/PhotoViewScreen.aspx?PID=607.

"Simpson Mine, Erie/Lafayette, 1909." Ed Tangen, photographer. LPL, LP02910.
http://www.cityoflafayette.com/PhotoViewScreen.aspx?PID=605.

"Sister Carmen Community Center." In *Lafayette, Colorado*, T104. BCLHP-SCW-176.

"Six children in doorway." Photo taken at migrant farm east of Longmont, off highway 119, May, 1990. Denisse Yamashita Allaire, photographer. LM, 2014.002.009.
http://longmont.pastperfectonline.com/photo/F554CC40-CECD-4D21-9E0B-072378257150.

"Sorrow, anger, hope fill meeting," *Longmont Times-Call*, Aug. 19, 1980. BCLHP-MKM-232.

"Spanish speakers sign national charter of American GI Forum," *Longmont Times-Call*, Feb. 18, 1961. BCLHP-SCW-022.

"State police sent to beet area," *Longmont Times-Call*, May 20, 1932. BCLHP-MKM-269.

"Sugar beets brought early Hispanics to Longmont," *Longmont Times-Call*, March 28/29, 1981. BCLHP-MKM-239.

"Suit filed to improve migrant workers' lot," *Longmont Times-Call*, Oct. 5, 1971. BCLHP-MKM-226.

"Summary, Occupational Analysis of Latino-Surnamed Adults, 1926-1975." Compiled by BCLHP from *Polk's City Directories*.
Boulder, BCLHP-Occ-009
Lafayette, BCLHP-Occ-008
Longmont, 1BCLHP-Occ-007

"Summary of the Principles of the Knights of the Ku Klux Klan," pp. 2-4. Issued by the Boulder Klavern of the KKK, undated, but 1920s.

BCLHP-MKM-459-461. For p. 1, see Illus. 4.3.

"Swearing-in, Lafayette City Council, 1989." Sharon Stetson, personal copy. BCLHP-FP-198.

"Swimming Pool." In *Lafayette, Colorado*, T46. BCLHP-SCW-169.

Tafoya, Mary Gonzales. Interview; Oli Duncan, interviewer, 2009. Transcript. BCLHP Collection, Carnegie Library. BCLHP-MKM-387.

"Ted Aragon in military uniform." BCLHP-LHS-338.

"Ten Day War." In *Lafayette, Colorado*, T26. BCLHP-SCW-162.

"Terry Aragon as soldier in Berlin, early 1960s (text)." Dixie Lee Aragon, personal copy. BCLHP-FP-159.

"Three boys in matching plaid jackets" in front of car. BCLHP-LHS-190.

"Three men with shocks of grain," Longmont, 1900-1920. LM, 1975.085.206. http://longmont.pastperfectonline.com/photo/5E3FB245-CD9B-4AAC-9D4A-432120071579.

"Tipple and tracks, Standard Mine," Lafayette, 1935? LPL, LP02960. http://www.cityoflafayette.com/PhotoViewScreen.aspx?PID=623.

"Tipple at Shamrock Mine," Lafayette, 1918. LPL, LP02800. http://www.cityoflafayette.com/PhotoViewScreen.aspx?PID=601.

"Tipple at Standard Mine," Lafayette, 1935? LPL, LP02950. http://www.cityoflafayette.com/PhotoViewScreen.aspx?PID=622.

Toledo, David. Oral history interview; interviewer unknown, c. 1978. Audio and summary, MROHP. http://oralhistory.boulderlibrary.org/interview/oh0080.

"Train load of Mexicans will leave for homeland tonight," *Longmont Times-Call*, May 17, 1932. BCLHP-MKM-210.

"Turkey plant workers," 1960-70. LM, 1995.028.005. http://longmont.pastperfectonline.com/photo/68F113A6-D2E2-41E0-A3EF-544715660390.

"Two men standing in front of a car." BCLHP-LHS-546.

"U.S. Attorney General asked to investigate shootings," *Longmont Times-Call*, Aug. 21, 1980. BCLHP-MKM-234.

Valdez, Emma Suazo. Oral history interview; Oli Duncan, interviewer, c. 1987. In Duncan, ed., *We, Too, Came to Stay*, pp. 49-50. BCLHP-MKM-710.

"Valenzuela, Francisco ("Frank"), Obituary," *Boulder Daily Camera*, Jan. 9, 2014. BCLHP Collection, Carnegie Library. Not online.

"Valley farmer charged with mistreating aliens," *Longmont Times-Call*, Sept. 23, 1971. BCLHP-MKM-224.

Velasquez, Maria. Interview; Rudy Zuniga, Alex Gomez, and Andrew Valencia, interviewers, 1979. In *El Aguila*, pp. 8-11. BCLHP-MKM-620.

"Victor David Romero in the Navy," 1940s? Janet Romero Perez, personal copy. BCLHP-FP-071.

"Victor Martinez in the military," 1940s. Tom Martinez, personal copy. BCLHP-FP-059.

"Vietnam War." In *Lafayette, Colorado*, T78. BCLHP-SCW-174.

Vigil, Jennie, Angela Apodaca, and Shirley Trevino. Oral history interview; Anne Dyni, interviewer, 2001. Video and transcript, MROHP. http://oralhistory.boulderlibrary.org/interview/oh1022.

"Vigil, Rudy and Theresa. Biography," in *Lafayette, Colorado*, F431. BCLHP-SCW-208.

Villagran, Lucia and Lily. Oral history interview; Esther Blazón, interviewer, 2013. Video and transcript, MROHP. http://oralhistory.boulderlibrary.org/interview/oh1884.

"Walking to School." In *Lafayette, Colorado*, T40. BCLHP-SCW-167.

"White sheet business brisk during KKK's Boulder reign," p. 1, *Boulder Daily Camera*, Jan. 30, 1976. BCLHP-MKM-359.

"Why bilingual, bicultural education?" by Esther Blazon, p. 1, *Longmont Times Call*, March 1-2, 1975. Esther Blazón, personal copy. BCLHP-FP-023.

"Winter looking bleak for migrants," p. 1, *Longmont Times-Call*, Oct. 18-19, 1969. BCLHP-MKM-221.

"Woman of purpose: Esther Blazon," *La Luz* magazine, Aug., 1974. Esther Blazón, personal copy. BCLHP-FP-030.

Young, David Atekpatzin. Oral history interview; Margaret Alfonso, interviewer, 2013. Video and transcript, MROHP. http://oralhistory.boulderlibrary.org/interview/oh1898.

B. Other Books, Articles, and On-Line Materials

2001 Latino Task Force of Boulder County Community Assessment. Longmont, CO: Latino Task Force of Boulder County, 2001.

2013 Boulder County Latino Community Assessment. [Boulder?], CO: Latino Task Force of Boulder County, 2013.

Abbott, Carl, Stephen J. Leonard, and Thomas J. Noel. *Colorado: A History of the Centennial State.* 5th edit., Boulder: University Press of Colorado, 2013.

Actual, Factual St. Vrain Valley. Longmont Times-Call Community Review, March 25, 2012.

Acuña, Rodolfo F. *Occupied America: A History of Chicanos.* 7th edit., Boston: Longman/Pearson, 2011.

Adelfang, Karen, ed. *Erie: Yesterday and Today.* Typed report, Eric, 1974. Copy at Carnegie Branch Library for Local History, Boulder.

Aguayo, José. "Los Betabeleros (The Beetworkers)." In Vincent C. de Baca, ed., *La Gente: Hispano History and Life in Colorado.* Colorado Historical Society, 1998, pp. 105-119.

Alamillo, José M. *Making Lemonade out of Lemons: Mexican American Labor and Leisure in a California Town, 1880-1960.* Urbana: University of Illinois Press, 2006.

Aldama, Arturo, ed., with Elisa Facio, Daryl Maeda, and Reiland Rabaka. *Enduring Legacies: Ethnic Histories and Cultures of Colorado.* Boulder: University Press of Colorado, 2011.

Allport, Gordon W. *The Nature of Prejudice.* Reading, MA: Addison-Wesley Publishing Co., 25th anniversary edit., 1979.

Almaguer, Tomás. *Racial Fault Lines: The Historical Origins of White Supremacy in California.* Berkeley: University of California Press, 1994.

Alvarez, Luis. *The Power of the Zoot: Youth Culture and Resistance during World War II.* Berkeley: University of California Press, 2008.

"American FactFinder, U.S. Census Bureau," Boulder County, 1910 and 1920. http://factfinder.census.gov/faces/tableservices/jsf/pages/productview.xhtml?src=CF

Andrews, Thomas G. *Killing for Coal: America's Deadliest Labor War.* Cambridge, MA: Harvard University Press, 2008.

Angel, Ronald, and Jacqueline Lowe Angel. *Hispanic Families at Risk: The New Economy, Work, and the Welfare State.* New York: Springer, 2009.

Atkins, James A. *Human Relations in Colorado—A Historical Record.* Denver, CO: Colorado Department of Education, 1968.

Balderrama, Francisco E., and Raymond Rodríguez. *Decade of Betrayal: Mexican Repatriation in the 1930s.* Revd. edit., Albuquerque: University of New Mexico Press, 2006.

Barrera, Mario. *Race and Class in the Southwest: A Theory of Racial Inequality.* Notre Dame, IN: University of Notre Dame Press, 1979.

Benavidez, Dan. *For All the Wrong Reasons.* Allen, TX: Del Hayes Press, 2013.

Boulder County TRENDS 2011: The Community Foundation's Report on Key Indicators. Boulder, CO: The Community Foundation, 2011.

Boulder County TRENDS 2013: The Community Foundation's Report on Key Indicators. Boulder, CO: The Community Foundation, 2013.

Brooks, James F. *Captives and Cousins: Slavery, Kinship, and Community in the Southwest Borderlands.* Chapel Hill: University of North Carolina Press, 2002.

Cadava, Geraldo L. *Standing on Common Ground: The Making of a Sunbelt Borderland.* Cambridge, MA: Harvard University Press, 2013.

Campbell-Hale, Leigh. "Remembering Ludlow but Forgetting the Columbine: The 1927-1928 Colorado Coal Strike." Ph.D. thesis, University of Colorado at Boulder, 2013.

Carrigan, William D., and Clive Webb. "The Lynching of Persons of Mexican Origin or Descent in the United States, 1848-1928." *Journal of Social History*, 37 (2003): 411-438.

Castañeda, Antonia, ed., *Gender on the Borderlands: The Frontiers Reader.* Lincoln: University of Nebraska Press, 2007.

Chalmers, David M. *Hooded Americanism: The History of the Ku Klux Klan.* New York: Franklin Watts, 1965.

Chávez, Ernesto. "*¡Mi Raza Primero!": Nationalism, Identity, and Insurgency in the Chicano Movement in Los Angeles, 1966-1978.* Berkeley: University of California Press, 2002.

Chávez, John R. *The Lost Land: The Chicano Image of the Southwest.* Albuquerque: University of New Mexico Press, 1984.

Chavez, Rebecca D. "Making Them Count: A Baseline Study of the Latino Community in Longmont, Colorado, 1910 to 1940." M.A. thesis, New Mexico State University, 2014.

Cohen, Deborah. *Braceros: Migrant Citizens and Transnational Subjects in the Postwar United States and Mexico.* Chapel Hill: University of North Carolina Press, 2011.

Cohen, William M. "Blast: The 1936 Monarch Mine Explosion." Louisville Historical Museum, Louisville, Colorado, 2006. http://www.louisville-library.org/Portals/1/Museum/monarchminenarrative.pdf

De Baca, Vincent C., ed. *La Gente: Hispano History and Life in Colorado.* Denver: Colorado Historical Society, 1998.

De Onís, José. *The Hispanic Contribution to the State of Colorado.* Boulder, CO: Westview Press, 1976.

Delgado, Richard, and Jean Stefancic. "Home-Grown Racism: Colorado's Historic Embrace—and Denial—of Equal Opportunity in Higher Education." *Colorado Law Review*, 70.3 (1999): 703-811.

Deutsch, Sarah. *No Separate Refuge: Culture, Class, and Gender on an Anglo-Hispanic Frontier in the American Southwest, 1880-1940.* New York: Oxford University Press, 1987.

Donato, Rubén. *Mexicans and Hispanos in Colorado Schools and Communities, 1920-1960.* Albany: State University of New York Press, 2007.

Donato, Rubén, and Jarrod S. Hanson. "Legally White, Socially 'Mexican': The Politics of De Jure and De Facto School Segregation in the American Southwest." *Harvard Educational Review,* 82.2 (2012): 202-225.

Echevarria, Evelio A., and Jose Otero, eds. *Hispanic Colorado, Four Centuries: History and Heritage.* Ft. Collins, CO: Centennial Publications, 1976.

Escobedo, Elizabeth R. *From Coveralls to Zoot Suits: The Lives of Mexican American Women on the World War II Home Front.* Chapel Hill: University of North Carolina Press, 2013.

Falicov, Celia Jaes. *Latino Families in Therapy.* 2nd edit., New York: Guildford Press, 2014.

Foley, Neil. *Mexicans in the Making of America.* Cambridge, MA: Harvard University Press, 2014.

García, Matt. *A World of Its Own: Race, Labor, and Citrus in the Making of Greater Los Angeles, 1900-1970.* Chapel Hill: University of North Carolina Press, 2001.

Garcilazo, Jeffrey Marcos. *Traqueros: Mexican Railroad Workers in the United States, 1870 to 1930.* Denton: University of North Texas Press, 2012.

Goldberg, Robert A. "Denver: Queen City of the Colorado Realm," in Shawn Lay, ed., *The Invisible Empire in the West.* Urbana: University of Illinois Press, 1992, pp. 39-66.

Goldberg, Robert A. *Hooded Empire: The Ku Klux Klan in Colorado.* Urbana: University of Illinois Press, 1981.

Gonzáles, Deena J. "Gender on the Borderlands: Re-Textualizing the Classics." *Frontiers: A Journal of Women Studies,* 24:2/3 (2003): 15-29.

Gonzáles, Gilbert G. "A Critique of the Internal Colony Model." *Latin American Perspectives,* 1:1 (1974): 154-161.

Gonzales, Manuel G. *Mexicanos: A History of Mexicans in the United States.* 2nd edit., Bloomington: Indiana University Press, 2009.

Gordon, Linda. *The Great Arizona Orphan Abduction.* Cambridge, MA: Harvard University Press, 1999.

Guerin-Gonzales, Camille. *Mexican Workers and American Dreams: Immigration, Repatriation, and California Farm Labor, 1900-1939.* New Brunswick, NJ: Rutgers University Press, 1994.

Gutiérrez, David. G. *Walls and Mirrors: Mexican Americans, Mexican Immigrants, and the Politics of Ethnicity.* Berkeley: University of California Press, 1995.

Hafen, LeRoy R. *Broken Hand: The Life of Thomas Fitzpatrick: Mountain Man, Guide, and Indian Agent.* Denver, CO: Old West Publishing Co., 1973.

Hafen, LeRoy R., ed. *The Mountain Men and the Fur Trade of the Far West*. 10 vols. Glendale, CA: A. H. Clark Co., 1965-1972.

Hafen, LeRoy R., and Ann Hafen. *The Colorado Story: A History of Your State and Mine*. Denver, CO: Old West Publishing Co., 1953.

Hamilton, Candy. *Footprints in the Sugar: A History of the Great Western Sugar Company*. Ontario, OR: Hamilton Bates Publishers, 2009.

Hart, John Mason. *Revolutionary Mexico: The Coming and Process of the Mexican Revolution*. Berkeley: University of California Press, 10th anniversary edit., 1997.

Hayes-Bautista, David E. *El Cinco de Mayo: An American Tradition*. Berkeley: University of California Press, 2012.

Hays, David. "'A Quiet Campaign of Education': The University of Colorado and Minority Rights, 1877-1945." Unpublished typescript kindly provided by the author.

Hernández, Sonia. *Working Women into the Borderlands*. College Station: Texas A&M University Press, 2014.

Jacobs, Janet L. *Hidden Heritage: The Legacy of the Crypto-Jews*. Berkeley: University of California Press, 2002.

Jaramillo, Nash. *Spanish Civilization and Culture of the Southwest*. Santa Fe, NM: Privately published by the author, 1973.

Katz, Friedrich. "Labor Conditions on Haciendas in Porfirian Mexico: Some Trends and Tendencies." *Hispanic American Historical Review*, 54.1 (1974): 1-47.

Knox, Peter. "The Campus and the Klan: A Classic Lesson in Civility." *[University of] Colorado [Magazine]*, Dec., 1997, pp. 10-11. BCLHP-MKM-366.

Kulkosky, Tanya W. "Mexican Migrant Workers in Depression-era Colorado." In Vincent C. de Baca, ed., *La Gente: Hispano History and Life in Colorado*. Colorado Historical Society, 1998, pp. 121-133.

LARASA (Latin American Research and Service Agency). "Contributions of the Spanish Surnamed American to Colorado." Denver, CO: LARASA, 1976.

"La Raza de Colorado: La Historia," and "El Movimiento." Two DVDs produced by Rocky Mountain Public Broadcasting Network, 2005 and 2006.

Lecompte, Janet. *Pueblo, Hardscrabble, Greenhorn: The Upper Arkansas, 1832-1856*. Norman: University of Oklahoma Press, 1978.

Longmont 125th Anniversary. *Longmont Times-Call*, June 16, 1996.

Lopez, Jody L., and Gabriel A. Lopez, with Peggy A. Ford. *White Gold Laborers: The Spanish Colony of Greeley, Colorado*. Bloomington, IN: AuthorHouse, 2007.

Lucero, Anne. Aguilar and Its Western Valley of Trujillo Creek. In José De Onís, ed., *The Hispanic Contribution to the State of Colorado*. Boulder, CO: Westview Press, 1976, pp. 163-182.

Maes, Arthur F. *Following in the Footsteps of our Ancestors from Santa Fe to Maes Creek*. Colorado Springs, CO: Earth Design Systems, 1995.

Martin, Desirée A. *Borderlands Saints: Secular Sanctity in Chicano/a and Mexican Culture*. New Brunswick, NJ: Rutgers University Press, 2013.

Martinez, Oscar J., ed. *U.S.-Mexico Borderlands: Historical and Contemporary Perspectives*. Wilmington, DE: Scholarly Resources, 1996.

McIntosh, Marjorie K. *Latinos of Boulder County, Colorado, 1900-1980*, Vol. II: *Lives and Legacies*. Palm Springs, CA: Old John Publishing, 2016.

McLean, Polly E., ed. *A Legacy of Missing Pieces: The Voices of Black Women of Boulder County*. Boulder: University of Colorado, 2002.

McLean, Robert. "Mexicans in the Beet Field (1924)." In Evelio A. Echevarria and Jose Otero, eds., *Hispanic Colorado, Four Centuries: History and Heritage*. Ft. Collins, CO: Centennial Publications, 1976, pp. 77-81.

Montoya, María. *Translating Property: The Maxwell Land Grant and the Conflict over Land in the American West, 1840-1900*. Berkeley: University of California Press, 2002.

Muñoz, Carlos, Jr. *Youth, Identity, Power: The Chicano Movement*. Revd. edit., London: Verso, 2007.

Murray, Douglas L. "The Abolition of El Cortito, the Short-Handled Hoe: A Case Study in Social Conflict and State Policy in California Agriculture." *Social Problems*, 30.1 (1982): 26-39.

Newby, Betty Ann. *The Longmont Album: History and Folklore of the St. Vrain Valley*. Virginia Beach, VA: Donning Company/Publishers, 1995.

Noel, Thomas J., and Dan W. Corson. *Boulder County: An Illustrated History*. Carlsbad, CA: Heritage Media Corporation, 1999.

Perks, Robert, and Alisdair Thomson, eds., *The Oral History Reader*. 2nd edit., London: Routledge, 2006.

Polk's City Directories for Boulder [and adjoining communities], 1904, 1916 (Polk's Boulder County Directory), 1926, 1936, 1946, 1955, 1965, and *1975*; *Polk's City Directories for Longmont, 1965* and *1975* (R. L. Polk & Co., place of publication not given).

"Population Estimates Program, Population Division, U.S. Census Bureau," Boulder County, 1990.
https://www.census.gov/popest/data/counties/asrh/1990s/tables/co-99-11/crhco90.txt.

"Race Matters." Power Point presentation produced by the Annie E. Casey Foundation, no date, to go with the Race Matters Toolkit.
http://www.aecf.org/resources/race-matters-powerpoint-presentation

Ramirez, Albert. *The Profe Files: Social Psychological Perspectives on Power, Pluralism, and Chicano Identity.* Smashwords ebook, 2013.

Ramirez, Albert. *Vera's Journey: Across Generations and Beyond Borders* (Smashwords ebook, 2013).

Ramirez, Catherine S. *The Woman in the Zoot Suit: Gender, Nationalism, and the Cultural Politics of Memory.* Durham, NC: Duke University Press, 2009.

Rees, Michael J. "Chicanos Mine the Columbine, An Hispanic Workforce in Northern Colorado: 1921-1928." Undergraduate Honors Thesis, University of Colorado at Boulder, 1995.

Rosales, F. Arturo. *Chicano! The History of the Mexican American Civil Rights Movement.* 2nd edit., Houston, TX: Arte Público Press, 1997.

Rosales, F. Arturo. *¡Pobre Raza! Violence, Justice, and Mobilization among México Lindo Immigrants, 1900-1936.* Austin: University of Texas Press, 1999.

Ruiz, Vicki. *Cannery Women, Cannery Lives: Mexican Women, Unionization, and the California Food Processing Industry, 1930-1950.* Albuquerque: University of New Mexico Press, 1987.

Ruiz, Vicki L. *From Out of the Shadows: Mexican Women in Twentieth-Century America.* New York: Oxford University Press, 10th anniversary edit., 2008.

Salas, Elizabeth. *Soldaderas in the Mexican Military: Myth and History.* Austin: University of Texas Press, 1990.

Sandoval, David A. "Recruitment, Rejection, and Reaction: Colorado Chicanos in the Twentieth Century." In Arturo Aldama, ed., *Enduring Legacies: Ethnic Histories and Cultures of Colorado.* Boulder: University Press of Colorado, 2011, pp. 239-255.

Scamehorn, Lee. *Colorado's Small Town Industrial Revolution: Commercial Canning and Preserving in Northeastern Colorado.* Indianapolis, IN: Dog Ear Publishing, 2011.

Segura, Denise A. "Challenging the Chicano Text: Toward a More Inclusive Contemporary Causa." *Signs*, 26:2 (2001): 541-550.

Smith, Phyllis. *Once A Coal Miner: The Story of Colorado's Northern Coal Field.* Boulder, Colo.: Pruett Publishing Company, 1989.

Sykes, Hope Williams. *Second Hoeing.* New York: G. P. Putnam's Sons, 1935.

Taylor, Paul S. *Mexican Labor in the United States.* Vol. I, Berkeley: University of California Press, 1930.

They Came to Stay: Longmont, Colorado, 1858-1920. St. Vrain Valley Historical Association, Longmont, CO: Longmont Printing Company, 1971.

Travis, Merle. "Sixteen Tons," 1946; recorded by Tennessee Ernie Ford, 1955. https://www.youtube.com/watch?v=zUpTJg2EBpw&feature=player_embedded.

Tushar, Olibama López. *The People of "El Valle": A History of the Spanish Colonials in the San Luis Valley.* Denver, CO: Privately published by the author, 1975.

Ubbelohde, Carl, Maxine Benson, and Duane A. Smith. *A Colorado History.* 9th edit., Boulder, CO: Pruett Publishing Co., 2006.

"UMAS y MEChA," Latino student organization at the University of Colorado at Boulder. http://www.colorado.edu/StudentGroups/UMAS-MEChA/history.html

Vargas, Zaragosa. *Labor Rights Are Civil Rights: Mexican American Workers in Twentieth-Century America.* Princeton, NJ: Princeton University Press, 2005.

VFW [Veterans of Foreign Wars], Mile High Post, no. 1771. *Service Record Book of Men and Women of Lafayette, Colorado and Community.* Includes World Wars I and II. No place or date of publication. Available at Carnegie Branch Library for Local History, Boulder.

Vigil, Charles S. "Mexican Land Grants in Colorado." In José De Onís, ed., *The Hispanic Contribution to the State of Colorado.* Boulder, CO: Westview Press, 1976, pp. 65-77.

Vigil, Charles S. "Spanish-Surnamed Americans in the First Hundred Years of Government." In José De Onís, ed., *The Hispanic Contribution to the State of Colorado.* Boulder, CO: Westview Press, 1976, pp. 183-189.

Vigil, Ernesto. "Rodolfo Gonzales and the Advent of the Crusade for Justice." In Vincent C. de Baca, ed., *La Gente: Hispano History and Life in Colorado.* Denver: Colorado Historical Society, 1998, pp. 155-201.

Weber, David J. *The Mexican Frontier, 1921-1846: The American Southwest under Mexico.* Albuquerque: University of New Mexico Press, 1982.

Weber, David J. *The Spanish Frontier in North America.* New Haven, CT: Yale University Press, 1992.

Weber, David J., ed. *Foreigners in Their Native Land: Historical Roots of the Mexican Americans.* 30th anniversary edit., Albuquerque: University of New Mexico Press, 2003.

White, Frank A. *La Garita.* La Jara, CO: Cooper Printing, 1971.

Zambrana, Ruth E. *Latinos in American Society: Families and Communities in Transition.* Ithaca, NY: Cornell University Pres, 2011.

Index

CPSIA information can be obtained
at www.ICGtesting.com
Printed in the USA
LVOW01*0807040216

473659LV00001B/1/P